SOLUTION PAKISTAN

VOLUME I

MEEM ZAAL JEEM

NAWA
PRESS

Solution Pakistan
Volume I

Copyright © Meem Zaal Jeem (pseudonym), 2013
Published 31August 2013. Paperback reprinted 2014.

A CIP catalogue record for this book is available from the British Library.

ISBN: 978-0-9576924-0-4

Nawa Press Ltd
145-157 St John Street
London, England
EC1V 4PW

www.nawapress.co.uk

Contents

Preface

1366 years after Hazrat[1] Muhammad[(PBUH)] founded the first Islamic State in Arabia, Quaid-e-Azam[2] Muhammad Ali Jinnah[(RA)] founded the second Islamic State, Pakistan, on 14th of August 1947. Pakistan is not only the second Muslim state in the world, but it is also the second largest Muslim country by population. It is the 7th nuclear power in the world. But now it is under immense pressures from within and without, and it is in danger of economic, social, and political collapse.

Pakistan faces many problems but there are three issues that threaten its survival the most; terrorism, absence of law and order, and a failing economy. Unfortunately, the leading Pakistani experts have failed to provide a comprehensive solution to these three problems. They can correctly identify the problems, but provide the same

---

[1] Hazrat is an honorific title reserved for messengers of God, and other notable Muslims who had contributions for Ummah. **PBUH** means, *Peace be upon Him*, reserved only for Hazrat Muhammad[(PBUH)]. **RA** has two slightly different meanings. The higher title **RA** means May *God be pleased with him/her*, which is reserved for messengers of God except Hazrat Muhammad[(PBUH)], Wives and Companions of Hazrat Muhammad[(PBUH)]. The lower title **RA** means *May God have mercy on him/her*, which is reserved for notable Muslims, such as, Quaid-e-Azam.
[2] Quaid-e-Azam means *Great Leader*. This title is reserved for founding father of Pakistan, Muhammad Ali Jinnah[(RA)]. Most Pakistanis refer to Muhammad Ali Jinnah[(RA)] with his title only because it is readily understood.

solutions, which have failed over and again. There are some easy solutions that the past and current government or any expert has not considered. These solutions do not require the government to pass many new bills, but they can utilise the current laws differently for desired result. In this book, I will explain my proposed solutions in depth, why they will work, what could be their consequences, and how we could minimise any undesired outcomes. If the government adopts these solutions, then we will be able to break the backs of terrorists and criminals without firing a shot, eliminate bhata mafia, eradicate kidnapping for ransom, and establish a lasting peace. We would be able to prevent drone strikes, pay off our domestic and foreign national debts without any expense, and we will not need to beg IMF for a few billion dollars. Our treasury will be brimming with extra cash to spend on the development and prosperity of our people without raising any new taxes. In fact, my proposals will allow the government to reduce taxes. However, the tools that I am proposing are extremely powerful, and there is a danger that these could be used against citizens. They have the power to make the entire nation hostage to a handful of men in the government. So we need to build some safeguards before implementing them.

I have two purposes in writing this book. Firstly, to provide our politicians some easy to implement innovative solutions, which will help solve the problems of terrorism, law & order, and economy in a short time possible. Secondly, the most important purpose is to educate Pakistanis with the ideas for change, so they demand of politicians the changes which will transform their lives for better. There is always a danger that the government, having received suggestions, only adopts those ideas that strengthen its power, and not adopt those which empower its people. So by writing this book, I am trying to ensure that people will understand and demand of politicians what is good for them.

You may be wondering how this book came about? Well, I had been researching and writing since 2008, and I planned to write a comprehensive volume covering many issues which I had identified in Pakistani political, economic and social life, and it was to be published in 2014. Unfortunately, Pakistan is going through a difficult time now, and there will be many troubles ahead when the American forces pull out of Afghanistan. So I decided to write a shorter book now covering the very important issues that need urgent attention. Further, the new government coming to power recently, and then taking some positive steps in the first few days of taking office created a hope. So I felt obliged to write this book to help the new government, which seems serious so far in tackling the issues Pakistan is facing. Let us briefly survey the main issues facing us presently.

The mother of all problems in Pakistan is that we lack a real, honest, and effective leadership following the deaths of our founding fathers. People leading the country were military dictators, feudal landlords, or industrialists. Their visions only went as far as their power, landholdings, and wealth. Even if some of them had intentions of doing good for the country, they were compromised by the very people who put them in power. Unfortunately, this is all caused by the outdated parliamentary democracy, which most of us think as a god of politics! Even though we have a president, and a senate, the actual power rests in the hands of one person, the prime minister. This is no better than a mob rule because there is no check and balance. Political system is in need of major overhaul and we must make it a real republic for a stable political system. Further, we must produce new and young political leadership who could take this country forward and upward.

Our political leaders so far, had planning horizon[3] set at next elections only. That is, how they could win them and come to power again. To make Pakistan a powerful and successful nation, we must start with long planning horizons. That is, we must plan where do we want to see Pakistan in 1000 years from now? Then work backwards to present in decrements of 500, 250, 100, 50, 25, 10, and 5 years from now. We must plan where would we be in relation to the rest of the world at these stages in future? What would be the condition of our people? Would Pakistan be the richest and most powerful nation in 100 years from now? Would it have acquired more territories, such as, entire Jammu & Kashmir, UP, Hyderabad, and a few islands around the world? Or would it be broken into several countries with Punjabistan and Pakhtunistan being landlocked?

Before I go on to explain the ideas to solve our country's major issues, I must bring your attention to the level and quality of debates taking place in our media. There is a sort of "Janu German Effect" in our debates in media, which is confusing and manipulating our people. I want you to beware of *Janu Germans* in our political parties and technocrats. Many of you may be wondering what I mean by Janu German Effect? Let me explain it briefly.

Some of you may remember a TV series on PTV called *Choti Si Duniya*, meaning, *A Small World*. This TV programme was set in a small village, in Sindh, where almost all the people were illiterate. In one of the episodes, an English speaking competition took place between Murad Ali Khan and Janu German. Murad Ali Khan was an English gentleman like figure who had spent many years in England, and could speak very fluent English, albeit with strong accent. But Janu German on the other hand knew only a handful of English words, such as, "that, why, where" and some English numbers. Villagers gathered around to watch the English speaking

---

[3] Planning Horizon refers amount of time the leaders will look into future when developing their strategic plans.

competition. Both sides had their supporters who provided encouragement to both competitors. There were three elders who acted as judges, but none of them knew English. The rules of the competition were that each competitor would ask three questions of his opponent, which the opponent must answer. This would then be followed by each opponent telling a story in English. Judges point to Janu German to ask questions first.

Janu German's first question contains only a single word 'that.' At this Murad Ali Khan got confused and people started shouting Janu German has confused his opponent. Anyway, Murad Ali Khan asks him – What do you mean by word 'that?' At this everyone thinks that Murad Ali Khan had answered Janu German's question.

So Janu German is told to ask his second question. At this, he again asks a single word question "Why". Murad Ali Khan gets confused at his single word question again, but he asks him 'I don't understand your question.' In this manner, Janu German is told to ask his final question. Again, his final question contained a single word 'where.' Murad Ali Khan clearly gets annoyed at this and says 'Oh my God- Are you a crazy man?' The competition continues and it is Murad Ali Khan's turn to ask questions. Here things get crazy!

Murad Ali Khans asks 'What is your name?' But Janu German quickly retorts '1,- 2, - 3.' At this Murad Ali Khan is confirmed that Janu German doesn't know any English apart from a few words. He protests to Janu German and asks 'But it is not the answer of my question.' But again, Janu German quickly retorts '4, 5, 6, 8, 8.' Everyone thinks that Janu German has the upper hand because he answers Murad's questions quickly and fluently. Even Murad's supporter, Ramzan, thinks that Murad is losing the competition, and he offers him to cool down with water, or to drink some milk. Murad tells him off at his suggestions. Clearly annoyed, Murad asks him 'Please give me a proper answer' but again Janu German quickly replies with '11, 28, 99, 100.'

Now the judges tell the competitors to move on to second stage of telling a story in English, and Janu German gets the first go. Janu German gets up and laughs loudly and then starts telling a story by just uttering '1 – 1, 2, 3, 4, 5 - - 5, 8, 9, - - 99, – 100, - 112, - 12 and 33, - 33 and 44, - 44 and 45, - thank you – very much, - that , - why, - where, - goodbye, goodnight, - half mind.'

After this, Murad Ali Khan is asked to tell a story in English. Murad Ali Khan gets up and starts saying 'Few moments before, my good old friend, **Ramzan**, has been telling me that I should drink a **glass** of milk. Then I would be able to fight with a person who don't even know a word of English. *So* please, why don't you excuse me on this occasion – that's all – my good old justice.'

After Murad's speech the three judges tell the audience that they have made the decision on who has won the contest, but would like to ask audience a few questions to ensure justice. Audience agree. The judge asks them, while telling the story, didn't Murad Ali Khan say three words 'Ramzan, glass, and so.' They all agree. At this the judges say aren't these three words from our language? They all agree. Please note that Urdu has adopted the word "glass" meaning the same thing, and the word "so" in Urdu sounds like word for number '100.' They then ask the audience that when telling the story in English, did Janu German use any word of our language? They all agree that he didn't use any non-English word. So the judges declare Janu German the winner.

Similarly, there are some politicians, technocrats, experts, anchor persons, and columnists who are actually no different than Janu German. They will try to confuse, manipulate, and deceive you with Janu German tactics. So I ask you not to rely on anyone else to tell you the truth, but try to spot the Janu Germans in our political life, so that you could distinguish truth from lies.

I hope this book is source of information and inspiration for ordinary people, professionals, and political leaders of Pakistan, so they could change their country for the better.

God Bless Pakistan!

Meem Zaal Jeem

1st of Jinnah, 66 AP[4]

---

[4] AP stands for 'After Pakistan' and it is a Pakistani calendar which started on 14 of August 1947 at the birth of Pakistan. So 14th of August 2013 CE would be 1st of Jinnah 66 AP. The months of Pakistani calendar are Jinnah, Iqbal, Zaffarullah, Aga, Fatima, Jung, Jauhar, Khaliquzzaman, Huq, Nishtar, Mandal, and Turner.

Organising Economic Fundamentals

Almost all of the serious crimes could be traced back to the failure of an economy, and poverty is the sign of a mismanaged economy. These facts become clear when we take a closer look at the economy of Pakistan. It is full of natural resources and a population necessary for economic growth and prosperity, but more than half of the population remains below poverty line. The reason for our economic failure and mismanagement is that our politicians do not understand the fundamentals of economics. They make decisions that effect every single person in their domain, but their decisions are just as good as their incompetent or naive advisers.

Unfortunately, our education systems is so dated that it produces economists, who are at least a century behind. Their ideas about economics are not suited to modern world. On the other hand, those economists who know the modern world are the advocates of international organisations, such as, IMF or World Bank. It seems that these economists are on the payrolls of these organisations, because they suggest policies to our politicians, which increases the powers of international organisations, and creates an uncontrolled poverty. These policies ensure that the taxes are increased, so that the wealth of our nation is transferred to IMF, World Bank, or other international institutions. From the published figures, you could easily see that more wealth has been transferred from the poor nations to the rich, instead of other way round. So it is important that our politicians understand the fundamentals of economics themselves instead of relying on experts, so they could make better decisions to create growth and prosperity for their people. I have tried to simplify economics in the next three chapters so that anyone could understand it without reading complicated formulae or charts.

Let us now turn our attention to the single fundamental of economics, *Money*, which many economists fail to understand, and its power is not utilised fully. Money is the basis for any economic system. If you take money out of an economy, then the whole country would grind to a halt, even if you have all the resources of the world. For example, if you do not have money to buy fuel then you cannot run your car. Without money you cannot buy food. If an employer does not have money to pay its workers, then his factory will stop. If you take money out of the system then your population may die of hunger, even when your shops may be full of food. This is because you have taken the means of exchange, the money, out of the system. This is how powerful the Money is! If you let your imaginations run wild for a while, then you will realise that the Money is much more powerful than a superior army!

The root of all of our economic and social problems is that we have not organised our Monetary System[5] properly. I will show you how we could organise and modify our monetary system to achieve many other goals apart from economic goals. When used properly along with other techniques, monetary policy becomes more powerful than a well trained army. It can be used to starve the terrorists of cash without which they cannot operate and launch attacks. You could disable Bhata Mafia[6] and kidnapping for ransom by using monetary

---

[5] A monetary system is a collection of policies and institutions through which the government supplies and controls money.

[6] Bhata Mafia (extortion) historically referred to gangs supported by political parties, who collected protection money from traders and the

policies coupled with other techniques. You could get rid of black economy and bring every product and service into mainstream economy. You could automatically collect taxes by fusing monetary and fiscal policies. You could eliminate corruption from entire economy by using monetary policy with other techniques. To eliminate corruption further, you could get rid of most of Inland Revenue department, which is responsible for most corruption. By adding a zero on the right hand side of the *Fractional Reserve Requirement* for our banking system, you could eliminate entire governmental domestic debt. In fact, by the force of this single zero, you could shift the entire debt onto commercial banks, which means the government will now receive interest on loans instead of paying it. I will also be discussing inflation in detail, which is the result of mismanagement of monetary system. How the inflation is responsible for widespread poverty and how to control it?

Other solutions in this chapter include ideas on how the government could erase its entire IMF debt with the flick of the pen, if it wanted to. If it wanted, it could teach the corrupt politicians a lesson by declaring its foreign loans *odious*. This is because by doing this, we will force the international institutions and other countries to go after the corrupt politicians to repay their loans, who took out these loans for public welfare, but filled their own bank accounts instead. These international institutions and other states have the powers to recover their money even if it is hidden in Swiss Banks. We will then discuss the natural disasters which are draining our wealth. We lose billions of rupees and precious lives each year in floods, which could be easily controlled. Our economists forget about the importance of *National Savings* and *Multifactor Productivity,* which drive a lasting growth. We will discuss these in this chapter and many other economic issues in the other two chapters

---

rich. But this is now the tool of choice for terrorists to fund their activities along with kidnapping for ransom.

But before we could discuss solutions, we need to identify and understand our economic problems properly. I will explain each economic issue briefly as I am discussing the solutions. Some solutions may have negative consequences, which I will point out along the way, with some ideas to reduce these risks. For simplicity, I will not use the complex calculations and terms, but where they may be necessary, I will try to explain them.   Another thing to bear in mind is that, almost all the figures the government publishes could be safely rejected, because these figures are manipulated by every government, so things look good to its voters at home, and lenders abroad. If we are to believe the government figures, then there should be prosperity everywhere. According to government, the inflation is around 9%, then why hundreds of people each year are committing suicides due to financial troubles? If unemployment is less than 6% then why many people are jobless and unable to make ends meet? If our economy is growing more than 2% a year then why there is poverty everywhere?

Money, Banking, & Economy

Money and currency are not the same things, but everyone seems to think that they are. Let me explain how they are different. Money is intangible, so unreal. But the currency note is tangible, so real. You cannot touch money, hold it, or keep it, but you can always touch or hold currency notes.   However, the money and currency are interlinked. Money is linked to currency in the same way the human soul is linked to its body. You cannot see or touch the soul, but you can always see or touch the body.   So think of money as the soul, and currency its body. To keep things simple, I will use the word 'money' to represent currency and also money, because this is how they are understood in society. But I hope you will keep in mind the distinction between money and currency.

But before we move on to the importance of money, we must understand what money is? Money is a Social Good[7] and it must always be used for the benefit of the public. You accept money for your goods or services because you know that everyone else will also accept the money you have, to sell their goods and services. Money comes into existence by the law of the country. The only authority that can ever create money is the state. Unfortunately, our private banks are also creating vast amounts of money, right under the nose of the state. That is the reason the bankers are so rich. I will explain a little later in this section how the banks create money. But the state must take away this power to create money from the banks, to establish its ultimate sovereignty, and for the good of the country.

Now let us see why money is so important for a country? We know that almost everything depends on economy, but the economy in turn depends on a nation's currency. If currency or money fails in its functions, then the economy will suffer and the whole nation. If the economy is failing then no one will invest in that country, which means there will be no jobs for the people, causing widespread poverty. On a closer examination, you will find that almost every aspect of life depends on economy. And if everything depends on economy, and economy in turn depends on money, then we must first make sure that our monetary system is functioning properly.

In any economy, the currency is the single most important and powerful tool, which if used properly will bring prosperity, but if used incompetently will ruin that country. At present, there is only one country in the world which uses its currency competently, so rules the world. Yes, it is America and its dollar. It is a different matter that America does not own the Dollar. I will explain later in this section that it is not the American military power, which maintains its hegemony on the rest of the world, but it is the dollar

---

[7] Social Good is a good or service that benefits the largest number of people in the largest possible way.

and other international organisations that help America to keep its economic and military dominance in the world. So we must learn about the power of our own currency, so we could utilise it for our prosperity and power. But we first need to look closer to home, how do we use our Rupee? Why are we in an economic mess and cannot survive without aid from America or IMF? I will then suggest some practical solutions to get out of IMF debt without paying them a dollar, paying off our bilateral debts quickly by adopting monetary policies, which will bring economic growth and prosperity to our people.

Currently, our rupee has devalued a great deal. Every time Rupee is devalued, our foreign debts increase. This is because most of our foreign debt is denominated in US Dollars, so we would need more rupees to buy the same number of US Dollars to pay off our debts. This is one of the reasons that IMF demands the borrowing country to devalue its currency after giving them a loan, so the debt increases straight away for the borrowing country, from which it becomes difficult to get out. This puts the borrowing country in constant need for IMF loans, and this is how the IMF enslaves those countries who borrow from it. Other conditions the IMF puts on the borrowing country are that the Finance Minister and governor of State Bank should be of their choosing. So IMF could control whole of our monetary systems and economy! If you don't believe me then just take a look at the Finance Ministers and State Bank's governors after we borrowed from IMF. You will find that they were all pro IMF. I will discuss IMF a little later in detail, and how to get out of its claws without paying them a dime. But let us see why Rupee is devaluing and how to stop this process?

Ever since the Gold Standard was abolished in 70s, any country now could print as much money as it wants. So why not print a lot of money and get what we want from the rest of the world? Well, things are not that simple. If we print a lot of money, more than our

Gross Domestic Product[8] (GDP), then there will be an excess of Rupees in the economy, which will decrease its value. In any economy the currency also behaves like a commodity, such as, flour and sugar. If there is a lot of flour and sugar produced, more than what everybody needs, then the price of flour and sugar will drop in direct proportion to how much was not needed. Similarly, if we print a lot of money, more than our GDP, then its value will also drop in direct proportion to the excess amount of our GDP. But there is another factor which affects currency value, perhaps more than the quantity of our currency we print, and that is the perception of the world about our monetary policy. If the world thinks that we are adopting a reckless monetary policy, then they will devalue our currency, more than they should have. Therefore, it is important that we control how much currency we print, and keep a well functioning monetary system.

Almost all economists agree that the price inflation, that is, the increase in prices of goods and services, is directly related to money supply in a country. This means that if a country prints too much money, then it will cause price inflation in its economy, which also means the value of the money has reduced. On the other hand, if a country restricts its money supply, less than its GDP, then the prices will fall creating a deflation and increasing the value of money. I know what you may be thinking. Why not reduce the money supply to control inflation and increase the value of our rupee?

I wish things were this simple! World has had a bad experience with deflation, because when deflation starts then it tends to get out of control. This is what happened during the Great Depression[9] in America in 1930s. Banks went bankrupt; factories and businesses

---

[8] The value of all the goods and services produced in a country in a year is called Gross Domestic Product or GDP.

[9] The Great Depression was an economic crisis which started in USA in 1929 but quickly spread to Europe and the rest of the world, causing massive levels of poverty, hunger, unemployment and political unrest.

closed down, and people were out of jobs, and there was no money to buy even food. So now every country prefers a little bit of inflation than deflation. To understand why deflation gets out of control when it sets in, let us consider the following example.

Suppose prices are falling weekly, then you would want to wait for another week or two for the prices to come down even further. Obviously, you can only delay buying the non-essential items, such as, cars, TV, etc. You have to buy the essential items like food, no matter what is happening in the economy. This delay from public to buy non-essential goods will put pressure on businesses to reduce prices even further, because they need money to pay their workers and suppliers. People would then notice that the prices have come down more than they expected, so they start to think that if they waited a few more weeks, then the prices will come down even further. This will increase more pressure on businesses to reduce prices even further, creating an unending cycle of businesses reducing prices, and buyers delaying purchases. This vicious cycle will reduce prices further, but this time they will stop buying from factories because they cannot sell the stock they already have. When this happens, then the factories will lay off people, who now do not have enough money to buy anything, adding to the problem. If the government did not act to break this cycle of price deflation, then it will cause widespread closures of businesses causing redundancies, bankruptcies, and poverty. So when there are a lot of people who are out of jobs then they cannot even buy the essential goods, so the prices spiral down and deflation sets in. That is why no country wants deflation. But let us now discuss how could we control price inflation and devaluation of our currency without causing a deflation?

The simplest thing to do is to stop printing any more money, and then try to match our money supply with our GDP. You may protest that it is easier said than done. The government needs money for its operation and they have to print it when no one is willing to lend them. I would say if this is how the things are then when will we stop printing money? Will we stop when our currency is devalued like Zimbabwe or 1940s Germany, that is, when you will need a wheelbarrow full of notes to buy a loaf of bread? Or will we dollarize[10] our economy? Both of the above options are bad for the people and country. However, I have another suggestion which will not only resolve the issue of government not having enough cash, but it will also provide a long term regular income to government. But this decision needs a great degree of courage from the politicians, and they will have to anger some of their friends who are bankers. So it will be a testing time for the politicians. Will they stand with the people, or their friends? But I can say with certainty that if they stood with the people, then they will come out as winners, because they will have the people on their side who will put them in power again and again. But if they stood with their friends and ignored the people, then the politicians will have no place to hide!

My proposal will require the government to do two things simultaneously. Firstly, it needs to make the State Bank fully independent and give it a single task of ensuring price stability in the economy. Secondly, it needs to implement a 100% *Fractional Reserve Banking* for all banks. This will create a huge shortfall of money in the banks, which the state bank could fill by lending money to banks by just writing the amount in its ledger. There is no need to print any new money. So when the state bank lends to banks, then it can charge interest on that money to earn a regular long-term income. Let me first explain in detail, the changes to our central bank.

Most advanced nations of the world who have a strong economy and low inflation, have independent central banks. The central bank

---

[10] Dollarization of an economy is a situation where the citizens of a country officially or unofficially use a foreign country's currency, such as US dollars, as legal tender for everyday transactions.

usually has a single task of ensuring Price Stability[11]. In theory, our central bank is also independent, but not in practice. In Pakistan, the central bank is a tool that the politicians use for their political and financial benefits. But if we are to make our central bank truly independent, then the State Bank of Pakistan will not print any money just because the government asks it to. Such a system will ensure Price Stability, which will drive economic growth and prosperity for its people. The question arises, how do we ensure that the central bank is fully independent?

The central bank, which is our State Bank, can only be fully independent when its governor is free from internal and external pressures. The external influence can come from the international institutions, such as, IMF and the World Bank. The internal pressure comes from the ruling elites who control his posting, tenure, and his safety. Here we must not ignore the risks attached to a fully independent central bank governor. The central bank, in a way, controls the entire nation's economic life by controlling money supply and other policies. So if he makes a mistake then the whole nation will suffer. But if he is not honest and does things to benefit himself and his friends, then it will destroy the whole nation! Therefore, it is utmost important that we have checks and balances on the governor while making him independent.

There are two possible ways to ensure the independence of governor; elect him through direct public elections, or select him by inter-party consensus. Whichever method we choose to elect a governor, we must ensure that he is capable to do the job and he has the same guarantees given to the chief justice of Pakistan. That is, his tenure in the office is secure, and he cannot be removed just because the new government does not like him. To ensure the governor is free from external and internal influences, we could set

---

[11] Price stability simply means that the prices of goods and services should remain stable. That is, the prices either change very slowly or do not change at all in an economy.

the criteria of eligibility to become governor, and place limits that the governor must not breach. For example, to ensure that no foreign influence is effecting governor's decisions, the eligibility criterion for the governor must include that he has never been associated with any foreign country or institution, such as, IMF and World Bank, etc. He must remain in Pakistan during his full tenure, unless the government gives him permission to go abroad, in which case he must report fully who he had met, purposes of his meetings, and details of the things discussed etc. He must never contact any foreigner during his tenure unless he has specific permission from the government. Similarly, to ensure that he is free from internal influence, he must declare his interests and links with other interests through his relationship, friendship, or otherwise, as part of his eligibility. During the course of his duty he will need to meet several interests, but he must be required to gain permissions from government and provide full details as mentioned previously. The importance of his job may create risks for him and his family's lives, so he must be protected during and after his retirement until his death. A constitutional cover must be placed for the state bank's governor. If he receives any threats to his or his family's lives then it may affect his decisions. In all of such cases, he is required to notify the government or other authorities to ensure all such threats are removed and no such threats arise in future.

The governor of the state bank should be given a single task of ensuring price stability, that is, to control inflation. The target inflation should be no more than 2%. But it is utmost important that the governor is given a realistic amount of time to achieve this objective. Otherwise, to meet his target, he may make serious mistakes destroying our economy. The tools he has at his disposal are the control of money supply and setting of interest rates. The simple solution adopted by many central banks in the developed nations to control inflation, is to keep increasing interest rates because it reduces the disposable cash in the economy. Such a method will achieve the target of price stability, or controlling inflation, but it will destroy businesses and put people under financial burden. Therefore, the goals of target inflation should be realistic, so the governor is not put under undue pressure, so he could come up with solutions to create price stability while the economy runs smoothly.

Now let us turn to the second solution I suggested of implementing 100% Fractional Reserve Banking[12] , and how it could provide all the money the government needs for its operations. Our banking system is the same as what the West uses, that is, it is a Fractional Reserve Banking. This kind of banking system is an encroachment on the sovereignty of the State, because the private banks create money, which is the sole right of the state! Because the private banks create money, which is the reason they are filthy rich! That is why no one else apart from the friends and families of the top politicians can start new banks. Most of us think that the banks are rich because they invest in good businesses which make profits, but this is a fallacy. Let me clarify here that the private banks do not actually print money, but they create money just in their books, which has exactly the same effect as if the government issued new notes. This is one of the main reasons that the people, or the state, does not detect that anyone else is creating money apart from the state, so they cannot stop it. Some people may already know how the banks are creating money, but my job is to explain it in an easy to understand manner so everyone can understand it.

In most fractional reserve banking system the bank only needs to keep about 10% cash for all the money on its books. The central bank, that is, the state bank of Pakistan in our case decides the Reserve Requirements. This 10% limit was set in the West because they knew from their banking experience of several centuries that

---

[12] Fractional reserve banking is a system in which only a fraction of bank deposits are backed by actual cash-on-hand and the rest of the money is lent out.

this amount is more than enough, because people do not draw out all of their money at once. The reason the private banks can create money is because the state bank has set the reserve requirement to 10%. Let me explain this with some imaginary figures.

Let's assume that you deposit Rs.100,000 in your bank. You may think the bank could lend out only Rs.90,000 to other customers because it must keep Rs.10,000 in its safe, as the state bank tells them to keep a 10% cash reserves. Unfortunately, you are wrong in thinking that because the banks could lend out Rs.899,990.79 for your deposit of Rs.100,000. This means the banks could lend out almost nine times the actual deposit anyone makes. So in this example, they had created about Rs.799,990.79, which did not exist before, but we cannot see it because it only exists on the books of the banks. Now you may want to know, how do they actually create money? It is a complex process so I will not go into too much detail. The main reason that the banks can create money is because they do not lend once but many times. So in the above example where you deposited Rs.100,000, theoretically the bank could lend 109 times from this deposit. Let us do some calculations based on your deposit of Rs.100,000.

In the first instance you deposited Rs.100,000, so the bank could lend Rs.90,000 against it, and keeps reserves of Rs.10,000. But now the Rs.90,000 that was lent out, becomes banks new deposit, because the bank argues that it will eventually be repaid. So the bank makes an entry into its ledger with a new deposit of Rs.90,000, which does exist. So against this new virtual deposit, the bank can lend Rs.81,000 and keep Rs.9,000 as reserves. Similarly, this Rs.81,000, which were just lent out, again becomes bank's new reserve. This means that it could lend a further Rs.72,900 against another virtual deposit of Rs.81,000, while keeping Rs.8,100 reserves. This process continues until there is no virtual deposit left to be lent. The total lending possible is Rs.899,990.79. This means there is now Rs.799,990.79 of new money in existence, which was not there before. It does not end here, because the bank will also receive interest on the loan it has issued. If the interest rates were 10% then the bank will receive an extra   Rs.89,999.08. The bank would have made a profit of Rs.989,989.87 in just one year if all the loans were paid back in a year. This is how the bankers get rich!

The above example shows us how the banks make huge profits and also increase our money supply which leads to further price inflation. I am not concerned with the banks making profits, but they must not have the power to create money, because it also creates inflation in our country. The power to create money is the sole right of the state, and if anyone else has the same power then that is challenging State's sovereignty. Would it not be better if the state made all the profits that the banks are making? This way, the government will not need to borrow money or raise our taxes to run its operations.

So how could we resolve the banking issue without causing any financial upset? The simple answer is to take away the function of money supply from the private banks by increasing the Fractional Reserve requirements to 100%. This is also called Full Reserve Banking. The changing of fractional reserve requirement does not need passing a new bill because our state bank has the power to alter it. When the full reserve banking is implemented then the private banks will be unable to lend any money, because they need to keep all the cash deposits in their reserves, available for withdrawal by their customers. This makes the banks just Deposit Institutions, which the bankers are not going to like, and start charging their customers fees for their accounts and transactions etc. They may even want to come out of banking because it will not be profitable anymore. I will discuss how we could tackle this issue later but we need to consider first some of the important issues arising out of implementing full reserve banking.

I can see three important issues developing if we implemented full reserve banking; the bankers with their political and financial connections will try to force the government not to implement full reserve banking; they will call up all of their loans early to cripple our economy; or they may argue on the finer points of full reserve banking with regards to loans to avoid paying the government interest. Let us consider each issue in detail.

We know the bankers have political and financial links with powerful politicians, so they will try to force the government not to implement full reserve banking. As I mentioned earlier that the politicians need to decide to either stand with the public who are many, or stand with their friends who are only a few. Politicians will definitely benefit by standing with the people, because they are too many and if they were to turn against the politicians, then it will be the end of their politics. On the other hand, their powerful banker friends are only a few in numbers, and if they are made poor with new banking rules, then they are unable to harm politicians anyway. Another thing that the media could do is to create public awareness about this important issue, so to create a public pressure on the government to implement full reserve banking.

The second issue is that the bankers may decide to cripple our economy by calling up all loans early. This will create widespread bankruptcies, businesses closures, unemployment, and above all shrinking our money supply to a level where the country will go into a spiral of deflation. They will have a perfect excuse to call up their loans earlier, because they could say that under new rules we need to have all the money in our vaults available for withdrawals. If they called up all of their loans, that is, if they asked all their borrowers to repay their loans earlier, then this would mean many businesses and individuals will not be able to repay their loans, so their assets will be auctioned off. This will cause widespread business closures, which will cause unemployment. This will also create deflation because a lot of things will be for sale but many people will not have money to buy these assets. This problem could be resolved easily but it must be done in advance. I am not a lawyer or a parliamentarian so I am not sure which route we will need to take. But I can say this, that we just need a simple law or condition on the banks which will prevent them from asking their borrowers to pay back their loans earlier than their original term they had agreed with borrowers. Perhaps, the state bank has authority to issue a notice to all banks that no loan could be asked to be repaid before its original term. If the state bank has such an authority then all is well. But if it does not, then we may have to pass a bill in the parliament under banking laws. Whichever method we need to use, we must ensure this before even thinking of implementing full reserve banking to avoid economic collapse.

But the bankers will protest that if the government prevents them from calling up their loans earlier, then how could they ensure they have all the cash in their vaults available for withdrawals? The simple answer would be that 'we cannot let you put financial burdens on businesses and individuals, because when they took out loans, they had not thought that you will ask them to repay their loans earlier, even though you may have the right to ask them to repay loans earlier according to terms and conditions of loans.' Secondly, we will help you fulfil the full reserve banking requirement by lending you the money you need on reasonable interest rates. But our condition is that you reduce the interest rates of your existing loans as we dictate. We do not need to worry about where the government is going to find money to lend to bankers, because the government is the sole issuer of money, it only needs to add an entry to its ledger that it has lent money to these banks. This will not create any new money or inflation because that money was already created by the banks, but now only the ownership of that money has been transferred over to the state.

Here, a very important thing to remember is that the banks created a lot of loans, so created a lot of money in the process, but they had very little deposits from the people and businesses. So it would not be difficult for them to fill up their vaults with the cash to cover people's deposits, or it will only be small gap, which they will be willing to borrow from the government. So this way they will try to relinquish their major responsibility of full reserve banking by not covering the loans, because they will argue that it did not come from anyone's deposit. But we need to remind them that the loans they issued under Fractional Reserve Banking were created by them for which they did not have authority. The money they created, actually belonged to the State. So you must also fund all those loans running into billions, and not just the actual deposits. Since these loans are so large that it will be impossible for the bankers to fulfil, even with new deposits, this is because the new deposits create new responsibilities. The only solution for the bankers is to borrow this money from the State Bank and pay interest on it. They will need to pay the capital slowly, which could only come from their profits which would shrink under new full reserve banking. It would be better for state that the bankers never paid the capital, because this way the state will have a constant income from interest on this loan to banks. The bankers will have no options but to accept. The government can then reduce the financial burdens of thousands of businesses and millions of individuals by reducing their loan interest rates, which will win the government many more votes in the next elections. However, the government must ensure two things; it does not cause inflation by reducing interest rates too quickly, and it does not encourage new irresponsible borrowing because the interest rates are lower now.

If the government reduced the interest rates too quickly then it will increase the disposable income of businesses and individuals, because now their loan payments have reduced. This has an effect of increasing money supply, which creates inflation. We do not want to help people and business by reducing their interest rates, and then take that money away from them by creating inflation. This will also be bad for the government from a political perspective. The government could reduce interest rates by small fractions, such as,

0.5% reduction or 0.25% reduction every few months. While these reductions may be excellent from the financial point of view, they are not very effective politically, because the reductions in loan payments will be so small that people will not notice them. So to help politicians win more votes, I would suggest on 1% to 2% reduction every six months or so, with bigger reductions just a few months before general elections. If the government spreads out benefits to public over a long period of time, then people will remember the good things the government had done for them, and may vote for such a government!

The other issue I mentioned above is that more new borrowers will come to market when the interest rates are lower. We do not want people to be indebted too much because it is bad for people, and bad for economy. Musharraf's government tried to create fake growth by increasing lending and spending, which put more people in debt and increased inflation without any lasting growth. We do not want such superficial growth, so we must control our credit by tightening up our lending policy. The state bank should issue guidelines on lending to prevent bad loans. Further, because the banks cannot lend now from their deposits and they must borrow it from state bank, then the state bank could control the money supply. It could work out how much money it will increase every year, and then issue monthly figures to banks telling them how much they could borrow to lend out.

Lastly, as I mentioned earlier that with the introduction of full reserve banking, the bankers may impose fees on accounts and transactions. They may also want to get out of banking. When I suggested the full reserve banking, then I never had any bad intentions towards bankers, because they serve an important role in our economy. So we need to ensure that they remain profitable and stay in business to help our economy. But how do we make the banks profitable when there is full reserve banking?

All we have to do to help banks is that the banks could lend money, but any money they lend must be borrowed from state bank, on which the banks will pay an interest. We could make a compromise that the banks could charge no more than 2% or 3% interest rates on top of the interest they pay to state bank on that loan. The exact appropriate interest rates could be worked out by the experts. This will give bankers profits. Good news will come to bankers when the government implements electronic money, which I have discussed in the next section. With the introduction of electronic money, every transaction will be done through banks and the banks will be able to charge businesses for their services. But these charges should be small and fixed, so the businesses stay profitable and the prices do not go up for customers. However, the banks should never be allowed to charge individual banking customers. This will greatly increase banker's profits.

Finally, the government must sell all the commercial banks it owns, but it must not privatise them because it is not good for the people. Instead the government must sell them to public by converting them into POCs which will reduce poverty. I have discussed POCs elsewhere in this book in detail. Another benefit of private banking with full reserve banking is that it will end corruption automatically from banking. In the past, the corrupt politicians borrowed money from banks with the intention of never paying them back. They then had those loans forgiven by just paying the 10% of loans. Have you noticed that the banks were happy to accept only 10%? This is because under fractional reserve banking system, 10% was the only money that the bank gave out from their deposits, and the rest of the 90% was created from thin air by the banks. But that money came into circulation, causing inflation. This type of corruption will end automatically in a full reserve banking system because when the banks will give anyone a loan then they borrow it from state banks, which should be returned. If that money is forgiven then where the banks are going to find any money to pay back the state bank? They cannot give it from their deposits because they must keep 100% of deposits all the time. But for this to work, the government must not own any banks, because they will forgive loans of politicians because the government will be responsible for all loans.

Electronic Money

As I mentioned previously, we could solve many problems just by adopting a cashless economic system, that is, an electronic money system. An electronic money system is where we do not use cash notes for our everyday transactions, but instead we use bank cards. When no one uses cash then it is impossible for anyone to dodge their taxes. In fact, the tax could be collected automatically through banking systems and transferred to tax office daily. This way we could get rid of more than 80% of tax office employees, saving us large sums of money, and eliminating huge amounts of corruption which the tax inspectors were engaged in. We could get rid of Bhata Mafia by adopting electronic money, because there will be no cash to pay them. The only way they could get money is by traders transferring money into the accounts of Bhata Mafia. If they accept money into their banks, then it is easy to catch them and freeze their accounts. We could eradicate kidnapping for ransom, because there will be no cash available to pay the kidnappers. Similarly, the terrorism can be reduced drastically and we could break their networks by starving them of cash, without which they will be unable to operate. Terrorist get their funds from kidnapping for ransom or bhata, both of which can be eliminated by using a cashless system. Everyday crimes will also reduce by using electronic money. There are many more benefits for such a system, but how do we ensure this system works as it is intended?

Electronic money is already in use in Pakistan but only at high end retailers. In the West, I think more than 60% of transactions are done using bank cards. We need to develop a system where we reduce the cash available to bare minimum. First thing we need to do is to buy the very best, and fail safe banking technology, and then improve it to make it forgery proof. For example, the current systems either use customer's signatures or a Personal Identification Number (PIN), either of which could be forged or discovered by thieves. If we are going to implement a full electronic money system, then our systems must be much more sophisticated than above mentioned system. We should verify the cardholder's identification with three methods. By identifying cardholder with his Iris, fingerprints, and PIN. We need to have a PIN so that if there is a failure in the system then the transactions could still continue. However, our PIN numbers must be more than four digits. The Point of Sale (POS) terminals must have a camera and a scanner built in, as well as the PIN entry system. The camera should be angled in such a way that it could easily detect the Iris of the user. The card should not have the full Biological Data (Iris and finger prints) in them for security reasons, but it should only have part of the biological data. The terminal will connect to remote systems and will send the part biological data, which the system will match with the rest of the data to authorise transactions. I think the architects will come up with some better solutions, but we need to bear in mind that the data must be safe, and it could not be stolen or copied by anyone, in case someone loses their cards etc. What about very small businesses, such as, peddlers, plumbers, labourers, buses etc? They should all be issued with small mobile POS terminals with the same features and safety mechanisms, but they should work on mobile phone networks. The busses are a special case because they cannot wait for everyone to put their cards in the terminal and make a transaction. We need a contactless system for buses, which is currently used in the West for small transactions. All we have to do is to set a maximum amount for contactless system. The banks must provide small businesses these devices free, and charge small transaction fees. In fact, the state bank must regulate such prices in consultation with businesses and banks, so while the banks make profits, the businesses do not need to increase their prices, and the individual customers do not lose out. The individual customers must never be charged for accounts or transactions. The most important of all, we need to have an emergency plan and a system, in case an enemy attacks our electronic money system. The aim of this emergency system should be to protect businesses, banks, and customers, and the normal business operation must not be interrupted. Any small interruption will cause a loss of billions of rupees and halt the entire nations' life. We should have security specialists whose job is to disrupt the system. They must be given all the information of the system to break it. Then they should attack in a small town with full permission from the team responsible for implementing and testing emergency measures. This way we will continue to find weakness and correct them, and this will test our emergency plans. Let us now briefly discuss, how we will implement the system?

As we are issuing POS terminals to businesses, we need to issue bank cards to everyone in the country, even the children. But the parents could set a daily limit on children's bank cards for safety. Once all the people are issued cards, then we need to slowly remove cash from the system. All we have to do is to remove the large notes from the economy of Rs.5,000, Rs.1,000, Rs.500, and Rs.100. First month, remove all the Rs.5,000 notes by making a public announcement that police will have the power to confiscate anyone carrying Rs.5,000 notes. But the police must give them the serial numbers for the notes confiscated. Everyone is scared of police, so no one is going to carry any notes at all. Next month we need to remove Rs.1,000 notes and so on until the biggest denomination note left in the system is Rs.50. So after removing all the large denomination notes, we need to announce that anyone carrying more than Rs.500 will have the extra amount confiscated. At this stage, all the banks must ensure that anyone with no matter how many bank accounts with so many banks could not take out more than Rs.500 a month from their machines. Perhaps, a central system will ensure the compliance of this rule. I think that we could be fully functional with electronic money in about six months. Two to three months will be required to develop and manufacture the POS terminals and opening accounts for all the populations, and the next four months to remove cash from the system.

Foreign Exchange Reserves

There had been much talk in media about our foreign exchange reserves (Forex reserves) depleting fast, and a need to go to IMF for a loan to correct this position. The issue of our foreign exchange reserves depletion is similar to our circular debt crisis of electricity. Every time the government pays off and clears the circular debt, it starts to build up again, because the government does not correct the issues with the NEPRA. Similarly, every time we will get a loan from IMF, the foreign exchange reserves will start to reduce again as we pay IMF, or import non-essential goods, and do not increase our exports. Let us first try to understand what foreign exchange reserve is, and why we need it?

When we buy goods and services from other countries, then we need to pay them with their currencies. For example, if we buy petrol from Saudi Arabia then we need to pay them in Saudi Riyals, because they cannot use our Rupee there to buy goods and services. In reality, things are not as simple. Countries usually trade with one another without exchanging currencies for each transaction, but instead, at specific periods, they calculate how much one owes the other, then the owing country pays the other with their currency. So if we import more than we export, as we do, then we need foreign currency with which to pay them. However, we do not hold the currency of every country we trade with. Instead, we hold a Foreign Exchange Reserve Currency with which to pay other countries. There are really two major reserve currencies, US Dollar and Euro. There are a few other reserve currencies but they are not significant.

As you can see that we have no choice but to hold US dollars as our foreign exchange reserve, if we want to trade with any other country. But the foreign exchange reserves do not really mean the dollars or Euros. Strictly speaking, foreign-exchange reserves should only be made up of foreign currency deposits and bonds. But it also includes gold reserves, and special drawing rights (SDRs). This is what we call Official Foreign Exchange Reserves or International Reserves. Generally the central banks hold foreign exchange reserves for at least three months worth of imports. Even though we still have more than the minimum requirement of foreign exchange reserves, but to the rest of the world it seems that we would not be able to pay them for their goods. So it drives down the value of our rupee, which adds more burden on the rupee, because we now need more rupees to buy the same amount of US dollars or Euros to pay with. Let us now try to understand what are the main reasons we need the foreign exchange reserves?

Even though the foreign exchange reserves are used to pay for the imports but this is not its only purpose. The real purpose of foreign exchange reserves is to defend the value of its domestic currency. By buying its domestic currency with the international reserve, the central bank can maintain and stabilise the value of its domestic currency. Further, by keeping enough reserves, the central bank can avoid currency attacks which could bring down an entire economy like the Asian Financial Crisis, which started in Thailand in 1997. They did not have enough foreign exchange reserves to pay the short-term investors, who pulled their investment out of the country on a short notice. This is one reason we should monitor our stock exchange closely because it is the weakest link, and we will discuss it in more detail in another chapter. Anyhow, there is a strong need to hold enough foreign exchange reserves to preserve the value of local currency, and to avert any currency attacks. But how much should we hold?

To avoid any currency attacks, experts say that we should hold Forex reserves equal to short-term foreign investments. But things are not as simple as that, and we should look at other ways to protect against currency attacks. For example, as I mentioned elsewhere, we could avoid any currency attacks by discouraging foreign investors pulling their investment out, all at once. We should require a 30 days' notice if anyone wants to sell their investment on the stocks market of a value of more than Rs.1,000,000. You can set a different amount but this is just an example. This does not mean they would have to wait for 30 days, but we should strive to let them sell in minutes. However, this will give us an early signal of a likely currency attack because many people would want to sell their investments if an attack is likely. But because everyone will know they need to give a 30 days' notice, they will never even try such a thing in the first place. These are the things that have already happened, so no one will try the same tricks again. So we should be alert to any crisis developing using different methods, because people would want to make quick profits, or to achieve a specific objective for international institutions.

Experts would want us to keep a higher forex reserve so we could avert currency attacks, and preserve the value of our currency. I would argue against it because there are other factors that will keep the value of our currency, and there are drawbacks to a high amount of forex reserves. About 70% of world reserves are in US dollars, rest in Euros, but some in other currencies. But we know that the value of US dollar has been decreasing for many years. This means that if we keep a large Forex reserves like China, Japan, or Saudi Arabia, then we will lose our wealth, because the value of our reserves would be decreasing even though the amount does not decrease. We should aim at developing a Sovereign Wealth Fund (SWF) for stability and liquidity and at the same time controlling inflation. Let us take a look at the historic facts and analyse how they affect us and what we could do about them.

Since 1944, when the Bretton Woods Treaty was signed, a few organisations were born, which now severely affect every individual on this planet. For example, UNO, IMF, World Bank, BIS, WTO etc are all evil organisations who enslave the entire world. Most people are led to believe that these organisations are divine institutions, but they do not tell us, which divinity these organisations worship? They worship a divinity called USA.

Under Bretton Woods, the US Dollar became the world reserve currency. But America further enslaved everyone on this planet by forcing the OPEC to price and sell petroleum in US dollars. At first sight, you may not understand the implications of this act - what does it mean for the rest of the world? But we know that every country on this planet needs petroleum, without which everything stops. But to buy petroleum, they all need US dollars. Where are they going to get these dollars from? They will have to get it from US because that is the only country who could issue them. This has created an artificial but a permanent demand for the US dollars. So every country in the world who imports petroleum is forced to trade with the USA. This gives USA the greatest advantage of consuming the world's products in return for dollar notes, which they constantly print. USA has achieved with this permanent demand of US dollars, what the Romans, Muslims, or Mongolian empires could not achieve with their blood. They were unsuccessful in conquering the wealth of entire world, but USA has done it with the help of its dollar. Let me explain. Most people consider the diamond, gold, and silver to be the wealth of a nation. For example, Indians protest that their largest diamond, Koh-i-Noor, has been stolen by the British. But there is no wealth in these metals. The real wealth of a nation is its labour, without which a country cannot produce anything. What the Indians and others, who were under British Empire, should complain about is the theft of their labour. Without the labourers who worked in sugar plantations or produced other goods, the British could not have gained any wealth. But the America is a strange and a sad phenomenon, because its wealth was built with the theft of the labour of African slaves and slaughter of millions of Red Indians. It continues to adopt the same policy of stealing the labour of the rest of the world by forcing them to trade their goods for paper dollar notes! Wealth of the nations is constantly transferred over to USA without them physically conquering the world!

Well, until the world stops using US dollars, we have no option but to be slaves of Americans, and give up our labour of sweat and blood for a few US dollars, so we could buy petroleum! If the Pakistanis do not want to be slaves of Americans, then they need to give up on the luxuries of imported goods and reduce our petroleum use. Until we decide what we may do in future, but we still need American dollars. But how do we get them? There are three main ways we can get the dollars. By borrowing, Pakistani expats sending dollars back home, or by trading our goods with the USA. As I mentioned before, the foreign exchange reserves will always be a problem like the circular debt of our electricity, until we make fundamental changes to our imports and exports, reduce reliance on petroleum, and make our currency a world reserve currency. I have suggested several solutions to address these issues elsewhere in this book, but here I will concentrate on the foreign exchange reserve. See other solutions I suggested, such as, Alcohol for Oil Programme, start trading with poor countries using Pakistani rupee as Reserve Currency to move it towards a full reserve currency status, and making rupee stronger by reducing inflation and economic growth.

The best solution is to address the fundamentals. Our imports are far higher than our exports. If we can equalise our exports and imports then we will not have any foreign exchange liability, and we will not need any US dollars. But it is difficult to increase our exports quickly to match with the imports, but we could always reduce our imports by convincing our people to make and use local goods until we can afford imported goods. Without going into the breakdown of each item that we import, we need to discuss just a few major items which can lead towards solutions.

Our trade deficit was $21 billion last year. This means that we imported a lot more than we exported. Most of this was made up of petroleum and fertilizers imports, but other large imports included cell phones, palm oil, make up items, and tea etc. We would need a certain amount of petroleum because most of our electricity is produced with it. But in the short run we could increase tax on the petroleum to discourage its overuse. This may help reduce some imports. But in the long run we need to provide safe, clean, and punctual public transport to encourage people to give up cars. We need to run media campaigns to encourage people to reduce consuming imported goods, such as, palm oil, make up, and tea etc. If every person gives up one cup of tea every day, then we could reduce our tea imports significantly. But this is a short term measure and we need to permanently reduce this reliance on imported tea by planting our own tea. Several studies have been carried out that suggested some of our land is favourable for tea production, which could produce much more than the country needs, and of high quality as well. We imported about $700 million worth of cell phones in 2012. If we can produce our own cell phones then it will not only reduce our import bill, but also provide jobs to thousands of people, and it could also be a source of export income. I have discussed only a few items, but we should also adopt similar approach for other items that we import. So we could turn our dependence on imported goods into self-reliance and a source of wealth.

Another way to solve the lack of forex reserves is by encouraging our expat Pakistanis to use Pakistani banks for saving and current accounts. If our banks play right then it is possible to have a large enough forex reserves than we need in a matter of a few months. But the banks will have to match their services to that of UK or USA banks before Pakistanis could be convinced to use Pakistani banks branches abroad for their everyday use. The banks will have to get rid of bureaucracy and treat their customers with respect and care. I would guess there are perhaps about 10 million Pakistani adult expats around the world, and if everyone deposited just $1,000 in their savings accounts then that is $10,000,000,000. By depositing $2,000 will instantly double this forex reserve. But if they all had their salary paid into current accounts of Pakistani banks, then we will have hundreds of billions of dollars of forex reserves. But the government must never deceive expats like they did to foreign exchange account holders in past.

Controlling Inflation

Everyone knows what inflation is and why it is bad? When the prices of goods and services rise in a country over a period of time, then we need more money to buy the same things. But if our incomes are fixed, then we do not have enough money to buy the things that we need, and we have to do without some of these things. This causes hardship for the poor, and to some extent for the middle class. In fact, our middle class is becoming poor due to high inflation and their fixed incomes. Let us discuss how the inflation is measured, its causes, and how we could control it.

Inflation is measured through Consumer Price Index (CPI). That is, it measures the rise in prices over a period of time of the goods and services which an average family usually buys. The state bank listed the inflation rates between 9.7% and 13.3% per annum between June 2011 and June 2012, with an average of about 11%. This rate of inflation seems to be manipulated by the government and the real rate of inflation is definitely much higher. But even if we accept the published rate of inflation, it is still too high. And if we do a crude mental calculation using the *Rule of 72*[13], then it takes only about six years for the prices to double at this rate. To keep pace with price increases, the wages will have to double every six years at this rate. If the wages were increased at the same rate as inflation then there will not be a problem, but the wages are slow to increase than the inflation.

Now let us see how the inflation occurs? Almost all economists agree that the increase in the money supply, above and beyond its GDP, is the root cause of inflation. It means that if the GDP has not increased, but the government has decided to increase the money supply by printing more money, then the inflation will occur. We know that our government is running its printing press on full speed!

As I explained earlier that the government is not the only entity which increases our money supply, but the banks also increase our money supply by providing loans on the money they do not have, with the magic of Fractional Reserve Banking System, which is even dangerous than the government printing money. But why does the government prints money? There are two major reasons. Firstly, the government does not have the money it needs for its operations, and it cannot get it by any other means. Secondly, inflation is the easiest way for the government to tax people without them realising it. You can call it *Inflation Tax* or *Seigniorage*. Inflation is a clever way for the government to take money away from people. Let me explain how the government confiscates your money through inflation. Suppose that you have Rs.3,000 in your bank and the price of 20 kilo flour bag is Rs.300. You can buy 10 bags of flour with this money. But suppose the government doubles money supply which reduces the value of your money to half. This means that the

---

[13] The Rule of 72 is a crude method of estimating the number of years required for an investment to double at a given interest rate. It can be used for many quick calculations. For example, if the inflation was about 12% a year, then you can calculate how long it will take to double the prices, simply by dividing 72 by 12.

price of 20 kilo bag has now increased to Rs.600. The amount of money in your account has not changed because of inflation and it is still Rs.3,000, but now you can only buy 5 flour bags with it. The government has taken the other 5 flour bags of you in *Inflation Tax* and you did not even realise!

The governments, which are inefficient in collecting taxes, rely on inflation to get money from the people. But this is very cruel method for the government to collect taxes, because inflation does not distinguish between rich and poor. The poor pays exactly the same amount of inflation tax as a rich man, but the poor man does not have the same income. That is why, you see many middle class people becoming poor with inflation, and poor becoming the poorest!

I have already explained that the banks also create inflation by giving out loans under Fractional Reserve Banking System. This is because they create money, increasing our money supply. So to stop inflation, we will also need to get rid of Fractional Reserve Banking and replace it with Full Reserve Banking.

Apart from the government and private banks responsible for inflation by creating money and increasing our money supply, there is one more group of people who creates price inflation. That group is of large traders who monopolise production of commodities. They are engaged in price fixing so people have no option but to pay a higher price. Secondly, they increase prices by hoarding. Unfortunately, Pakistan suffers from both the monopoly and hoarding. We do have laws against monopoly and hoarding but they are never implemented. We need to have an independent department, which has honest inspectors who cannot be corrupted, to implement these policies throughout the country.

Retailers are also a problem because they never have fixed prices for any goods, so they charge what they like. Further, they sell low quality goods disguised as high quality. There are so many fake products in the market that the buyer cannot distinguish between the real and fake goods. This is known in economics as the problem of *Imperfect Information* because the buyer is not aware of the quality or durability of the products sold, but the retailer is fully aware of them. There must be some rules which require all the retailers to publish their prices by putting the price tags on each item, so public is aware of prices and does not need to bargain. We need to try different things to get rid of Imperfect Information from our retail sector to make our markets efficient. Imperfect information may not have direct links to inflation, but it does play a role.

To sum up, the inflation could be controlled by the government implementing Full Reserve Banking and adopting electronic money. Because this will produce huge sums of tax revenue for government, so they will not need to print any more money. This will also prevent private banks to increase our money supply. These are the real cause of inflation and if these are addressed then there will be no inflation. As discussed above, other indirect forms of inflation are monopoly, hoarding and imperfect information. We need to implement rules to tackle these problems to prevent indirect inflation.

Domestic & Foreign Debts

According to the State Bank's annual report of January 29, 2013; in June 2012, Pakistan owed Rs.6,460.2 billion (in 2013 prices) to rest of the world, while it owed Rs.7,638.3 billion to Pakistani banks including other liabilities. I noticed three important things when reading the report's section 7 titled Domestic & External Debt. The government was moving towards debt trap[14], it paid nine times more interest to local banks than the foreign banks for almost similar

---

[14] Debt Trap is a situation where you add on a new debt in order to pay an existing debt. This creates a situation where the debt will never be repaid and the government will continue to pay interest.

amount of loan, and there was a clear transfer of wealth from the poor to the rich!

The report admits that government persistently spent more than it earned, for the last 6 years. It borrowed money from local private banks at higher interest rates to cover government spending, and now the Governor of state bank thinks that Pakistan could move into a debt trap, meaning, it will never be able to repay its debts and continue to pay interest forever.

According to report, the government paid Rs.811.2 billion in interest to domestic banks, while it paid only Rs.89.8 billion to rest of the world. So the biggest problem is not the interest payment to the rest of the world, but is to our domestic banks. Now let us compare the domestic interest payment with direct tax we collected. FBR [15] collected Rs.731.9 billion from all of us, but the government took that money and gave it all to domestic banks. Then they paid another R.79.3 billion to local banks. Do you see something strange here? Well, I see a clear transfer of wealth from public to the owners of private banks! It seems the government is acting like a tax collector for the bankers!

But then our politicians talk about collecting more taxes from everyone. What for? So the government could give it to the bankers who are their friends? I have already mentioned above how we can pay the domestic debt off just by setting the Fractional Reserve Requirement to 100%. This will pay off all the government debts, and it will be a way for the government to earn hundreds of billions of rupees every year. So they will not have to raise more taxes, and leave the people to have more money in their pockets.

---

[15] FBR stands for Federal Board of Revenue.

Paying off Foreign Debts

According to the State Bank's annual report 2013, in June 2012 Pakistan owed $65.8 billion dollars to the rest of the world. The three major lenders are Multilaterals, Paris Club, and IMF, to whom we owed $25.4, $15.0, and $7.3 billion respectively in year 2012. These three lenders together make up 72% of our external debt. The report then goes on to say that our debt servicing was reduced due to two important factors among others, the exports being lower and devaluation of Pakistani rupee. The above three debts can easily be paid off legally without us paying a single dollar. If we adopt the legal position I am proposing, then we will also prevent future rulers from borrowing from abroad, which will keep Pakistanis free from foreign debt. If we decided not to use this method then I can show you a method which will allow us at least to repay IMF loan without paying a dollar, using SDRs, the currency with which they gave us the loan.

I do not know how anyone defines debt, but it is clear to me that, the debt is an instrument with which the wealth is transferred from the borrower to the lender! Let me show this with a simple example. Suppose someone borrows Rs.10,000 on an interest rate of 10% for ten years. By the time he had paid off his loan, he would have paid an extra Rs.5,858 to the lender. That extra Rs.5,858 was earned by the borrower with his blood and sweat, but he transferred this wealth to the lender. This is the reason I am against government borrowing money from internal or external banks or institutions. If we look at the IMF and the countries who borrowed from it, then we will find there had been a *Net Transfer of Wealth* from the poor countries to IMF. Are we prepared to transfer our wealth to rich nations who do not need it?

Apart from the transfer of wealth through debt, there are two other major problems with borrowing from IMF and other foreign nations or institutions. Almost all of these debts are denominated in US dollars. When the dollar increases its value against our Rupee, or our

Rupee loses its value against US dollar, then our debt increases automatically, because we need more rupees to buy the same amount of dollars

On the other hand, when IMF gives loan, it imposes conditions, which ultimately destroy the borrowing country's economy. For example, these conditions state that the borrowing country should reduce public spending, increase taxes, remove all subsidies, remove trade tariffs, adopts market economy, privatise state enterprises, and devalue its currency to improve exports etc.   Other conditions dictate, directly or indirectly, that the borrowing country should appoint two important officers of the government on the recommendations of IMF to oversee IMF conditions are being met. These two posts are the Governor of State Bank and the Finance Minister, which are usually IMF's cronies. As I mentioned already that these two officers have the power to create prosperity or cripple the economy, depending on how they run their departments. Why do we give so much power to IMF to dictate our elected Prime Minister, who to appoint?

Another condition the IMF imposes is to devalue our currency to help our exports. But improving export is not the IMF's true intention. There are two hidden agenda's behind this. By devaluing our currency, we make things cheaper for US, so it buys things from us at rock bottom prices. This is the main reason that the US is consuming more than its global share of the world's products! The second thing is that by devaluing our currency, all we do is increase our debt which is denominated in foreign currency. Let us take a quick look at how does devaluing currency affects the loans.

Suppose we took out a loan of Rs.50 billion from a local bank and then devalued our currency by 100% then it would not matter much, because all we need to pay back the loan is Rs.50 billion, which is exactly how much was borrowed. In such a case, the government wins but the bank loses out because the value of Rs.50 billion it received is now worth only Rs.25 billion. So this tells us that a loan taken out by the government in its own currency is easier to pay no matter what is the value of underlying currency. But on the other hand, when the loan is denominated in US dollars then devaluing our currency has adverse effect on our debt.

Suppose that this time we do not borrow from local banks but from IMF. Even though the IMF does not give us US dollars, but it requires that we pay them back in dollars. Suppose we borrow $50 billion and the value of our currency was Rs.50 to $1 dollar. If the value of our currency decreases and now we need Rs.100 to buy the same $1 dollar, then our debt has doubled in reality. The important thing to note here is the amount of loan does not change but it remains $50 billion. Instead, by devaluing our currency, our ability repay is reduced. So when IMF tells us to devalue our currency to improve exports, the primary purpose is to reduce our ability to repay the loan. So that the constant transfer of our wealth to IMF continues forever!

By the way, if we take a look at our imports and export then it is apparent that we are a net importer country. We have nothing to gain by devaluing our currency, because we do not export to the rest of the world very much like other countries, such as, China and Asian Tigers. But by devaluing our currency, all we do is reduce the value of our exports, creating a bigger gap between our import/export balances. Those economists who tell us to devalue our currency are actually on the payrolls of IMF and other foreign institutions. Let me break this myth of devaluing currency to improve exports with another example.

If a country needed to devalue its currency to sell more goods, then why the USA or Europe does not devalue their currencies because we buy a lot of their goods, from shampoos to cars? We are a poor country, but we still buy the expensive items from the rich nations whose currency is much stronger than ours. If the IMFs prescription of devaluing our currency to increase exports was true, then the USA, Europe, and Japan would not be able to sell their shampoo, make-up, chocolates, and cars to us because their currency value is higher. The rich nations do not devalue their currencies because they are not stupid like us!

Before I could propose a solution for how to pay off our foreign debts including IMF, we first need to understand how the IMF works. There are 188 countries who are members IMF, but there are 29 founding countries. Like UN, and World Bank, IMF is also located in USA. Usually, wherever an organisation is located, it usually serves that country, and IMF is no exception. IMF allocates Special Drawing Rights (SDR) to its member states. As the name implies, it is just an allocation and nothing else. It's just another form of children's board game, *Monopoly*. In theory, if Pakistan is allocated 1 billion SDRs, then Pakistan should be able to convert them into US dollars, Japanese Yens, British Pound, or Euros. But these four countries are not obliged to give Pakistan their Dollars, Yens, Pound, or Euros for the SDRs we have. In reality, the SBP has directly converted SDRs to rupees according to IMF exchange rates. How clever? Converting SDRs to rupees is just a self-deception because what did the SBP do, is to print money against SDRs. Then why not just print money without having SDRs? By converting from SDR, we owe Real Money to IMF, but if we just printed money, then we did not owe anything to IMF! Both methods create exactly the same amount of inflation.

On the other hand, if Pakistan uses these SDRs, then it must return these SDRs with only US Dollars, Yens, Pounds, or Euros. You cannot take these SDRs to a currency exchanger to convert them into dollars or into any other currency. IMF says that SDR is not a currency but it still publishes an exchange rate for it. How strange? If it is not a currency then why there is an exchange rate for it?

From the above discussion, you would have gathered by now that when we get a loan from the IMF, we do not get actual money. But instead, all the IMF does is create an entry into its ledgers that it has given us money. Our state bank then makes an entry into our ledger that we have received a loan from IMF without ever receiving a dime! I am not sure who shall I congratulate, IMF for its cleverness, or our government for its self-deception?

Let us now discuss how we could repay these foreign loans easily, or without paying them anything. There are three methods to repay these loans, including one special method reserved for IMF. We could repay in the old fashion way by paying them cash for everything that is deemed owed; we could declare our foreign debt as Odious and not pay anything; or in the case of IMF, we could create large enough money and then convert them into SDRs and give it to IMF. Let us now briefly discuss each method.

Our major foreign loans are made up of loans from IMF, Paris Club, and Multilaterals. Loans from Multilaterals means there are many countries involved in these loans, and we may not want to spoil our relationships with some of them, so we may need to just pay them what we borrowed. This would mean we would have to come up with cash to pay them. But if the government implements full reserve banking, as I proposed, then we will have plenty of spare cash to repay our foreign loans. We must get rid of all of our loans, only then we could grow economically.

The second method is to declare all of our foreign loans as Odious, because this loan money was not spent on people, but it went into the pockets of politicians. This is my favourite method because it will prevent all future politicians from getting foreign loans to fill up their pockets. It will become clear, how it will prevent corruption by politicians, as we discuss this further.

Many countries, including USA had declared their debts as odious, and not paid a penny. Odious Debt is an accepted theory in International Law. A debt is odious if a regime borrows money, but does not use it for the welfare of its people, instead uses it to oppress its people or to fill its own pockets. If a debt is declared odious, then the nation is not obliged to repay the loan. Instead, the loan is considered a personal loan of the regime members. The interesting fact is that if we successfully declared some of our loans as odious, then the IMF and other lenders will go after our corrupt politicians for the money they borrowed on behalf of our country, because now that loan is considered their personal loan. In such a situation, there will be no escape for corrupt politicians, because IMF and other foreign lenders have the power to cease their Swiss Accounts and other assets around the world. If this happens then no politician in right mind, will borrow money from abroad and fill his pockets.

However, we have to satisfy certain conditions before a debt could be considered odious. The most important condition, as mentioned above, is to prove that the loan was not used for the welfare of people but to fill the pockets of regime members. To this, the lenders could always argue that they did not know how the money was going to be used for their defence. However, the law requires lenders to carry out due diligence before giving loans. So if they given loans to a regime, whose members were known in the international community with their nicknames, which suggested their corrupt nature, then the lenders will not have any defence. They knowingly given loans to corrupt regime and cannot enforce repayments. Anyway, this is just a single argument to declare our foreign debts as odious, but we will have to prepare a watertight case with lots of solid arguments, if we want to go down this route.

The third method is reserved only to repay our IMF loan. For this, all we have to do is to increase our money supply to match that of IMF loan, and then convert these extra rupees into SDR using IMF's published exchange rates for SDR to Rupee, and then tell IMF that we have all the SDRs which were issued to us. So we do not owe IMF anything and do not need to pay any interest. By the way, we do not need to print any money to increase money supply, but it only has to be done on paper, just as the IMF allocated SDRs to us. Then we should cancel our IMF membership. IMF is going to make noise that we cannot convert our rupees to SDRs, and that we should pay back in US dollars. We just need to remind them that they did not give us any US dollars but all they did was made an entry into their ledger of our SDR allocation. They have published an exchange rate from SDR to Rupee and we converted your SDRs to rupees according to this rate in the past. Now all we did is to use the exchange rate issued by them, to convert our rupees into SDRs and paid them back. If the SDRs can be converted into Rupees, then why they cannot be converted the other way around?

Natural Disasters & Economy

Pakistan has been suffering from natural disasters for the last few decades, be they earthquakes or floods. More than 100,000 people died in earthquakes since 1974, and nearly 4 million people were made homeless. The floods have also killed many people, and made hundreds of thousands homeless. The economic cost of 2010 floods alone was $43 billion, never mind uncountable human suffering. Since then, we had floods almost every year, and as I am writing this, people are suffering from floods. The economic cost of earthquakes and floods runs into hundreds of billion dollars, and the human cost cannot be measured. But the government has not taken any precautionary measures to reduce the impacts of floods and earthquakes. It is nonsense to talk about economic growth, but not stop the leakage of almost half of our GDP due to floods and earthquakes!

There are no defence against earthquakes, as yet, but we could make laws, that require building of houses, which will withstand earthquakes and reduce the number of lives lost. But as far as the floods go, they could be controlled easily by employing different methods, such as, dams, dikes, reservoirs, lakes, and floodway etc. But why no Pakistani government tries to control floods, or reduce the impacts of earthquakes? They instead, send help after the event. Why don't they build flood defences and save its people and economy? The reason is simple. The politicians want you and me to be dependent on them for food, clothing, and housing. Because if we have plenty of food to eat, clothes to wear, and a houses to live in, then how would they ask us to vote for them? So they let these floods out on us to take away our food, clothing, and homes, so we beg them for help. So when they help us, then they can remind us on next elections 'Didn't we help you when you had no one to help you.' Floods are the best friends to politicians, why would they keep them away with the flood barriers?

Unfortunately, this is how the politics work in Pakistan. But if it had worked in any other way, then they would think of how many lives are lost to floods? They would think how much it had cost the economy? But, until the politics changes in Pakistan, we will keep seeing the floods. People will die and those who survive will keep becoming homeless and helpless!

But if the politicians are serious then they could build flood defences within a year, to dramatically reduce the floods. Flood defences are the fundamentals of economics in a country like ours, which suffers from such natural disasters. We must save our production (crops) that we have first, before looking to increase our production. So if we save our crops from floods, then we will be able to provide food and clothing to our people. So we will not have to spend our foreign exchange reserve to buy food and clothing from abroad.

If the government is looking to build flood defences, then they will have to take simultaneous actions. For example, to prevent our cities from flooding, they need to look to unblock the natural waterways that existed for thousands of years, but now people have illegally built on them. In the current floods of 2013, the Lahore city was also under water. Some people have pointed out that Lahore had not suffered from floods in olden days, because there were many natural waterways, known as "Nalay" in Pakistan, which used to take flood water away from the residential areas. These natural waterways run right through cities. I am not familiar with the geography of Lahore

that much, because I only stayed there for a few months, but I do
know about the natural waterways in Rawalpindi, where I spent
most of my childhood. I still remember clearly that we used to live
in military quarters on the edge of Nala Lai. There was a large house
belonging to Air Chief Marshal, Asghar Khan just behind us, and
there were three cinemas across the road from his house. On the
other side of Nala Lai, was the famous Liaqat Bagh. The water in
Nala Lai was always black and filled with rubbish, but flowing and a
stench smell filled the air. In heavy monsoon season, my father used
to go to the bridge to read the scale printed on bridge wall, to see
how high the water was. I cannot remember a year, when the Nala
Lai caused flooding. According to some people, the Lahore city is
flooded because of two reasons, which the provincial government
must investigate. They say that people have built houses illegally on
all the Nalays in Lahore, blocking the natural waterways. Similarly,
the river Ravi is usually dry, so a lot people have built their homes
there illegally; this diverts water out of river into the city. Another
dangerous thing which came to light this year was that someone had
farmed about two hundred alligators in Lahore, which are now
spread all around the country, because that farm was flooded and
water took away alligators with it. If all of those alligators are not
caught, then we will have a real problem at our hands from the
missing alligators breeding and creating bigger problem for the
entire population. Similarly, there are people in Pakistan, who breed
tigers and lions. How on earth, these people are allowed to breed
such dangerous animals? The person who owned alligators must be
fined heavily first and then put to death for causing this mayhem.

For flood defences, the government has many experts who could
advise it better. But I will only say the plans should first concentrate
on preventing the major floods, and then moving onto preventing the
smaller floods in all areas of Pakistan. When building flood water
dams or reservoirs, we should try to build them upstream (higher
grounds) first, so we could also use them to irrigate our lands for

crop productions, without using pumps. Wherever possible, we should try to work with nature to our advantage, and not try to work against it.

National Savings & Economy

Pakistani politicians keep wishing that foreign companies invest in Pakistan, and they believe this is the only solution for Pakistan's economic problems. Other politicians rely on US, China, IMF, and World Bank for financial assistance to run their government. A common theme emerges from these views, that is, the solution lies only outside of Pakistan for its economic success. If our leaders carried on with these views and wishes, then Pakistan will keep on falling towards economic crisis and failure. Unfortunately, our leaders are living only on hope that someone, someday, will sympathise with Pakistan and come to its assistance. This is a pipedream[16]. But there are others, who believe that due to Pakistan's geopolitical importance and its nuclear arsenal, the superpowers will not let Pakistan become a failed state, and surely will come to its rescue. This view is even dangerous than those of pipe dreamers. If at any time, the super powers believed that Pakistan should not have nuclear arsenals, then they will unite and force Pakistan to give up its nuclear weapons, which will not be a good outcome for Pakistan.

Pakistan has everything that it needs for economic growth and prosperity, such as, it is full of natural resources and labour. On the other hand, Japan had no natural resources but it became the second largest economy of the world. Japan is an example we should follow for economic prosperity with a few changes according to our unique position in the world.

---

[16] Pipe dream is a term to describe a vain but fervent hope for an impossible or unlikely situation. Hallucinations or dreams caused by smoking an opiate pipe.

Let us see how Pakistan could rely on itself to achieve economic success? There are many steps we need to take, but the national savings is the most fundamental requirement for economic success, because without it no factory or business could be organised. Savings are the lifeblood of economy because it provides the needed capital for the businesses to create new businesses, or expand the existing ones. Banks play an important role in this respect because they gather savings from the people and make them available for business to borrow. The national savings has three components; personal savings by the public, savings by corporations, and savings by the government. Before I discuss savings any further let me show you how important the national saving is for economic growth.

Before Japan started off with its economic growth, their national savings were more than 40% of GDP. China was saving over 50%, and Hong Kong over 30% of their GDPs respectively. When we compare national savings data for the rich nations to that of poor ones, it becomes obvious that the rich nations save more than the poor ones, and this is one of the fundamental reasons for their economic growth and prosperity. Unfortunately, Pakistan's national savings linger around 10%. If we are to create economic growth, then we will have to increase our national savings similar to that of China and Japan. Without enough savings, we will not be able to grow. But if we borrowed money from abroad for this purpose, then we will be burdened with debt, and any economic growth will need to be transferred over to the lenders in the form of interest payments. The question arises, how do we save money when there is none?

As mentioned above, we could save money in three areas; personal, corporation, and governmental savings. Now let's look at each one in some detail. Personal or public saving is the money you and I save in a bank. The Bank could then lend this money to corporations, who invest it to produce goods and services, which provides employment to people. Pakistanis, like other Easterners, used to live within their means, and save. But the easy credit availability which started in Musharraf's time had changed all that. People now live beyond their means, and buy cars, appliances, and houses they cannot afford. If people are living beyond their means then there will be no savings. So to save more, we will need to move people away from taking out loans for luxury items. The government needs to tighten its credit policy, and enforce it through state bank, which regulates the commercial banks. At the same time, we need to ease people out of their existing loans by reducing their interest rates as I mentioned previously.

The second cause of people not saving more is high inflation and devaluation of our currency. Inflation has eliminated most of our middle class by moving them into poor class. So we have either the rich, or the poor. The poor obviously have no money to save because they cannot even buy their life essentials due to inflation. But the middle class is not any better off because their incomes hardly cover their expenses. So they cannot save anything. This leaves us with the third group, that is, the rich and the very rich. Even though they have a lot of money to save, but they still do not save because the continuous inflation and devaluation of our currency reduces the value of their savings. So to guard against such problems, they save their wealth in foreign currency accounts, which Pakistan cannot use for its economic growth. This money could only be used by those countries whose currencies these accounts are in.   The simplest solution to stop this money flight, is to reduce inflation and improve our currency value. I have already discussed the steps we need to take to reduce inflation in an earlier section.

To increase our governmental savings, we could try several alternatives. The first thing that we could do is to reduce governmental expenses by selling state enterprises to the public. Our government pays a few hundred billions to keep running the state enterprises, and if we have sold them then we could save a lot of money. I have discussed in detail elsewhere in this book, a better alternative to privatisation, by converting our state enterprises into

POCs, which will create a public ownership with the government still owning the 20% of shares. By selling the state enterprises, we will get at least a few hundred billions, which we could use to pay off our foreign debts. By paying off foreign debts, we will reduce the government's burden even further, because it will not need to make interest payments to foreign financial institutions. Both of these steps will create more than enough space for governmental savings, which could be used for economic growth.

Another unnecessary governmental expense is to run three levels of governments, national, provincial, and local governments. The national and local governments are necessary and useful for an effective political system, but the provincial government is not only unnecessary, but also dangerous for the stability of our country in the light of new NFC Award[17]. The provinces have become much more powerful and wealthy than the federation, which will eventually cause them to leave the federation. Devolving powers to provincial governments has always created further desires for cessation from the central government. For example, the UK government devolved power to Scottish government and now they are asking for a cessation from the UK and there is referendum to decide this in 2014.   We must learn lessons from other's experiences. But unfortunately, a provincial form of government suits the two largest political parties in Pakistan, because they are guaranteed to have their provincial governments in their respective provinces despite their failure in the national elections. Now a third political party has emerged and it has found its roots in another province and formed their government there. Will they allow the provincial governments to be dissolved? I doubt very much. But the provinces are a danger to our federation and a financial burden on its people. If we dissolved the provincial governments or reverted the

---

[17] NFC Award stands for National Finance Commission Award, which is a series of planned economic programme enacted in 1951.

NFC award, then we will be able to save a lot of money, which could be used for the growth of whole country.

Lastly, the government must plan to save money by bringing efficiency within all of its departments including military. However, we must be cautious and not become overzealous by wanting to save too much, in too little time. This will disrupt the whole system. Instead we should aim to save just 1% in year one, 2% in year two, 3% in year three and so on. This must be a never ending process but obviously we cannot save 100% so the goals must be realistic, small, and achievable.

Multifactor Productivity (MFP)

The single most important element in GDP growth is the productivity in an economy. Productivity is the single factor that makes the rich nations rich, and lack of it makes the poor nations poor. All it means is that we increase output through different means. For example, if a mason and labourer takes 4 hours to build one square meter wall, but after we train them in new building techniques, they could build the same wall in 3 hours. This means that we have increased their productivity. Suppose we now give them better materials to build the wall with, such as, washed sand and improved bricks etc. Suppose this reduces the time from 3 hours to 2.5 hours to build one square meter wall. We could further, increase their productivity by giving them better tools, such as, a cement mixer, a wheel barrow to carry bricks, and new type of trowel, chisel, and hammer. These will increase their speed and quality of work even more. These new tools may reduce the time to build the same wall to only one hour. So by providing training, materials, and equipment, we have increased their productivity four fold. In economics, the training is called *Labour Input*, materials is obviously *Materials Input*, and the new tools and equipment are called *Capital Input* because you need capital (money) to buy them.

These together are called multifactor productivity. For a true growth, we must have increased all levels of productivity. However, if an economy has not increased its MFP, but their growth is dependent only on one factor, such as, capital, then that economy would not have really grown. If you remove the capital from such an economy then the whole growth is gone. For example, some economists argue that the Asian Tigers' growth was such a growth.

In Pakistan, there are about 54 million males and 49 million females of working age, out of 180 million population. If these 103 million people increased their multifactor productivity only by 10%, which is easily achievable, then they would be doing the work of 113 million people in the same number of hours worked. But if everyone worked just 2 more hours each day over a five day week period, then this is like there were 109,000 extra workers in our economy. The possibility of growth is enormous if we only look. However, the productivity is not the concern of building trade only. But the productivity could be achieved in every walk of life, for example, in manufacturing, transport, healthcare, education, management, government, and even in household work. Apart from training, materials, and capital investment, the other main drivers of productivity are innovation, technology, and competition. Pakistan has not fully utilised all the tools of productivity so it has great potential for real growth.

To create a real economic growth, we must put economic fundamentals right first by concentrating on improving Multifactor Productivity. To achieve MFP, we must invest in new tools, equipment, and machinery from the first world, instead of reinventing the wheel. And we must stop the use of outdated tools, equipment, and machinery. We must hire the best trainers from abroad to increase the workers efficiency. We must adopt the best management methods and practices from the developed world. We must not try to do everything ourselves, because we will waste a great deal of time and energy in reinventing the things which have already been invented elsewhere. We must acquire whatever is necessary for our growth from abroad first, and then improve on it. To enter world leaders club we must develop the latest technology, and promote innovation and competition.

... and ... invested elsewhere. We must acquire whenever ... oxygen from ... growth from above us, and ... in ...
... to ensure we ... their ... which ... must ... to those effects ...
... probable to ... discoveries.

Resolving Economic Policy Issues

There is widespread poverty in Pakistan: about 70% of the people live below poverty line, or on less than one dollar a day. Inflation is rife and increasing daily, making people poor on fixed and low incomes. The official figures show an inflation rate of 9% but the actual inflation is likely to be much higher. There is a growing national debt for which we pay an interest payment equal to 25% of country's yearly income. Our foreign debt is growing due to the devaluation of our currency on a daily basis. As I will show you that all the above issues are interlinked, but at the core of these problems is the way the government is handling our money or currency.

The two main reasons among others, for a high rate of unemployment, are a lack of electricity and law & order in the country. So the industries are moving out of the country at a fast rate. These two issues are interlinked and are also related to widespread poverty in Pakistan.

The government's expenditure is more than its income, which is directly linked with the mismanagement of our national corporations, government debts, and uncontrolled corruption. Corruption needs some time before it could be fully controlled, but I will propose some easy solutions that could limit the corruption to a manageable level quickly. But the mismanagement of our corporations such as PIA, Pak Steel, Railway, and WAPDA, etc can be easily turned around, if we converted these state corporations into

Publically Owned Corporations (POCs). Then we will not only reduce the burden of government, but also bring widespread prosperity to our people. Let us now discuss some of the policy issues that must be clarified and resolved before we could create economic growth.

Population & Economy

A few so called thinkers in Pakistan are making noise about overpopulation. They are spreading fear among people that we will not have any food and other resources left if we did not control our birth rates. Our economy will collapse, they claim. It seems that they are now reading something that was written more than 200 years ago. In 1798, Thomas Malthus, a British political economist, wrote an essay titled *Essay on the Principle of Population*, which later became known as Malthusian Trap. These so called thinkers who spread fear and worry about population are either misguided, or they are working on someone else's agenda.

Let me quickly explain what a Malthusian Trap is? Thomas Robert Malthus was an English economist and he was convinced that population was growing faster than the sources of food. He argued that humans are growing *geometrically* (by multiples, 4, 8, 16 ...) while the source of food is growing *arithmetically* (by addition, 4, 6, 8 ...) so the population is heading for resource extinction. He was convinced that the global population had reached its natural peak at a population of 980 millions, meaning the population will start to decline after this. But after two centuries, we have 7 times more population than what Malthus predicted. That is, now there are about 7 billion people in the world, but we have not run out of food or other resources. In fact, we are better fed and healthier than the time of Malthus. Where Malthus went wrong was that he did not account for human innovation. Our so called thinkers are fear mongers and do not believe in human innovation. Further, they lack the knowledge of positive effects of a bigger population on economy.

Despite what I have said above, I do have a concern. Currently, the fossil fuels, petroleum, gas, and coal are supporting the large population and economic growth, which are finite resources, and will become extinct eventually. Let us suppose, tomorrow we run out of all of the petroleum, gas, and coal resources in the world, what will happen then? The entire world's economies will grind to a halt. Food and other commodities could not be transported for consumption by others and population will start to starve and die. To complicate things even further, the current food production increases depended largely on fertilisers and genetic modifications. Fertilisers are derivative of natural gas, so without fertilisers the food production will drop dramatically. A Malthusian nightmare can ensue if we did not innovate before we run out of natural resources, but I am optimistic about human innovation.

In contrast to our thinkers who are 200 years behind, the thinkers in the developed world are concerned more about their declining birth rates. Ironically, the same developed nations tell the Third World to reduce their population, and they provide free contraceptives to Third World to reduce their population. Why is there so much conflict and hypocrisy in their views? I think, they know that their population is declining, which will reduce their economic and human power which comes from large numbers. So by reducing the Third World's population they could keep their financial and economic hegemony. This is because if the Third World population kept on growing then they will have more workers to create economic growth. On the other hand, if the developed nations lost their population then they will also not matter much in the world due to their small population. Some of the developed world has a birth rate so low that they cannot sustain their population number, that is, more people are dying than are born. So their population is declining.

A bigger population has two major advantages. A large population matters on world stage than a small country, and the larger the population means a large workforce which will create economic growth. But to create economic prosperity from a large population requires an environment, which provides opportunities for the entire workforce to be employed in work. A large population not employed in work, can become a political and social hazard.

Lastly, I want to warn people of what might be happening on world scale. The sperm counts have decreased at an alarming rate just in less than fifty years. But in evolutionary terms fifty years is just a blip, meaning that nothing should change biologically in humans or animals in such a short time. Evolutionary changes require not thousands of years, but hundreds of thousands of years, or millions of years for such significant changes in biology of humans. Then why in less than fifty years, human sperm count has decreased significantly? The only plausible explanation is that it is manipulated somehow by someone!

Many people believe the West wishes to reduce the developing world's population and is doing everything to achieve its goal by hook or crook. There are likely to be some conspiracy theories floating around, but I will let you be the judge of them. The fact is that the West is providing condoms and contraceptive pills free to the Third World, but some believe that these condoms and pills contain drugs that could create infertility in men and women. Our foods have pesticides sprayed, which mimic estrogens, perhaps the very reason for male reduced sperm count? Fluoride and chlorine is added to water supply to kill germs, but they have been known to alter *Thyroid Functions* in humans, which also have negative effect on sexual organs in humans. Interestingly, these chemicals are also the ingredients for psychotic drugs for mental health patients. Some believe the major drinks companies put these chemicals in their drinks. Further, there are only handfuls of drug companies in the world, who dominate the world drugs. Some theorists believe that they introduce chemicals in the drugs that are used often in the Third World, such as pain killers. They claim that these chemicals in these drugs are designed to reduce human fertility of the Third World.

Finally, our religious leader's position on birth control had been positive from an economic point of view. But this does not mean we put our women through unnecessary burden of one pregnancy after another. The easiest and the most natural way for a woman to ensure that she does not get pregnant just after giving birth is to breastfeed her baby. Breastfeeding mothers do not get pregnant, but here the women are to be blamed, because they stopped breast feeding their babies under Western influence to preserve their youth and slender shape by not breastfeeding their babies. The breast fed baby is much healthier and does not need many doctor visits like a bottle fed baby and it keeps the mother healthy as well.

Fiscal Policy & Taxation

In Pakistan almost every politician says that the cure for all of our economic problems is to collect more tax. But can any politician provide guarantee that all of our economic problems will be over when we started collecting more tax? No one has given a figure, how much tax we should collect? But it seems the politicians only want quick solution to their problems without any regard to how much the public will suffer from new taxation. We have to decide, how much taxation is fair because it is the money earned with people's sweat and blood. The reason that people of Pakistan are unwilling to pay more tax is that they have seen politicians filling their own pockets with the public money instead of running the government honestly.

We know the government's income come from ordinary people. All of us give part of our income to government in the form of tax. History tells us that those nations which could not collect taxes were dominated by those nations which could collect taxes from their people. This was because the nations which were efficient in collecting taxes, could afford standing armies that were well equipped and well trained. Apart from security, a nation needs a lot of money so it could organise a well functioning society. Every country has its unique issues and Pakistan is no exception. But we need to understand what the government's needs are, and where the money is being wasted, so we could stop leakage? We need to understand how much tax we should impose on people and why?

Pakistan has over 70 direct and indirect taxes. This system needs a lot of workers to calculate and collect taxes for which the government spends a large amount of money. Further, the people who suppose to collect taxes make themselves rich through corruption, and the government gets very little. So there is a strong need for simplifying the tax system and eliminate tax theft. So if we simplify tax into 3 or 4 taxes, then this will reduce the number of people needed to calculate and collect taxes. We get two benefits from simplifying taxes; it increases government's income while reducing its spending. This is because we will need less people in tax office, which will reduce government spending. This would also mean there will be less tax theft by the tax collector, and the government will collect more. I will explain how we could simplify the tax system, which will give us the greatest amount of taxes without making the people poor.

But first we need to calculate how much tax we need to collect and how we could eliminate the unnecessary expenses forever. I will propose a method which creates government income from sources other than taxes, so we will have a very small tax need, about 5%. Now let us see how much money our government needs each year so we could decide on the fair amount of taxes?

According to State Bank of Pakistan's (SPB) 2013 report, in year 2012, we collected a total of Rs.2,566.5 billion but we spent Rs.3,936.2 billion. We will use 2012 expenses as our baseline for our national budget and our calculations. Bear in mind that in 2012, all provinces spent an extra Rs.279.3 on developmental projects due to upcoming elections. Year 2012 expenses also included interest payments of Rs.811.1 billion to domestic banks. But I have already explained how we could easily eliminate interest payments to domestic banks. So in future we will not have this expense. Therefore, we could easily deduct the extra developmental and interest expenses from the 2012 budget, which reduces our total expenditure to Rs.2,845.8 billion. As I mentioned earlier in this book that by implementing full reserve banking, we would shift all the government debt onto private banks that will have to pay interest to government. Let us assume the interest income for government is Rs.800 billion a year. This will reduce the government budget to Rs.2,045.8 billion. Assuming all the expenses remained the same, then this would mean the government will have an extra Rs.520 billion. If the government implements my other proposals, such as, selling all state enterprises to public, then we will also save a few hundred billion a year, which we used spend to run our PIA, Railway, and Steel Mill etc. I think that we could easily save another Rs.300 billion a year from this to give us an extra Rs.800 billion a year above and beyond budget.

For a healthy and educated population we ought to spend a good amount of money on health and education, but we spend very little. Spending more on education will create an upward social mobility[18], which in turn will increase our GDP. Similarly, spending more on health will reduce infant mortality and create healthy population that is happy and productive, which will also raise our GDP. So I suggest the federal government spend an extra Rs.200 billion each year on health and education, on top of what the provinces are spending already. This will have two positive effects. Firstly, the education and health of the people will improve dramatically in a short time with this much investment. Secondly, the federation would have

---

[18] Social mobility is the movement of an individual from one class to another.

gained some power back from the provinces in these two important areas and could create central policies for both the education and health.

The most important thing for economic growth is the internal and external security. To create a secure environment within our country we will need to give extra funds to Police, Intelligence Agencies, and Courts. I suggest that we should give all these three departments at least Rs.100 billion each every year until our country has been made secure. This extra money in these three departments will greatly help our law and order situation very quickly.

Finally, we need to reduce our reliance on foreign military technology due to their huge expense and unreliability of delivery due to foreign policies. So we need to manufacture our own latest weapons, aircrafts, ships, submarines, and spy satellites etc. We must be self-sufficient in military technology. To achieve this goal, we need to invest at least Rs.100 billion a year on research and development. Even after all these new critical and important expenses I suggested, we will still have some left over. Anyhow, I have kept my calculations simple for our discussion, but the actual calculations will need to take many other factors into account for budgeting.

Now let us discuss the government revenue, that is, taxes it imposes on people. In developed nations, people pay almost 50% or more of their incomes in different taxes, such as, income tax, National Insurance Contributions, VAT on already taxed income, local government taxes, capital gains tax, and Inheritance Tax on death, and many more. There is much double taxation going on. In Pakistan we have more than 70 different taxes but only the employed people pay most of the taxes. The rich and the businessmen almost never pay any tax. On the other hand, the poor pay taxes in the form of high inflation tax, and many taxes levied on their utility bills. The whole system of taxation is not only inefficient, but is also unfair. Would it not be better if there was a single tax, which no one could avoid, and at the same time it is not imposed on the poor people?

I strongly believe that people should be able to keep most of their income, and only a small amount should be taken by the government in taxes, and there should be no double taxation. I propose that we reduce the income and corporation taxes to 1% over time. Then we should introduce VAT of no more than 15%, while phasing out Sales Tax and reducing other taxes. For example, we could introduce the VAT of 3% while reducing the Sales, Income, and Corporation Taxes by 3%. We could then increase the VAT by 1% each month while reducing all the other three taxes by the same amount. No one will object to this because they could see the government is reducing a much more tax than it is introducing, and the net effect is that the government is reducing taxes. We must run this process slowly to avoid any disruptions. I prefer the VAT because it cannot be avoided like the Sales Tax, and it is transparent. There are many other advantages of VAT over Sales Tax but the important one is that no one will be able to escape it, especially when we have switched to electronic money. In this system the government will know exactly who has spent how much, and when? The banking systems and Point of Sales Terminal (POS) must be organised in such a way that each transaction must calculate and display the VAT element clearly on receipts and banking accounts. And the VAT element is automatically transferred to the Inland Revenue account of that bank. The banks must automatically report to Inland Revenue of the collected VAT at close of each business day, which should be midnight instead of actual closing of the banks, because the transactions continue long after the banks close. By implementing such a system, the government will be getting tax revenue automatically and every day, without waiting for months or a whole year for the businesses to send their tax returns. Let us now discuss, why I am proposing a gradual decrease in income and corporation taxes as well as eliminating Sales Tax?

Currently the maximum Corporation Tax is 39% in Pakistan. Most of these corporations pay bribes to Tax Officers to reduce their tax bills so the state never gets much tax this way. But if we reduce their final tax to 1%, then all the corporations will happily pay this tax, and then they will not need to pay bribes to tax officers. This way, the corporations will send their true accounts to the state. We can then reduce the numbers of people we employ in the tax office, and reduce corruption and state expenses enormously. But this is not the main reason for me proposing to reduce corporation taxes: there are two other important reasons. Firstly, by reducing corporation taxes, we will create incentives for businessmen to invest more in new businesses or expand the existing ones, which will create thousands of jobs and we could move towards full employment. When this happens then not only the GDP of the country will increase, but people will also prosper and the poverty will be eliminated. Secondly, when the corporations are paying higher taxes then the goods and services they produce reflect tax expense in the final price, meaning the goods and services will be expensive. So when we reduce corporation tax, then the prices of goods and services will come down, and people will be able to afford food and other necessities which they could not afford before. They will also have more money in their pockets because of reduced prices, all of which is good for politicians to boast about in their next general elections. However, the government must ensure that it links the reduction in corporation taxes with them reducing their prices. This could be monitored by looking at the historic prices.

Similarly, by reducing the income tax to 1%, the government will win over the employed people who are unhappy with the current system because they know that they bear the burden of the whole nation. It will win the government more votes for the next elections. However, the government must bear in mind that any reduction in corporation and income taxes has the same effect as increasing the money supply, which will create inflation. If the inflation is increased then no one will be happy with the government even though it had reduced the taxes, because the public will not be better off. So, as I mentioned elsewhere in this book, the government must reduce these taxes slowly. Reducing taxes slowly has a political benefit as well, because it will seem to people that the government is merciful by constantly reducing public's tax burden.

As I discussed earlier, the sales tax is inefficient because it could easily be avoided and the retailers have no incentive in collecting it. But by introducing VAT, no one could avoid it. And with the help of electronic money, it will be collected instantly, reducing the accounting requirements for the businesses. That said, the VAT will require more training and accounting than sales tax. So we should have these in place before implementing it. Since no one could escape from VAT then how do we protect poor people from this tax?

To protect our poor countrymen, we could exempt the essential goods and services from VAT. For example, all raw food items should be VAT exempt while the restaurant food should have VAT. Clothing of low quality must be exempt while of high quality be charged VAT. To help the poor, the utilities, such as, water, electricity, and gas, should be taxed if used more than a certain amount. A higher usage of electricity and gas is a sign of abundance of money, so they should pay taxes, while the poor will be exempt because they use less of these utilities. Building a small house should be exempt from tax, while a larger house should be taxed. Similarly, we could come up with a list of twenty to thirty products which the poor use most, and then exempt them from VAT.

There has been much talk about imposing agricultural tax but it seems that no government will be able to impose such a tax because most of the powerful politicians are themselves agriculturists. They will never impose a tax on themselves. However, I do agree with those who argue for such a tax so we could eliminate black economy related to agriculture, and to know the truer sources of their incomes. For example, those in favour of agriculture tax, argue that some politicians who own agricultural land, hide their financial corruption by declaring that their lifestyle is being supported by the income from their agricultural land, which may not be true. Politicians are not the only ones misusing the system. Here we need to bear in mind that even the capitalist societies pay huge subsidies to their farmers to ensure food security. So we also should not be harsh on our farmers but we must maintain a balance. I think that a token tax of 1% with the option for full rebate for capital expenses incurred will be much easier to impose. Let me explain. We should impose a 1% tax on agricultural income. However, we should allow all agriculturists to reclaim whole of tax paid, if they have bought capital items, such as, equipment and machinery to be used for agriculture. This way they would not have paid a penny but this will document our agricultural economy fully, which will greatly reduce corruption.

Eliminating Corruption

Corruption is everywhere including the most advanced societies of the world, but the level of corruption there is very low when we compare it with Pakistan. Everyone knows that corruption is bad, but we perhaps are not clear what corruption is, and how it affects all of us? Let us define and categorise corruption before we discuss the ways to eliminate it.

Corruption can be defined as the abuse of entrusted power for private gain. For example, when a police officer takes a bribe to ignore an offence, then he is involved in corruption because he is abusing his power for private gain. However, political theorists categorise corruption into many types, but we will discuss only the four major types; Systemic, Political (grand), Petty, and Sporadic Corruption. When a government official takes bribe irregularly and only a handful of officials are involved, then this type of corruption is called *Sporadic Corruption*. This type of corruption doesn't threaten society and we should aim for achieving this level of corruption. You may protest, why should we not eliminate corruption altogether? I would say, that it is impossible to eradicate corruption altogether, because you will always find some people who have inclination towards corruption.

On the other hand, when more than a handful of public officials take small amounts of money as bribes from public, and it happens regularly, then this type is called *Petty or Bureaucratic Corruption*. This is also called *Low Level Corruption* because it happens at the implementation side of rules and laws. Examples of petty corruption include, a police officer taking bribe to ignore minor traffic offence, a teacher not teaching properly so students come to his private tuition centre, a doctor not seeing his patients so they come to his private clinic, or a tax officer helping someone forge their accounts if they pay him a bribe.

But when the politicians or their acquaintances misuse their power, to accumulate wealth by converting public wealth into private wealth, then this type of corruption is called *Political or Grand Corruption*. This is also called *High Level Corruption* because it happens at the rule and law making side. This type of corruption comes in many forms. For example, rulers make rules that only allow them to own and operate certain industries, such as, Sugar Mills, Cotton, and Car industries etc. According to Sheikh Rashid, an old face in Pakistani politics, twelve of the basic commodities, which everyone needs, are monopolised by a handful of powerful politicians. You may have seen this type of corruption behind many new laws that the parliament made in past. For example, privatising state enterprises and selling them to friends and family at rock bottom prices. It is the grand corruption that still happens even in the most advanced societies, but Pakistan obviously is rife with grand corruption. Political corruption causes misallocation of resources and drains public wealth. So everyone in society is affected adversely.

Lastly, when a society is suffering from Political and Petty Corruption simultaneously, and it has become an integrated and essential part of economic, social, and political system, then this type of corruption is called *Systemic or Endemic Corruption*. This type of corruption is usually embedded in wider situations that help sustain it. In this situation people suffer doubly because both types of corruptions have joined forces. Unfortunately, Pakistan suffers from Systemic Corruption.

So how can we treat this corruption disease? It is not difficult to eradicate corruption, but political corruption is very difficult to eradicate, but not impossible. To deal with the systemic corruption, we need a strong and honest government which has the majority in parliament to pass the necessary laws.

Fortunately, Pakistani media and Supreme Court have been very active in creating awareness and tackling of political corruption and many good things have happened. If these two pillars of state remained independent and autonomous then less political corruption will take place. Unfortunately, part of media itself is suffering from corruption, which needs urgent attention of theorists and law makers. Elsewhere in this book, I have proposed some suggestions to eradicate corruption from the media.

The current system allows the Prime Minister to allocate large amounts of money to their parliamentary members for development without any auditing. Many commentators argue that these are rewards given to party members by ruling party. Party members use these to rich themselves, and for pre-poll rigging. I think there is another problem with this system as well. That is, the funds are only given to party members, which means that if any money is spent on development, then that will only be in the constituencies of ruling party members. This would mean, the constituencies of opposition party members will remain undeveloped. This is a *collective punishment* to those people who did not vote the ruling party. To eradicate this type of corruption and uneven development, we must change the rules on how the development funds are distributed. We also need to make other functional changes in *Planning Commission of Pakistan.*

First of all, the Planning Commission must be made independent of Prime Minister and Federal Ministers, because their interference in Commission's work will cause an uneven development. Their roles must be only to monitor the Commission's work. Planning Commission has wide range of responsibilities, but here I am discussing only infrastructural development for which currently the party members (MNA/MPA) get funds. The Commission must be given a task to plan infrastructural development for the entire country without any prejudice. It must prepare a report which identifies at least three levels of infrastructural development needs. That is, the commission needs to identify the *Critical, Essential,* and *Desirable Developmental Needs* for the entire country. Then it is the job of the government to ensure the funds are released for critical development first for the entire country. Once all the critical developmental needs are met, only then the commission is allowed to proceed with essential development and so on. This way we could tackle the corruption for developmental funds allocated to party members, have an even development throughout country, and avoid collective punishment.

However, I need to digress a little and say that the current rules push the government to leave the developmental planning to provinces to decide, which is a great debacle in the name of power devolution. The main reason the provinces should not be allowed to decide developmental projects is because they will have a very narrow remit and view of development according to the areas they control. For example, if we are building flood controls, road and rail links, then the provinces cannot come up with the correct plans for development, because they will not be able to see the bigger picture. There are many other infrastructural development needs where a central planning is required. The best approach would be for every district or tehsil to send their developmental needs to planning commission, who should then include their needs within their grand plans for the entire country.

Let us now get back to how we could eliminate grand or political corruption that happens on the law making side. The best and easiest approach in my opinion would be an ability of the state to confiscate the assets and property of all government officials, which they gained through illegal means or corruption, anywhere in the world. If such ability is achieved by the state then it will create a threat for politicians and all government employees, which will prevent them from engaging in corruption. Let me explain how this could work.

A bill must be passed in the parliament, which declares that 'The government of Pakistan shall have the right to confiscate the assets and property (land, money, and investments etc) anywhere in the world, of all those in the service of Pakistan now, or in past. This will include all the civil servants, Judiciary, armed forces personnel's, members of parliament and senate. The law allows the government of Pakistan to gain access to (and/or recover) the financial affairs of all those concerned, provided there is investigation of corruption or crime, for which there exists a court order.' Once such a law is passed, then the government of Pakistan does not need to get agreements of all those in the service of Pakistan before the law applies to them, but it should issue a notice saying that anyone in the service of Pakistan, who does not wish to obey this new rule must resign from his position within 30 days. If no one resigns, then they have agreed implicitly. However, if anyone resigns, then we could single him out for investigation. However, the government of Pakistan should guarantee that no property will be confiscated unless it is proven that the property was obtained through corruption or illegal means. All legally earned property must be transferred to the legal heirs according to the government of Pakistan's property laws on the death of such personnel.

However, we may be depending on the mercy of politicians to pass such a law. Why would they shoot in their own feet? I am certain that any bill which also includes the members of parliament and senate is unlikely to have their support, because a significant number of them have gained their property illegally at some point in their lives. I am relying on the public to build up pressure on the politicians to pass such a law. But a much easier bill to pass is to exclude members of parliament, senate, and armed forces from such a law. The compromised bill will only apply to civil servants. This is still as good as including all the politicians, because the parliamentarians and senators do not get their hands dirty with corruption themselves but they get civil servants to do the corruption. And if the civil servants' hands are tied, then it will be difficult for any corruption to take place.

Let us now turn to petty corruption which is rife in our society. This type of corruption is very easy to eradicate very quickly. I proposed earlier in this book to introduce electronic money and to limit the amount of cash available for each adult to Rs.500 per month. By limiting the cash available only to Rs.500 a month, there will be no extra cash left over to be given in bribes to government officials. If they need to give bribe then they will have to transfer money into offending official's bank accounts. This is easily traceable and no one will take the risk of having money transferred into their accounts, or into their friend's bank accounts. To catch corrupt officials the Anti Corruption officials only need to look at the bank accounts where a lot of money had been transferred from many unrelated persons. This way, within no time, all petty corruption will be eradicated from the society.

Corporate Governance

Corporations around the world get audited by independent accounting firms. The main aim of such operation is to monitor the corporations. However, we saw how the ENRON, an energy giant, falsified its accounts which led to its bankruptcy in 2001. Arthur Andersons were the auditors for ENRON but they failed to detect accounting fraud on such a scale. It is impossible for them not to notice accounting fraud, the only plausible explanation is that they must have colluded with ENRON. This view gets it strength from the bankruptcy of another giant corporation WorldCom, which was also audited by Arthur Anderson. Why such collusions occur between corporations and auditors? And how do they affect corporations in Pakistan?

Let us understand how the auditing works generally around the world. Most governments require large corporations to have their accounts audited by independent auditors. A corporation employs an auditor firm to audit its accounts. The auditor is paid directly by the corporation it audits. For many auditing firms, the fees run into millions of dollars each year. This creates a conflict of interest for the auditors, who wish to please the corporation it audits, so it does not lose a regular fee income of millions of dollars each year. So they will ignore minor inaccuracies and perhaps collude with them if they are offered substantial sums of money to create fraudulent accounts. While this conflict of interest exists, there is no effective oversight of auditors by any authority. That is, the accountants and auditors usually self-regulate themselves. So how could they regulate properly? Self-regulation is like giving a prisoner keys, and telling him to stay in the prison, and then hoping he will not escape! In cases of bankruptcies, the auditing firms are sometimes sued for not warning ahead of time of any problems. The problem is intensified due to there being only four big auditing firms in the world. They have thousands of employees, so they cannot always ensure that their auditors are not colluding with the corporations they are auditing. The current system of auditing is severely flawed that has caused loss of billions of dollars for shareholders, and thousands have lost their jobs due to bankruptcies. Fraudulent accounting has even shaken the economies of countries.

Pakistan has similar auditing rules and there is a great danger that we may also suffer a scandal like ENRON and our people may lose billions of rupees, lose their jobs, or it destroys our economy. We should pre-empt this problem by modifying our auditing rules in such a way that it removes conflict of interest and collusion of auditors. The solution I am going to suggest is simple, and it will not only resolve the auditing problems, but also raise the standing of our corporations in the world. Further, if my suggestions are implemented then it will become a new source of governmental income, creating thousands of new jobs, and providing a new source of public income as well.

To resolve this issue, the government must make a small change to the rules of auditing corporations. Instead of corporations employing their own auditors, the government should employ auditors for every firm. The government will pay the auditors and collect that fee from the corporations. Under such a system the government becomes the single source of providing auditing contracts to auditors, so it can do it at a reduced cost than the individual corporations, and it must pass the savings on to the corporations. But the important thing that will be achieved with this change of rule is that we will have true knowledge about our corporations and their profitability. This will be good for everyone. The investor will know whether to invest in a particular firm. The government will collect right amount of tax, and it could ensure the corporations are not going to go bust causing widespread unemployment. This way shareholders will have accurate information about the corporations they own.

However, when these changes are implemented into corporate governance rules, then we are likely to find thousands of discrepancies in many corporations initially, which will temporarily damage the reputation of those corporations. But this will provide an opportunity for the shareholders to get rid of bad management and other problems from within their corporations, to make them stronger and profitable which will increase the longevity of these corporations. So we should not worry too much when we find many problems with our corporations. Once the problems are identified and remedied, then the confidence in Pakistani corporations will be restored among Pakistanis and around the world, which will lead to more investment, creating even stronger economy. But the benefits of new auditing rules do not just stop here.

We could create two new auditing firms, which will be Publically Owned Corporations (POCs), with the government keeping no more than 20% of shareholdings. I have explained in detail how to organise POCs in a later chapter. Good news is that these new auditing firms will be profitable from the day one, because they will have the captive business of auditing, provided by the government. The very best accountants and auditors from Pakistan and around the world should be hired for these two POCs and these two must compete with each other and other firms for government business. The government must not provide all the business to these two firms, just because it owns shares in them. But it must ensure that other private auditing firms are not disadvantaged, which should also be allowed to bid for auditing work from the government.

These two POCs must try to become the world's finest and largest auditing firms by continuous improvement in training and by keeping the highest standards. In a few years, they would be able to get new business from around the world. These corporations must operate in exactly the same manner everywhere even if the rules of auditing are different in the rest of the world. Initially, the foreign corporations will not want to hire an auditing firm which will expose its weakness to shareholders, or even report to the government of any discrepancies. But if we keep these standards in the face of strongest of opposition, then sooner many reputable large corporations will want to hire our auditing firms, because the shareholders will have much more confidence in the corporations, which were audited by our auditing firms due to our unwavering integrity. This, of course will raise the audited firm's prestige and they will become much more successful. But these benefits will not be obvious to many corporations at first and they will be afraid to hire our auditing firms. To counter this resistance, we must offer pre-audit consultancy to any prospective corporations, and tell them to put their act together before we audit them, because we will not care if they had any consultancy with us and paid us heavy fees. Our obligation is to the public and the relevant government for whose benefits the auditing report is prepared and we will not spare anyone for anything.

Stock Exchange Reforms

The performance of national stock exchanges is often taken as a proxy for the health of a nation's economy, or at least investor enthusiasm for the country's prospects. This rationale is deeply flawed because the stock prices can go up and down significantly without any real operational or strategic change in the underlying companies. It is just a giant casino and sophisticated method to lure investors in, and then steal their money! Stock exchanges were used to even steal the wealth of an entire nation, as we seen in the currency attacks, which caused financial crisis of Asian Tigers in 1997. Such an attack creates suffering on a large scale due to loss of jobs, inflation, and poverty that follows. So we should not leave this topic unaddressed.

The stock exchanges around the world have deviated heavily from their original purpose, that is, to trade stocks and shares. They have now become gambling houses, and we know the house always wins. Here, only the individual investors lose their money, but if it is played by the big foreign investors with the knowhow and backing of world finances and financiers, then it could cripple an entire economy in a day. This is usually an unnoticed aspect of a country's

National Security Doctrine. But like the physical borders of a country, the stock markets are its *Financial Borders*, which should be included in National Security policy and protected similar to its physical borders.

But being a Muslim country we have an added responsibility to prevent gambling within our borders. Further, from the point of view of law, if someone steals money using sophisticated methods then we usually do not prosecute them because we do not understand the dynamics of such theft. If we are to discuss how the money is stolen then it will need hundreds of pages due to complexity and sophistication todays' stock markets have. But I will discuss a few things briefly to explain my point.

Firstly we need to know that the world's largest stock exchanges such as, NYSE, NASDAQ, Tokyo Stock Exchange, London Stock Exchange, and Hong Kong Stock Exchange are all owned by private firms. Shanghai Stock Exchange is the largest of state owned stock exchange which is a non-profit organisation. Our Karachi Stock Exchange is owned by members and brokers, which is going towards demutualisation but it is not owned by the state. I am against governments owning corporations but there are certain functions that cannot be allowed to be owned by private individuals such as stock exchanges, because they determine a nation's economic destiny.

In stock exchanges, there is an important and powerful player, known as the *Market Maker*, which is the real culprit? A market maker is a company or an individual that quotes both a buy and a sell price in a financial instrument or commodity held in inventory, hoping to make a profit on the bid-offer spread. There are many ways the market makers and owners of stock exchanges steal people's money, but I will mention only three of them here; bid-offer spread, short selling, and IPO. Let's see the various ways the market makers steal public wealth.

On stock exchanges, there are privileges given to market makers which are instrumental in their theft. These privileges are not available to ordinary investors. So they are disadvantaged. At the time of writing, the market makers margin requirements were only 5%, while individual investor must keep 50% margins in their accounts. Margin requirement is the amount of money you must maintain in your account to buy the amount of stock you desire. This means that if a market maker wants to buy shares worth $1,000,000 then he only needs to have $50,000 in his account. But an ordinary investor must have $500,000 in his account if he wants to buy the same value of shares. This gives market makers huge advantage over any individual investor.

Further, if an ordinary investor wants to buy or sell large blocks of shares of stock in a certain company, then by law the market maker must be notified in advance. He cannot just surprise the market maker with large blocks of stock orders. So the market maker has the inside special privilege to know how much stock people want to buy or sell. With such knowledge, the market maker can 'move the market' in his stock and increase or decrease the price of his stock based on the law of supply and demand, and make huge amounts of profits.

Furthermore, when a company has important news announcement to make that will seriously affect the price of the stock; the company must tell the important news to the market maker 30 days in advance of releasing the news to the public. This gives market makers enough time to manipulate the market by advertising campaign or planted financial journalists etc.

The last two privileges, if used by individual investors, would be punishable by law under 'insider information' in some countries, but the market makers get away with it because they, along with private stock exchange owners, control the stock exchanges.

Let us now see how the Bid-offer spread works in favour of market makers. This is the easiest of the idea to understand. The stock market or market makers buy a share at a lower price than they sell at. For example, if they buy a share for XYZ Company for Rs.50 from you, then they could sell the same share for Rs.60. This is known as bid-offer spread. They have made an instant profit of Rs.10 per share in above example, and if they sell hundreds of thousands of these shares a day, then they make huge profits, and no one can protest against it.

Initial Public Offering (IPO) is another method of stealing people's money. It is a type of public offering where a company sells its shares to the public for the first time, and this process convert a private company to a public company. Please note that a company, which sells its shares, is never required to repay capital to public investors. The companies undertaking IPOs use the services of investment banking firms who tend to have their own brokerage houses. The investment banking firms create marketing campaigns, and are known to use the Boiler Room[19] Techniques to push the value of the stock as high as they can, from double to ten times its worth, like in the days of dot com bubble. Such an IPO is collusion between the IPO offering firm and the investment banking firm running its operation, to steal the wealth of ordinary investors. The investors later find that the investments they had bought were not worth tenth of the price they had paid for it. People lose billions in this way but they cannot do anything about it because law is silent on this.

We hear almost every day that billions had been lost on the stock markets, but have we ever thought where has all the lost money gone? Stock markets are *Zero Sum Games*[20] like the gambling, that

---

[19] A Boiler Room is usually referred to an outbound call centre that sells questionable stocks by telephone.
[20] In economic theory or game theory, the Zero Sum Game refers to a situation where, when calculated, the losses of losing participants equal

is, someone's loss is someone's profit. Let us suppose that a few people are playing poker for money. If someone loses fifty rupees then someone gains fifty. Similarly, if billions of rupees are lost in the stock market, then billions of rupees are gained by a few, who are likely to be the market makers or members of stock market. We must not allow such things to go on in our country, so to protect the wealth of our ordinary investors.

The easiest way to achieve this goal is to return the stock markets to its original role, of being a broker between a company selling its shares, and investors buying them. The gambling aspect could be removed by putting a small tax on each transaction, and a graduated tax on profits gained in short periods. Let me explain what I mean? Investment is usually defined as putting someone's money in stocks and shares of a company for at least five years, to profit from its growth and dividends[21]. Any investment less than five years is considered a *Speculation*. Speculation is just a respectable word for gambling. So if we put a small tax on each transaction, say 0.5%, then it will reduce the profit and discourage *Day Trading*, or short-term trading. Day trading means to buy and sell the same shares in a day. Short-term trading, as the name suggests, is to buy and sell shares in a short-term of a few days, months, or a few years. All of these types of trading are speculation or gambling. Graduated taxes that discourage gambling and encourage investment will be effective. For example, if someone buys and then sells the stock within 30 days, or vice versa, then we could impose a 10% tax on such transaction. This tax is then gradually reduced by 1% for every month they have held stocks. For example, if the stocks are bought and sold in the second month then the tax would be 9%, for third month 8%, and so on until in the tenth month when the tax would be

---

exactly to the gains of winning participants. In other words, if we deduct losses from gains, then the resulting sum would be zero.

[21] A Dividend is a payment made by a corporation to its shareholder, which is usually a distribution of profit.

reduced to 1%. It should then be 1% tax for all transactions until three years. If anyone keeps their stocks and shares for more than three years, then they should be able to reclaim any taxes they paid, so we could encourage investment and discourage gambling. This way, we have fulfilled the Islamic State's duty and protected novice investors at the same time.

Now let us discuss how we could protect our financial borders? Because others will attack our financial borders for various reasons, from making profits to doing the will of international institutions to push us towards IMF, World Bank, and others. You may wonder how they could attack our financial borders. The exact dynamics are quite complex of such attacks, but I will explain and simplify how the Asian Financial Crisis of 1997 occurred. There are many conspiracy theories, and some strong arguments, but I am not going to go into them and I will ignore why it happened. Instead, let us just take a look at how it happened. Much foreign capital flowed into South East Asia, which created growth in the receiving economies. We should be sceptical of growth in economies due only to capital, because such a growth is superficial. As mentioned earlier, the real growth comes from Total Factor Productivity[22] (TFP), which is also known as MFP. The large proportion of Asian Tiger's growth was due to asset appreciation, that is, the rise in house prices. These economies borrowed heavily apart from the short-term foreign investment in their stock and currency markets. Some, including the foreign ministers of these countries, say the crisis was created deliberately. But others say that a rise in interest rates in USA pulled investors back into USA for more profits from high interest rates there. These investors took most of their money out from Asian

---

[22] Total Factor Productivity (TFP) refers to a variable which accounts for effects in total output, which is not caused by inputs of labour or capital. In other words, TFP measures an economy's long-term technological change or its technological dynamism. TFP is also called Multifactor Productivity.

Tiger countries quickly, because most of investment was in the stock market and not in real factories or businesses. Most of the investment was in foreign currency so the Tigers needed to convert their local currencies to US dollars and other currencies, for which they should have had a lot of foreign exchange reserves. Unfortunately, they only had a limited amount of foreign exchange reserve and could not pay back the investors the needed dollars. This created a sort of bank run[23] on these economies and their currencies lost values. As investors learned that these countries do not have enough foreign exchange to pay back everyone, they all panicked and tried to sell their investments. This further devalued Asian Tiger's currencies, and investors could not convert their investments into enough dollars. If these investments were in local currencies then there would not have been a problem, because they could have just printed the needed money, but you cannot print foreign currency. Well, the real impact this crisis had, was the indebtedness of Asian Tigers. This was because these countries borrowed heavily from foreign banks and institutions and the loans were denominated in US dollars. So when the currencies of the affected nations were devalued drastically, their foreign debt increased phenomenally. This is because now they needed a lot of local currency to buy a few dollars. This was an attempt to enslave these nations to foreign banks and institutions?

Since Asian Crisis, many countries have learnt the lesson, and they have adopted a policy to tackle such speculative currency attacks, by holding foreign currency equal to short-term foreign investment. This means that the world is now holding hundreds of billions of US dollars. This has several implications. Firstly, the economies of the world are linked even more to USA, which means that any crisis in USA will have impact on the rest of the world. So it is in everyone's interest to keep USA afloat, no matter how irresponsibly it behaves

---

[23] A Bank Run occurs in a Fractional Reserve Banking when a large number of depositors try to withdraw their money simultaneously.

financially. Secondly, the dollar has gained hegemony at the cost of other currencies. Thirdly, USA receives a Seigniorage[24] on all the US dollars which the rest of the world holds in its reserves. Apart from Seigniorage, the holding country also loses out on currency price movements. Even though many countries prefer to hold US dollars in their reserves to thwart currency attacks, but I think such a policy is dangerous and costly for the reasons I mentioned above. Why should we not discourage the speculators in the first place and encourage more *Foreign Direct Investment* (FDI) in bricks and mortar, which cannot be taken out so quickly?

I do not disagree that we may have to keep foreign exchange reserve to trade with others. But would it not be better that our currency becomes the Reserve Currency of the world? Then we will not have a problem of foreign exchange reserve requirements. But in the short term, we could protect our financial borders by first requiring a notice period of at least 30 days, if anyone wants to place an order to buy or sell a stock or share for an amount larger than Rs.500,000. This will give us enough time to react. But we must make fundamental changes to our stock markets. We should firstly regulate them through Central Bank and then take them out of hands of a few individuals and make them true public companies by converting them to POCs as explained elsewhere in this book. We should not stop at these measures only, but the experts need to analyse our financial system for weaknesses and further reforms, because the future attacks will not be the same as previous ones.

[24] Seigniorage is the difference between the value of a currency and the cost to produce and distribute it.

Free Trade & Protectionism

Most mainstream economists advocate free trade[25] between states and no protectionist policies because it benefits all those who trade. In the case of two countries trading with each other, free trade means that they do not impose tariffs, taxes, or other policies which makes the imported products expensive than the local ones. Protectionism is just opposite of free trade. The reason economist give for free trade, is that it helps an economy through a concept, known as Comparative Advantage.   David Ricardo proposed the theory of comparative advantage in his book *On the Principles of Political Economy and Taxation* in 1817. Comparative advantage can be explained with a simple example.

Suppose, in a fishing village, Salma could make 4 loaves of bread and catch 2 fish in a day. But if she specialises, then she can either make 8 loaves of bread, or catch 4 fish in a day. But on the other hand, Ali can catch 6 fish and make 2 loaves of bread in a day. But if he specialises, then he could either catch 10 fish, or make 5 loaves of bread in a day. As you can see from this example that Salam is good at making bread, while Ali is good at fishing. In other words, Salma has comparative advantage over Ali when it comes to making bread, while Ali has comparative advantage for fishing.

Let us now consider how they both will benefit if they specialised and traded with each other.   Before specialising, they both could make 6 loaves of bread and catch 8 fish in a day, making the total units produced to 14. But if they both specialised, then Salma could make 8 loaves of bread, and Ali could catch 10 fish in a day, making the total units produced to 18. There are now 4 extra units, which mean that if they specialised and traded their products with each other, then both of them will have extra bread and fish. The same

---

[25] Free Trade is a form of international trade which is left to its natural course. That is, there are no tariffs, quotas, or other restrictions on trade.

principle could be applied to two countries that trade with each other and specialise in producing the goods they have comparative advantage in. For example, some countries can grow tea very easily because their soil and weather is suited to tea production. If other countries try to produce tea whose' soil and weather is not good for growing it, then they will waste time, energy, and capital, but they still will not be able to grow good quality and quantity of tea. These countries would be better off in specialising in the goods they could produce easily, and trade. This is the reason the economists stress that countries should specialise and trade with each other, because all the trading countries will mutually benefit. But any barriers that come in the way of two countries trading, such as, tariffs, then they both lose the benefits which could have been drawn from their specialisation. Large scale producers of goods and services who have influence and political links, push *Protectionist's Policies*[26] to impose tariffs on certain goods and services which they produce, to ensure they continue to make large profits. However, if the government did not impose tariffs on those goods and services, then all of its citizens will benefit from cheap and good quality imported goods and services. In other words, money is stolen from people's pocket by the government and given it to their friends who own these industries!

People, who are against free trade and favour protectionism, argue that this way they could save our infant industries and jobs. There is some weight in their arguments but in reality, they own industries which produce the same goods they want to impose tariffs and quotas on, so they could protect their profits. For example in Pakistan, people who are against importing foreign cars older than three or five years, have their own car assembly plants. This is because the cars built in Pakistan have lower standards, even by the same manufacturer, than the same car built in the UK or other

---

[26] Protectionist policies are policies that restrict international trade to protect local businesses.

advanced countries. If there were no age restrictions on car imports, then less new local cars will be sold in the country. These restrictions are the reasons the cars usually hold their prices in Pakistan, while they lose their values in other countries as soon as they come out of car showroom. The result is the low quality cars get expensive in Pakistan, and extra prices the buyers pay goes into the pockets of local car assembly plant owners! Let me digress here a little to point out an important issue in my mind. In the West most families have four members, that is, a father, mother, and two children. So a car that carries five passengers is suitable for West. But the average family size in Pakistan is perhaps eight or nine family members, that is, a father, mother, and six or seven children. But almost all of the cars sold in Pakistan have five seats, which are not suitable for Pakistanis. The cars that we need should have an extra row of seats so it makes it eight seater car. But if the design is changed slightly, then we could have three seats at front to make it a nine seater car. Our government must tell the car manufacturers abroad that 90% of the cars they will send to Pakistan needs to have nine seats but still the same design as a car. All the manufacturers have to do is to stretch the length of the car to add extra seats. The government could allow car manufacturers to add no more than 20% on the car price for such cars.

Imported cars are just one example but there are hundreds of other goods and services that have tariffs in Pakistan, which only make things expensive for Pakistanis. Everyone suffers because a few people with power want to make larger profits for themselves! Increased prices are not the only problem that comes from protectionist policies, but it also makes our local industries un-competitive with the rest of the world and they do not advance. So, in the long run, with protectionist policies our industries will be left way behind in technology and management than those who did not impose protectionist policies. This will eventually force us to import foreign made goods at higher prices. Let me explain my argument with an example.

Hindustan Motors of India was left way behind in technology by imposing protectionist policies. India restricted importing cars to help its motor industry, which meant the Hindustan Motors had captive customer base, who had to buy locally made cars. The Hindustan Motors did not have any incentive to improve their cars because they were sold to local people who had no choice but to buy them due to protectionist policies. So an Ambassador car built in early 80s would not be much different than its original, which came out of showroom in 1958. This was a loss of two decades of technological innovations and advance. India did eventually realise its mistake and it is now trying to catch up with the rest of the world. To go even a step further, it is buying the whole car brands to make its mark on the world car market!

Despite my stance against protectionist policies, I do understand that we need to protect our infant industries and jobs. But the argument of saving infant industries should not be misused for private gains. Instead, we need to come up with some concrete plans to grow our infant industries to maturity, by adopting advanced technology in a shortest time. The main hurdle for our infant industry is the lack of information of other technologies and financial resources. The government should hire experts, some even from the advanced nations into our Planning Commission who could guide our industrialists on new technologies. Then the government must provide these industries cheap loans to buy the new technologies. So the trade tariffs and quotas should be imposed only for short periods, such as, a year or two, until these industries have acquired technology and can compete with the most advanced nations. We must not keep on protecting our industries for a long time, because they will become lazy and left behind other nations like Hindustan Motors. We must not fear to compete with the advanced nations because competing with them will make us strong and resilient. It is the same principle that was proposed by our founding father, philosopher, and Thinker, Allama Muhammad Iqbal in his poetry 'Do not fear oh Eagle of the opposite winds – they only blow, so you can rise even higher'.

Price Controls

Ordinary people who do not understand economics believe that by fixing prices of the commodities, the poor will get all of what they need. Unfortunately, the opposite happens. By fixing prices the poor pay more, or they go without having what they need. The examples of price controls in Pakistan in recent history are Electricity Prices controlled by NEPRA, Sasti Roti Scheme by Punjab government, and federal government buying wheat on large scale to be resold to the public. As you can see all of these policies cause shortages. But why?

Let us first see what the price controls are. Prices could be controlled in two ways, by setting the maximum or minimum prices. Government could set a maximum price above which it must not rise. This is called Price Ceiling in economics. Similarly, the government could also set a minimum price below which it cannot fall, which is known as Price Floor. Let us consider some of the price control examples in Pakistan and their negative effects on Pakistanis.

NEPRA is the government department responsible for setting electricity prices. Historically, it has set prices of electricity lower than the cost of production. This meant the producers were making losses, which the government had to repay to producers. NEPRA's policy was not intended to provide cheap electricity to public, but due to its inefficiency and incompetence, the NEPRA prices behaved similar to Price Ceiling. The results are obvious: there is extreme shortage of electricity, causing widespread job losses, poverty, and human suffering.

Sasti Roti scheme by Punjab government is another example of government interfering with Market Forces[27]. This scheme failed, because no government is powerful than the market forces in a free market economy. Sasti Roti scheme, meaning *Cheap Bread* scheme, was introduced by the Punjab government, so the poor people could have access to cheap food. No one could doubt local government's good intentions but that is not enough. The good intentions must to be backed with sound economics. The basic economics tells us that if something is cheap then there will be greater demand for it. There will be more people buying than the producers could produce. In this example, the government was subsidising the scheme, which meant more and more money would be needed to fulfil the ever increasing demand. This makes such a scheme unsustainable, and that is why the scheme was abandoned. The chief minister of Punjab obviously was not an economist, but why none of his advisers warned him of the dangers of such schemes, which would waste a lot of money and still cause humiliation for him?

Let us now turn to an example of Price Floors in Pakistan. The government buys wheat from the farmers at a pre-determined price, that is, the minimum price the government will pay the farmers for their products. As far as I am aware the government makes this large scale purchase to ensure food security, so any needed grains are not exported. I am sceptical about this claim because if the food security was the main reason for such purchase then why millions of people are going hungry in Pakistan? I may be wrong, but I think the government buys large amount of grain to increase the price of grains to create large profits for large agro-businesses, which are owned by politicians, or their friends and families. The reason is simple. When the government holds almost all the grains produced in the country, then it is the largest monopoly. So it can set any price it likes. People are disadvantaged in two ways under such a system.

---

[27] Market Forces are the economic factors that affect the price, demand, and availability of a commodity

Firstly, the government pays higher prices for grains to large businesses from tax payer's money, which is a transfer of wealth from the poor to the rich! Secondly, by creating artificial food inflation, the government destroys the buying power of the public. So many will go hungry, or will not be fed properly. But there is another dimension to basic commodities in Pakistan.

According to Sheikh Rashid, an old name in Pakistani politics, a handful of politicians monopolise the twelve basic commodities in Pakistan. So they can charge any price for those basic goods, and people have no choice but to pay higher prices. If this is true, then the Pakistani politicians have gained full control over all of its citizens, and have made them slaves, politically and economically!

Pakistan works on the principles of free market economy, so the government must not interfere with market forces because it will always come back to bite them. However, they must take actions to make this free market economy efficient, by getting rid of monopolies, hoarding by traders, and price fixing. All of these three are bad for economy and people will pay higher than normal prices for low quality goods. The government's job should be just to ensure that the markets work properly and efficiently, and nothing more.

I think the government should let the market forces decide the prices of goods and services according to supply and demand. Most years, we produce more food than we need. This means the prices should be lower because there is an excess supply. But there are two things that can still increase prices despite the oversupply of food products. Firstly, there is war going on in Afghanistan, and they are willing to pay any price for food. This demand leads our people to smuggle food out of Pakistan into Afghanistan to make larger profits. Secondly, if there is oversupply of food products then the producers know they will get lower prices for their produce here, so they would want to export it, making the food prices higher at home. To keep the prices lower, the government should prevent smuggling of food, and then act as broker for farmers for export. This will ensure only the extra food is exported out.

One of the biggest consumers of food is our army. The government has a duty to keep it fully supplied with the food. Instead of government buying the food for the army, it could choose one of the two options for food supply to army. It could allow the army to buy food in the open market from its budget. This way they could get discounts on large scale purchases. On the other hand, the government could allow the army to create its own agro-business, giving them independence about food. Army has a large standing force, which could be used for this purpose when not at war. When at war, the army could use civilians for its agro business. The government has large unused farmland, which it could let the army to use. This may not be enough, so the army's agro business could lease large areas of agricultural land from other landlords. The army should be encouraged to produce more than it needs. So some of it could be stored for future when food is short, while the rest should be given out to poor on subsidised prices. This will increase the prestige of our army and government.

Interest & Islam

Holy Quran, the guidance from God for Muslims, forbids the taking of interest on money lent. Pakistan's constitution declares that, all laws in Pakistan will be made according to Quran and Sunnah[28]. But we have a banking system that charges interest on loans! Most Pakistanis agree that the interest based banking system is against the spirit of Islam. However, there are now some Middle-Eastern Muslims scholars, who defend charging of interest. I am not a

---

[28] Sunnah is the way of life prescribed for Muslims according to the teachings and practices of Muhammad(PBUH) , which was based on exegesis of the Quran.

scholar in Islamic jurisprudence so I cannot offer my input, but I will outline their arguments for our scholars and thinkers to debate on.

They argue that the word that Quran uses for interest is Riba, and Riba was actually an ancient Arab practice of taking the borrower and, or borrower's family into slavery if he could not pay his loan on a specified date. The borrower was usually given two chances before the lender would enforce slavery. At first failure to repay the loan, the lender would double the loan for failure to keep the promise, and then give another date to repay this increased loan. By doubling the loan, lender is actually ensuring that the borrower will not be able to pay the loan because he is already in financial difficulty. When the borrower fails to repay the loan for the second time, which is most likely, then his loan was re-doubled, and the lender would give a new date to borrower to repay. This doubling and re-doubling was guaranteed to put the borrower and his family into slavery because it was now impossible for the borrower to pay this extortionate amount, unless the borrower gets help from his rich relatives or friends. These scholars, point out that when Quran speaks of Riba, then it refers to this doubling and redoubling of loan. They argue that the Islam forbids the practice of Riba but not the modern banking interests, because the borrower is never penalised like Riba. At least in the West, the struggling borrower can always declare himself bankrupt and absolve himself of all financial liabilities. The borrower has never gone to jail for non-payment of loans in recent times. I could sense that these arguments could have been given by those who have a vested interest in charging interest by backing their deeds with some historical facts or fiction. However, I am in no position to reject their arguments because I am not an Islamic scholar. Unfortunately, we do not have a central Islamic institution which everyone accepts. So we will have conflicting views on many matters including bank interest.

Interestingly, the top leadership of the new government in Pakistan are practising conservative Muslims who try to follow the Islamic financial rules, but there seems to be some intellectual confusion among them about charging interest. This is because, during his first budgetary speech of new government, the Finance Minister, Ishaq Dar made a comment about charging a Mark-up rather than Interest on loans, because he believed that interest was forbidden (Haram) in Islam. His comments suggest then the mark-up on a loan must be allowed in Islam?

Mark-up on a loan achieves the same results as charging interest because a mark-up is added to the original amount of loan which the borrower must pay. This is like loading all the interest up front. I think just by changing the name and the shape of interest and calling it a mark-up, does not make it Halal[29]. A similar example of intellectual confusion comes from the late president Zia-ul-Haq era, who was also a conservative Muslim. In his era the banks started offering Profit & Loss Bank Accounts. But I am yet to find a person who lost any money from a Profit & Loss Account? They all made profit, which is just another name for interest. To digress a little, another thing that was distressing in Zia era was that many people started claiming to be Shia Muslims, when they were actually Sunni Muslims. So the government would not deduct yearly Zakat[30] from their bank accounts!

What do we do for money? I think that one should be clear in his faith and follow it wholeheartedly, instead of following what is profitable. I can understand the plight of the Finance Minister because if he implements an interest-free system at this moment in time, then the capital will take a flight, meaning it will flow out of country. This is because no one will earn any interest on their savings. So by keeping their money in the bank while the inflation is high, the value of their wealth without receiving any interest will

---

[29] Halal is an Arabic word for what is allowed in Islam. Haram is the opposite of Halal, meaning forbidden.

[30] Zakat is one of the five pillars of Islam, and it is the prescribed alms that the Muslims are required to pay from their wealth.

decrease drastically, and the rich will become middle class, and middle class will become poor, in a few months. In this situation, the best choice the people have is to take their money out of Pakistani banks and put it in foreign banks where they will earn interest. If such a situation arises, then the government, businesses, and people will have no access to any capital to borrow and the economy will go into a tailspin.

However, our Constitution requires that we have true Islamic banking, and it is also the responsibility of the government to provide an economic environment for all of its citizens to follow their faith. By not providing an environment to establish an interest-free banking the government is failing in its moral, legal, and religious obligations. To resolve this, the government could launch a pilot project running a parallel banking system which follows the strict Islamic rules. For it to be successful, the government needs to provide its full support and guarantee in case people lose their money. The best option is to run Islamic banks only in a few districts as pilot projects, and learn and fix any problems that come along the way, until we have found a way to run a successful true Islamic banking. Only then we should slowly roll it out in the rest of the country. We must never do it all in one go because an economic disaster will more likely to follow. Further, we should be keenly aware of what is happening outside of our borders and how it could affect our finances?

Minimum Wage

Capitalists and Free-Market thinkers are against government setting a minimum wage for the labour, arguing that it will lead to loss of jobs. While the socialists want the governments to set minimum wage, arguing that it stops capitalists exploiting the helpless workers. When the governments set a minimum wage that should be paid by the employers to its workers, then it reduces business profits.

But a capitalist is only in business because he wants to make more profit with least expense. And if he is forced to pay more wages for the same work, then he usually does two things. Firstly, to keep the profit levels same as before the minimum wage came into force, he reduces the number of employees, which causes job losses and poverty. Secondly, because he pays more now, he forces the existing workers to do the work of those who have been made redundant. Unfortunately, this scenario usually plays out in Pakistan because it is a Market Economy[31]. The loser in this scenario is the labourer who has lost his job. But the labourer who kept his job has also lost out, because he now does more work for a small increase in his wage. Currently, the minimum wage in Pakistan is Rs.10,000 per month, but the capitalists do not obey these rules. Many people are paid less than half of the minimum wage in Pakistan because people are grateful for just having a job so they do not complain. Further, the employers do not take their employees on permanent contracts to avoid giving them job security and other benefits, even when these workers had been working there for many years

Apart from the labourer losing out, there are two more problems. Firstly, the minimum wage laws hurt small businesses the most and they can no longer compete with large corporations who benefit from Economies of Scale[32]. Small businesses may go out of business if they have to pay a higher wage, worsening the problem of unemployment. The government loses out in revenue which used to come from taxing those who were employed. Large scale job losses could also add to the problems of government in the form of social unrest.

---

[31] Market Economy is an economic system that relies mainly on market forces to allocate goods and resources and to determine prices. This means that the government does not centrally decides on prices and allocation of resources.

[32] When a company produces goods in a very large quantity then it reduces its cost. This is called Economies of Scale.

The government could enforce minimum wage laws if they wanted to, but they cannot stop employers from shedding jobs. Minimum wage policy is bad for the economy and people because they will not have jobs. But the politicians like minimum wage policies because they can win more votes. However, the voting public may not understand the macro level economic consequences from such policies, such as, job losses. But they only see the government as on their side to force employers to pay them more. So they vote for such politicians. If the ordinary people understood that minimum wage policies actually hurt them, then they would not vote for those politicians who give them false hopes.

If the governments want more jobs for people then they should have no minimum wage policy and let employers pay what they want. The existing businesses will expand and new businesses will start to create a lot of jobs. But many fear that if there were no minimum wage policy, then the employers will make the slaves out of public by paying them meagre wages. Yes, there will be some employers who would pay small wages, but in the long run the employers will learn that a reasonable wage must be paid, because the quantity and quality of work is directly related to the reward an employee gets. There is an unspoken, unwritten universal law, that states 'The employer will pay just enough so the employee does not leave, and the employee works just enough so the employer does not fire him.' Further, the labour market also works on supply and demand principles. So initially, when there are many unemployed people, and there is no minimum wage law, the employers will pay lower wages. But as the economy improves and more and more people are employed, then this will create a shortage of workers, which will push the wages up. But the most important thing right now for our economy is to put our entire workforce in employment, producing goods and services to create economic growth. Instead of setting minimum wages, the government should ensure that the labour laws are satisfactory to protect its workforce. There should be a balance between protecting the rights of workers and not creating negative incentives for employers. The employers should be required to ensure the health and safety of its workforce and provide training and opportunities for their career development without any prejudice. The government on the other hand can set Guide Minimum Wages, not Minimum Wage, for major sectors of employment. It must stipulate that any companies wishing to get governmental contracts must be paying Guide Minimum Wages to all of its employees and not just at the time of tendering contract. But any breach by firms even after the contract is over, will incur heavy fines. These steps will ensure that major employers pay good wages to their employees and the best employees will go to work there. But other employers will also want the best employees so they will have to raise their wages as well.

Welfare Benefits

Since 2007 Pakistan had been paying welfare benefits to people below poverty line, and there were 70 billion rupees allocated for it in 2012-2013. I am amazed that how a country that has to borrow money every year to finance its budget, can hand out such a big sum of money, even when it may come from outside? While the intentions may be good - it is unsustainable and bad for people who receive them. What would poor people do who have become dependent on it when it eventually stops?

The developed nations, such as, UK and Europe are trying to move away from welfare benefits because it is becoming unsustainable without continuously increasing taxes. They are reducing benefits and making it difficult for people to get them. The welfare benefits are not the only public expense the government has to make, but there is also National Health which provides free healthcare to rich and poor. But why, we a developing nation, deeply in debt, are moving towards a welfare benefits system? Could it be just another copycat act like we did in 2002 by adopting Daylight Savings Time (DST) to look more Western?

There is a Chinese proverb that goes '*Give a man a fish and you feed him for a day. Teach a man to fish and you feed him for a lifetime.*' By giving people income support, we are feeding them for a day and making them dependent, which is not good for them. If we want to eradicate poverty then we need to teach them to fish, so they become independent. In the next chapter I have discussed in detail, how we could produce economic growth and eradicate poverty. We cannot wipe out poverty by giving people money. But if we want to eradicate poverty then we should create an economic environment which is suitable for new jobs and opportunities. We then need to ensure the extremely poor people will get jobs first, by offering incentives to employers to employ those who are living below poverty line.

Producing Economic Growth and Prosperity

In the previous chapter we discussed some of the important economic policy issues, which need to be resolved before the country could move towards economic growth. In this chapter we will discuss some of the things that are holding us back, so by resolving them we could move forward. Then we will discuss some of the ways we could actively create economic growth. But I believe that we should not just try to increase the GDP, because increase in GDP could be created without making the majority of the people better off. That is, we could have a few very rich industrialists increasing our GDP, but most people may remain poor. So there is an automatic increase in GDP without any real growth. The politicians also deceive us by telling us that our GDP has grown by quoting the Nominal GDP. The nominal GDP does not tell us about real growth because the way it is calculated. The nominal GDP is calculated using current prices of goods and services. But if the inflation is high then prices will be higher, and it will seem that our GDP is growing really fast. For example, if the price of a 20 kg flour bag was Rs.300 last year and it has increased to Rs.600 this year, then it will show as a rise in GDP, but in fact there had been no growth, only the prices of goods have increased. But many politicians confuse people by quoting a 3% or more GDP increase a year due to inflation, and they do not tell us that the increase in prices of goods and services increases nominal GDP, but this is not the real growth. To calculate the real growth in GDP, we need to deduct the inflation element from the nominal [33] GDP increase. Further, how is it possible to have economic growth when thousands of factories have closed down, and millions of people are unemployed? I cannot recall a year when Pakistan declared economic recession. In Britain, we had a few quarters of recession in recent years where most of the people are employed and there are no other issues, but Pakistani government has always posted GDP growth of around 3% or more. We would be lucky if we had a Hindu Rate of Growth [34] in Pakistan!

Instead of getting into a race with other countries in economic growth, we should create growth at the grass root level, ensuring that our people are out of poverty, into middle class, and finally rich. This is because if the majority of the people are rich in a country then the GDP would have increased itself. My point is to concentrate on eradicating poverty, rather than GDP growth because growth will happen as a by-product. To achieve our goals, we first need to tackle the energy shortage crisis, and then decide on the things to produce instead of producing just raw materials. This is because the richest nations of the world produce final products, while the poor countries produce raw materials for them. We will then take a look at reversing brain drain because that is our guarantee for economic growth.

We will then briefly discuss intellectual property rights and their importance in economic growth. We will look at some of the ways to reduce poverty instead of giving poor people handouts. The heart of our discussion on economic growth will be on the POCs, a special kind of corporation that will be owned mainly by the public with a

---

[33] Nominal GDP refers to gross domestic product (GDP) that has not been adjusted for inflation

[34] Hindu Rate of Growth refers to a very slow rate of per capita income growth of less than 2% in India between 1950s to 1980s.

small governmental share. These corporations, if started, will not only bring widespread prosperity, but will also provide funds for the government to run its operation, which will reduce the need to increase taxes. Finally, we will discuss the importance of water for our survival as a nation, and alcohol for oil programme to tackle our foreign exchange reserve issue.

Electricity Shortage

In Pakistan, there has been an electricity shortage since early 2008, causing rolling blackouts (load shedding) of more than 20 hours a day in many parts of the country. At the time of writing, according to Pakistan Electric Power Company (PEPCO), the electricity shortfall is between 2,500 to 6,000 megawatts (MW) depending on the season. According to some estimates more than 12,000 factories closed down in the last five years, making hundreds of thousands of people unemployed, which have caused a wide spread poverty. Further, if there is no electricity for 20 hours a day, then nothing could be done in any household, from cooking, cleaning, to children studying. People could not even sleep in hot summers because the fans or air conditioning cannot work without electricity. In fact, people's lives are turned upside down because of electricity shortage. But before we could find a solution, let us first discuss the reasons for electricity shortage?

Analysts will tell us several reasons for the consistent shortfall, but there is only a single basic reason, the wrong pricing of electricity units. Pakistan has three main sources of production of electricity, petroleum, gas, and hydro power plants, where each element makes up roughly one third of total production. The cost of production is highest using petroleum, and least for hydro power, while for gas it is in between. The matter is further complicated by having many companies within the power sector, including production and distribution companies etc. For example, there are power generation companies which rely on fuel supplying companies. Then there are transmission and distribution companies which supply electricity to our homes and factories. Finally, there is NEPRA which sets the price for electricity. NEPRA is constantly trying to figure out the right price per unit because the price of oil is volatile in international markets. Historically, NEPRA had been behind with the price change, so the cost of producing electricity was always higher than the price it was sold. This meant that someone had to pay the difference, and it was always the government who picked up the bill. By using simple arithmetic, we can easily see that if we produced more electricity, then the bill the government would need to pay due to wrong prices will be greater. So the last government decided not to pay the producers so they would stop producing more electricity. This kept the cost down for the government. But this strategy cost the last government the general elections in 2013. There was a real need to set the price of electricity correctly, so the cost of production was equal to or less than the cost of supply. The last government did not want to resolve the structural problems in electricity production because it meant increasing electricity prices, which would have been a problem for the government. But by not doing anything, it still brought a bad outcome for the last government.

However, the new government is trying to make some changes, and taking some positive steps. But ultimately, this would mean the price per unit will go up dramatically to cover the costs of new plants, and to equalise the production and supply costs. People at first, may not mind the higher cost of electricity, because they are sick and tired of not having any electricity. But as the time passes, the people will realise that they are paying a much higher price even when the electricity production is shifted to coal. The opposition, who lost the general elections from the new government due to load shedding, will certainly capitalise on the higher costs of electricity, which may, again decide the fate of incumbent government?

Further, the Prime Minister has made it clear that it will take about five years to get rid of load shedding completely, but others believe it is still not possible. Another issue is that some of the friends of the incumbent government, own electricity power plants, so the government is running the risk of bad public perception by giving favours to its friends, which will certainly go against the party in the next elections. If the government wants to lift this burden from its shoulders and wishes to stay in power in the next elections, then there is an easier solution, which will also bring prosperity to the public.

The easiest solution for the government to get rid of this responsibility is to sell the electricity production and distribution to public, by converting it into a POC, as detailed later in this chapter. Under this arrangement, the government will own 20% shares of the company, while the public will own the rest. This will be a profit making organisation. To streamline production and distribution, we would have to merge all the electricity corporations into one big corporation. To merge the private companies, we would have to make a *Compulsory Purchase Order* and then pay the market prices to them. We then should install a competent management team to run this corporation. By doing this, the government would have shifted its responsibility onto public, and if the prices go up then they cannot complain to government because now the public owns it. And if it takes longer than five years to remove load shedding, then it will not affect the incumbent government's political position. Further, if the CEO of this new corporation is not performing, then the public could get rid of him in the Annual General Meeting. On top of this, the government could call the CEO in front of the parliamentary committee, and tell him off now and then. This way the government and its ministers will absolve themselves of responsibilities for electricity. Another benefit to the government will be that it would not have to pay a subsidy of hundreds of billions rupees every year. However, initially the government should give it a grant to help it stand on its feet.

The government will always want to privatise state corporations by selling them cheaply to party workers or their donors to keep them happy.   But it would be dishonesty and would ruin the party reputation. The government must always stay clear of any privatisation, because the public has the first right to buy it because it is with their taxes, these companies exist in the first place!

Finally, there had been a lot of talk about energy mix, meaning that we should not rely only on petroleum based electricity but also use coal for electricity production. Coal obviously is cheaper than petroleum right now and should be considered. But I think we should take a long view of our energy production, a time when the world would have run out of fossil fuels. Where would we get our energy from then? I know the scientists are working on using energy from hydrogen cells, but all of these inventions are going to cost money and they will have inherent risks. Why don't we look to a source of energy which will not run out for at least a few billion years? That is, the solar energy. It is free and it is in plenty where we live. If we spend money on research and development to develop solar cells, which could store enough energy for a household for 24 hours, then we will not need expensive power plants, or extremely expensive electricity pylons running the length and breadth of the country. Or at least, we should aim to be able to store large amounts of energy in solar cells. I remember when I was in primary school, I asked my father who is an electrical engineer, why do we need these electricity pylons to distribute electricity? Why can we not send them over air, just like the radio signal? He answered with a question, suppose if we could transmit electricity over air like the radio waves, then what would happen to people and animals which will come in the way of electricity transmission, because the air waves will now have a lot of power? He did not have to go into details of problem of metering, and billing. But the answer to my childhood question could be that we may not need these electricity pylons if we created solar cells able to store enough energy to run a house for a week. Would it not be better if we could find a way to quickly collect and store 1 MW of electricity in a rechargeable battery cell that fits in a laptop computer? With a few of these cells, we could run our houses for months, cars for thousands of miles, and we could provide electricity cheaply to people living in remote places.

As we are talking about research and development, I will leave a problem for our scientists and engineers to solve. The biggest problem in electricity production is the inefficiency of power plants. Let me explain what I mean. Most power plants run at about 60% to 75% efficiency, even the hydroelectricity which should have been about 99% efficient due to its storage capacity, still does not achieve this efficiency. The reason the power plants cannot run efficiently is because it is impossible to match the production to demand, especially at night. Suppose the demand of electricity during the day is 18,000 MW but at night it is only 10,000 MW. So when we decrease the power production of a large plant to smaller production, then there is some loss of efficiency but this is not the biggest problem. The biggest problem is that, at night when the power plant is producing 10,000 MW, someone gets up in the middle of night and decides to have a cup of tea. As he turns on his kettle, it throws the whole of power production into a chaos because it now needs an extra 1,000 watts of energy. So the power plant needs to increase its production to cope with an extra 1,000 watts of electricity. In a population of about 200 millions, how many times will the power production has to be increased and decreased? That is anyone's guess. The constant effort of power plant to match the production to consumption is the major cause of inefficiency in power production and management.   To address this problem, many forms of electricity storage had been developed but no one so far has come up with a solution that is efficient and economical. This is the challenge that I want to leave for our scientists and engineers to solve, because whoever solves this problem, will be a billionaire overnight.

Raw Materials vs. End Products

Have you ever thought why the poor countries are poor, and rich remain rich? Well, there is one important difference among them but let us first see some of the reasons which keep countries poor. Constant war keeps a country poor, and a landlocked country has difficulty trading with others or at least it costs more to trade. Similarly, lack of natural resources, such as water, oil, or coal etc also plays an important role in a country becoming rich. If we accept these explanations given by economists, then Japan should have been the poorest and Saudi Arabia the richest nation. But we know that just until last year, Japan was the second largest economy of the world without having any natural resources. And Japan is a much more fascinating phenomenon if we consider that it was the only country in the world, which suffered two nuclear attacks by USA. Japan lost almost a million people in just these two attacks alone. Further, these two nuclear attacks came when Japan's population of the many major cities was reduced to less than half through constant bombing. Despite the severe devastation it suffered, Japan became the second largest economy of the world in a few decades after war. We must learn everything we could from Japan and not from USA for these reasons. On the other hand, when we consider Saudi Arabia, which never suffered devastation like Japan, but it has the second largest petroleum resources in the world, then it is still the twentieth on the list of rich countries. This comparison tells us that by just having many natural resources do not make a country rich. The fate of the nation depends on its leadership, its vision, and how it organises its economy!

We could find an answer to economic prosperity when we observe keenly what the rich countries produce, and what the poor ones produce? It is obvious that the rich countries produce technological goods, while the poor countries produce agricultural, miming or petroleum products. Almost all of the products the poor countries produce are the raw products, which need huge amounts of labour and resources, but they yield only very small profits. Further, if there had been floods or droughts, then these countries make huge losses due to inherent risks in producing such products. This way, the profits of the poor countries are never guaranteed. However, if the poor countries have received debts from IMF or World Bank, then those nations would surely be enslaved, because both of these organisations interfere with the economies of the countries they lend money to. Their prescription for every country is the same; devalue your currency, trade more so you can earn foreign exchange reserve to pay back the debt, increase taxes, and remove all subsidies etc. These policies, especially devaluing currency and doing more trade to gain foreign exchange reserves, ensures that the West receives the raw materials for their factories at rock bottom prices from the Third World!

West on the other hand turns this raw material into finished products, which it sells back to poor countries at higher prices. West's profits are guaranteed because they do not have to worry about their crops getting flooded or suffered from droughts etc. They spend the least amount of energy to produce these finished products for maximum profits. IMF and World Bank act as the brokers of rich nations to ensure the poor countries will remain poor and dependent, and continue to supply the raw materials needed for the West's factories at rock bottom prices. These two organisations achieve this goal through a complex system of giving out loans and then imposing *Structural Adjustment Programmes* etc. IMF and World Bank's methods may be complex but they are no different than the methods of sugar mill owners in Pakistan.

Everyone knows there are only a few sugar mills in Pakistan, which are owned by politicians, their friends, or relatives. No one else in Pakistan is allowed to open a new sugar mill, unless he is a powerful politician or his acquaintance. This is a high level corruption and monopoly because it takes place on the law making side of things. Poor farmers spend months in growing sugar canes, but when the sugar cane is ready to be sold, then no sugar mill owner is willing to buy their produce. Farmers do not have any alternative buyers because there are only a handful of sugar mills in Pakistan who all collude with one another. So after a few days, when the sugar cane starts to rot, the farmers become desperate to sell. So they accept rock bottom prices for their hard labour. However, the sugar mill owners or the monopolists do not put the farmers out of business, just like the worms which do not kill their hosts, but keep the farmers in a situation where they cannot afford to either leave farming, or make good profits. Using similar methods, the West keeps the poor countries poor and helpless through their institutions.

Let us now consider how the poor countries remain poor, and how the rich get rich with a very simple example. Cotton is one of the largest products of Pakistan. We grow cotton in our fields, which takes several months before it is ready to go to factories. To grow cotton, the farmer spends huge amounts of labour, fertilisers, and water etc, which are very expensive. The farmer then takes his cotton to the factories, which turn it into raw cloth. This also needs much labour and resources. We then sell this cotton cloth to America for example, for a low price because our rupee has been devalued. American branded companies design dresses, but they do not do any cutting or sewing etc to turn it into finished dresses. Instead, they send this cloth to China or Bangladesh, where poor women sew these clothes into dresses for pennies. They put the labels of American companies on these dresses and ship them to America. Then we, the fashion conscious, suffering from inferiority complex, buy these foreign branded dresses at much higher prices to impress others, than what our farmers or factory owners have sold their products for. Imagine, if we continue to produce raw materials to sell at low prices to advanced nations, who turn them into finished products, and then we buy these finished products at much higher prices, then can our fate ever change?

One of my proposals for economic prosperity is to produce what the rich countries produce, the finished products and stop relying on producing just the commodities. We in Pakistan produce the finest cotton in the world, then why can we not hire the best designers from around the world, to create our own brand names and sell our products at much higher prices? We should do this for every raw material we produce. Further, we should actually import raw materials from other countries to make other finished products. If we want to be one of the richest nations of the world, then we will have to stop producing raw materials but instead we must produce finished goods. To do that, we must buy technology instead of reinventing the wheel and then improve on it. But what should we produce? If we just take a look at two nations then the answer to this question will become obvious.

China with its huge population has become the Workshop of the World, producing labour intensive goods for Western businesses. On the other hand, Japan with a smaller population, decided a long time ago, to become technologically advanced by first buying the technology already in existence, and then improving it to become the leaders. Everything that Japan produces is expensive and well made, so they do not waste their time and energy on producing cheap goods for Western businesses. But they have decided to produce only the most expensive items, such as, cars, computers, TVs, and watches etc. Do you know who owns Lexus, Toyota, Nissan, Honda, Mitsubishi, Mazda, Yamaha, Suzuki, Sony, Panasonic, Toshiba, Hitachi, Canon, Nikon, Minolta, Fujitsu, Nintendo, Sharp, Seiko, Citizen, Casio, Bridgestone, Yokohama, and Toyo?

Reversing Brain Drain

As we discussed before that it is the leadership that decides the fate of a nation, whether a nation will be rich or poor? But the good leadership comes from the most intelligent of its citizens. When we take a stock of the most intelligent people, then we find that most of them live in the advanced societies. If we are to decide on a single most important factor which makes a nation rich, then it is undoubtedly the most intelligent men and women, most of them live in the West and not in the third world. The West attracts the most intelligent persons from around the world, especially from the Third World. This is because there are hardly any opportunities for intelligent persons in the Third World countries. If there were many intelligent people in the advanced nations than the Third World, then this must be the most important commodity in the world for economic and technological success!

But have we ever thought about why so many educated people leave Pakistan and head for the West? Here in UK, I see more Asian doctors than the English, and doctors are not the only professionals who come to West. These professionals only come to West because they want to advance their skills, and here they have the opportunities to grow professionally. They want to lead a safe and happy life. But they do not get this kind of environment in Pakistan due to widespread corruption, terrorism, and lawlessness. But have we ever thought how much the West profits from the investments of the Third World?

Like the other Third World countries, Pakistan also spends several hundred thousand rupees to produce a doctor, engineer, or a scientist. It then waits patiently for many years for these professionals to be ready to serve Pakistan. Unfortunately, as soon as they qualify, they leave for the West. We not only lose out several hundred billions every year, but we lose out many precious years, which were spent to prepare these professionals. On the other hand, the West spends nothing on these highly qualified and intelligent people, but it profits vastly from their services. On top of that, the West also taxes these professionals to make more profits. Why are we so stupid to lose these professionals?

Here, I would not go into the whys of our stupidity but let us discuss what we could do to plug this gap. First thing that we need to do is to make fundamental changes in our country, that is, eradicate corruption of every kind including barriers to career advancement, and create safety and security for all citizens. Then we need to ensure that our fiscal, monetary, and financial policies are fair for economic growth, which I have discussed in detail in this book. We then need to make a policy to produce and keep highly qualified and intelligent people in Pakistan, not by force or coercion, but with positive incentives. The urgent part of this policy should be to attract highly qualified persons from around the world for our economic and technological growth and prosperity. We could perhaps, follow the readymade programmes adopted by USA, UK, and Canada for this purpose? If we want to grow quickly then it is essential that we have highly skilled and intelligent scientists, managers, teachers, lawyers, doctors, and researchers, who could modify and improve our existing systems and structures, which are outdated. We could achieve this through several sources.

Our first priority should be to attract highly qualified Pakistanis living in the West and elsewhere. They would be the easiest to attract, but we must be careful and not disappoint them with our bureaucracy, nepotism, and patronage policies. The second easiest professionals to attract would be the highly qualified people from nations who are poorer than us, or have a similar sized economy. We could do this by offering them a good package and nationality. The most difficult people to attract would be the highly qualified westerners due to the law and order situation here and not much income that we could offer them. But I would argue and stress that we should at least attract professionals from at least two nations, Germany and Japan.

The reason is that the German engineering is still the best in the world, and if we go back in history after WWII, then we will find that it were not the American and Russian engineers and scientists, who were behind the space race between these two countries, but it were the German scientists who were captured following the Second World War. The Russians got the space scientists while the Americans got other experts. This was the reason that Russia won the space race from America. Further, we only need to look at the German cars or machinery: they are the best in the world.

Similarly, Japan was the most devastated country after Second World War, having suffered from two atomic bombs and losing more than half of its population. But in a short time, they became the second largest economy of the world without having any natural resource. The Japanese electronics and engineering are renowned in the world. As discussed in previous section, they make the most expensive items the world needs and not bother with becoming the labourers of the world. They have developed some of the most successful practices in manufacturing and management that we must learn. So we must attract professionals from at least these two countries to help us advance, even if we have to pay ten times more to professionals from these countries then it will still be worth it because it would be a long-term investment.

Intellectual Property Rights
Pakistan has its own Intellectual Property Office (IPO) but how many inventions have come out of Pakistan that have contributed to its technological advance or wealth? We have our own Copyright laws but the authors and artists have to pay fees and apply for copyrights of their works, while in the rest of the world, the copyright is automatic and no fees or registration is required. Has IPO protected the copyrights of our founder, Allama Muhammad

Iqbal? Billions of rupees worth of our founder's poetry is stolen by those who publish his poetry, without any permission from his heirs.

The only reason that I can see the patents exist in Pakistan is to protect the intellectual property rights of the rich nations, and to prevent us from gaining any benefits! At the time of writing, I checked the last four week's patents issued on IPO's website. I found all the patents that were granted, were to foreign corporations. We are not just the fools, but we are fools of a third degree! The reason we have patent laws in Pakistan is because of TRIPS Agreement (Agreement on Trade Related Aspects of Intellectual Property Rights). Whether we like to be part of the TRIPS Agreement or not, we are forced into this agreement because we are member of WTO (World Trade Organisation), so any decision they make, is automatically imposed on all member states. This book is not about the role and power of international institution, but I would like to digress a little to show you the level of our stupidity by being the members of these international organisations from which we gain no advantage.

There are many drawbacks by being the members of international organisations who act like concubines of USA, because they serve their master-lover. WTO is one of those organisations. By being the member of WTO, we give foreign corporations the same rights as Pakistani citizens. In fact, these corporations have the citizen's rights in every member state of WTO! The problem here is that by giving the citizen's rights to foreign corporations, among other powers, it gives them the power to challenge any laws which they see are damaging to their profits. So foreign corporations gain huge advantage over local corporations due to their size and advanced technologies. Could you or I, go to India, France, or USA and claim exactly the same rights as their citizens? Of course, they will tell us where to go. But these foreign corporations gain the same rights of citizens in every country they operate to dominate their economies, because the turnover of these corporations are more than the GDPs of many countries. Let me be clear here that I am not against patents and copyrights. In fact, I support these initiatives but they must be beneficial to Pakistan. But the current system is created only to make the WTO happy without any thought to what could we gain from it.

My first demand is that a special copyright, which will never expire, must be issued to our founder, Allama Muhammad Iqbal's poetry. Such a copyright will be first of its kind in the world. This copyright must go back to August 14, 1947. All future publishers of Iqbal's poetry must seek permission from his heirs and pay a royalty. Forgive my digression but I like to suggest that Iqbal's poetry is so important that all of his poetry should be organised chronologically, and every line of every poem should be numbered. Poems could be classed as chapters. This way, if we need to refer to a particular line in the poem then we could say chapter 6, line 17, or represent it like 6:17.

Now let us see how we could organise our intellectual property rights which will advance us in technology in a short time while helping economic growth. The first thing we need to do is to get out of TRIPS. I am not a lawyer but it must not be difficult for our lawyers to come up with a solution. The next thing is to look at the weaknesses of the patent offices of the developed nations, so we could exploit them and create an Intellectual Property (IP) system that will pull most of the world's best innovators into Pakistan. Then see how these innovators could help our technological advance and economical growth?

It is estimated that it costs on average about $30,000, and more than two years to get a patent in developed nations, that is, in USA and Europe etc. While the cost and time are the biggest hurdles for an innovator, but under patent laws he must also disclose full details of his invention, if he wants a patent. This way, others could copy his invention where there is no copyright protection. Further, the patent holder must pay a yearly fee or lose his patent. The patent holder also needs to issue civil proceedings against those who copy his invention. The court costs are very high for an individual going to courts. After crossing all these hurdles, he must find money to turn his patent into a product or a service.

Now we understand the issues an inventor faces in the West, we should also understand that people invent only for one reason, to become rich! If we could ensure that the inventor achieves his goal without any hassle, and in a shortest time possible, then we could attract many inventors and innovators in Pakistan. All we have to do is to address the issues which an innovator faces in advanced nations, which I have outlined above. Our patent and intellectual property rights system could work in the following way.

We could ensure that a patent will be issued within 30 days of application as long as they have fulfilled all the requirements. Our patent fees would be set in such a way that it only covers the costs of running its operation, making the process inexpensive for an innovator. We need to ensure we do not have too many layers of management, so we could reduce bureaucratic frustration and costs. IPO could employ patent lawyers who would provide their services on fixed or low costs to help innovators. We would issue the patents only for 10 years instead of the usual 20 years, so our companies can benefit from these innovations. But the other benefits to the patent holder would include a very important clause, in which the innovator does not need to disclose the details of his patent for one year, so it gives him time to create new products and sell them to make profits without worrying that anyone would steal his ideas in other countries. This would also give him a good idea of the efficacy of applying for a patent in other countries. He would have also earned cash from his invention at this stage to ensure his patent is protected worldwide. In addition, we should have a large enough fund, which should provide cheap loans to innovators to turn their innovations into products and services, to turn his dream into a reality. In other words, such a system will be much more beneficial to innovators and they will all head for Pakistan.

This system will probably bring more patents than we may be able to handle. Perhaps, half of those patents may be useless. So we need to come up with some advance solutions to such likely problems. We could make a list of the types of patents that we think are important for our economy, and then give such patents priority over the ones that are less important. For example, we are in desperate need of new medicines, machinery for industry and agriculture, electronics, weapons and satellite technology etc. But we should not discourage innovators of less importance things for us, but just give them a slightly longer time to get their patents. If these patents are registered in Pakistan, then they will produce their new products and services here as well, creating more jobs in Pakistan.

Reducing Poverty

Every government comes to power with the help of the poor, promising them the prosperity. But in reality, if there are no more poor people, then the current politicians cannot come to power again. So it is in their best interest to keep a large number of population poor, uneducated, and politically weak so they could not challenge the rich, educated, and politically powerful elites. To rule the rich, educated, and politically powerful population requires sophisticated politicians which do not exist in Pakistan yet. So the people in power keep things simple, so they could resolve the simple issues of the poor and uneducated people. They do not have any interest in making the large population rich and prosperous. All they want to do is to stay in power, and if the old ways work, then why change them? The only thing that we can do is, to pray that God sends us sincere and honest rulers who would work in the best interests of their subjects.

It is good to pray but then teachings of Islam tell us 'God helps those, who help themselves.' So I am hoping that our educated citizenry will push the politicians to reduce poverty in Pakistan. There are a few things that we could do, to reduce poverty and eventually eradicate it. But all of these things should be done simultaneously to be effective. We must continue these policies until all the people are above poverty line, and then, start new programmes to make them prosperous. However, the first thing that comes to mind to reduce poverty is to give money to the poor, so they could buy food, clothing, and housing. This model of social support is failing in the West, and more and more countries are moving away from it. Let us put this idea to bed before we could discuss more active ways to help our poor.

Most people would say that USA does not provide social support as good as Europe. But they ignore the enormous amount of money USA spends on healthcare, which is perhaps a larger bill than what the Europe spends on their citizens. It is true that USA does not provide long-term social support to its citizens like Europe, because it discourages them to be lazy. Europe on the other hand, provides a long-term cash support to its poor population. But there are two major problems with this method. Firstly, the money that is provided to the poor has to come from somewhere. This means the working class citizens pay most of their income in taxes to keep the system running, which I feel is not fair. Secondly, the poor who get cash benefits do not wish to go back to work because they get more money by not working. This is because if they are on social support then they get other benefits as well. For example, they do not pay for medicines or dentists. Further, they are guaranteed a certain amount of income. But if they go to work then all of their benefits stop, and their take home pay from employment is usually less than the social benefits they used to get. This is because they have to pay taxes now and all the other benefits stop. The UK government is trying to remove such negative incentives to work. And they are also moving away from social support because there is only so much they could tax their population, beyond which the public will not tolerate.

My main objections to paying social support in Pakistan are that we will make a large population dependent on handouts and they will not try to find a job. Their dignity will also suffer due to them receiving handouts. Further, the working population would have to pay high amount of taxes to support such a system. I think, instead of giving people handouts, the government will benefit much more if they spent extra money on their health and education, because an educated and healthy population is the requirement for economic growth. However, there will be some people who we must help, such as, disabled and very elderly who do not have family support. A poor country like Pakistan cannot afford to pay handouts while it is begging rest of the world to fund its budgetary deficit. Let us now discuss what steps we could take to reduce poverty without making poor dependent on government handouts.

As I mentioned before, we must reduce inflation because that has a direct effect on poverty. If someone is on fixed or low income but inflation is high, then he will only be able to buy a few things. But if the inflation is close to zero then the same amount of money in his pocket is worth more and perhaps he could buy most of the things he needs. Apart from the inflation, we need to work to raise the value of our rupee because this also has a direct effect on poverty. If our rupee is stronger in relation to US dollar, then we will be able to buy more petroleum with the same amount of money. The price of petroleum has a direct effect on prices within a country because of transport and other related costs to a business. So just by reducing inflation and increasing the value of our rupee, we will bring millions of people out of poverty.

However, as we make the above structural changes, we need to generate more jobs which depend on having enough electricity for our factories. I have already discussed how to resolve the energy crisis elsewhere, so I will not repeat it here. As the electricity problem is sorted out, we need to concentrate on relaxing our labour laws, such as no minimum wage, to encourage investors to invest their money to generate new jobs. I am all for the labours to have work rights, but if the labour laws are too tough, then no one would want to invest in new businesses, and there will not be many new jobs. Right now we need to get the economy moving, and get everyone in jobs. So we should delay imposing Western labour laws until our economy has become stronger. Even then we should only slowly make changes. However, at this stage, we must ensure workers safety because many people die each year at work. In most cases, these workers may be the only bread winner of their households. If they are dead, then their entire family is put into poverty and hardship. We must never compromise on *Safety Standards* because we have already lost thousands of our men, women, and children due to poor safety standards like in Karachi Factory Fire in September 2012. We need to ensure their safety while at work, when working with chemicals, machinery etc. I am going to digress here to discuss an important public safety issue that has not been resolved for many years. We hear almost every day that a bus had crashed killing all the passengers because the driver jumped out of the moving bus. These drivers are so heartless that they call the driver door 'Pilot Gate', meaning they will eject if there is a danger to their life. Most of these drivers are drug addicts causing accidents. Then we have rogue conductors who misbehave with women. The owners of bus companies are equally guilty because they do not cooperate with law enforcements to bring these drivers to justice. We have heard of taxi and Rickshaw[35] drivers colluding with others to rape young girls who use these vehicles. These are all safety issues for our people and we should protect them, especially the vulnerable women and children. The first and most important thing that we should do is to make it a requirement

---

[35] Rickshaw is a three-wheeled modified motor cycle used for carrying passengers.

to have a license from the local government for anyone who is dealing directly with the public. The license should be issued only to those who do not have a criminal record. There must be an easy method for the public to make complaints about the behaviours of such drivers or conductors. The second thing to reduce passenger deaths and injuries is to make it unlawful for any bus to have a driver door or large window from which the driver could escape. The buses that have driver doors should be welded completely and tested that they could not be opened. This measure will prevent many accidents because the driver cannot escape so he will not drive recklessly. Thirdly, we should require that all passenger carrying vehicles must install *Electronic Tachographs*, which measure vehicle speed and driver's activity. We should modify these tachographs to be able to send the data over mobile network, so the traffic police could monitor each passenger vehicle's speed remotely and stop and fine the offending drivers. This will greatly reduce road traffic accidents of passenger vehicles and help save thousands of lives. Tachographs could also be installed in the vehicles of persistent speeding offenders of private vehicle drivers to further improve road safety.

Let us get back to our discussion of health and safety of our factory workers. Apart from the safety standards, the government must make it compulsory for every employer to have adequate insurance to cover the injuries and deaths of their employees, so the victim's family could receive regular income or lump sum in case of severe disability or death at work. Such insurances must cover all types of workers including daily wage workers. But we should not stress on the minimum wages. I have discussed this elsewhere. A too high a minimum wage reduces the investor's profits, so it will discourage new businesses from starting. What we should do instead is to issue a *Guide Wage* for workers. This will give workers a negotiation power, but it will not discourage investors from investing because it is only a guide and not a requirement. Once we have these structural changes in place to help the poor employees, we then need to look at what direct support we could provide them?

To target any direct support to poor, we must know exactly the level of poverty, and who to help. This information gathering will cost much time and money. I believe some of the *Means Testing*[36] has already been done for *Income Support Programme* the government is currently running. I cannot comment on the data gathering methods because I have not seen the means testing forms and how accurately the information is recorded. But many commentators complain that the support is given only to those poor who were the last government's voters. There were also complaints of people charging the poor people to fill out their forms for income support, because many poor people are illiterate. We need to gather simple and essential information and avoid complicated forms which will only create bureaucratic mess. The best option would be to train the teachers to fill out these forms and then giving them extra duty to help gather this data in the areas they teach. They must be paid for their time so they provide us accurate data. If the government assures the public that financial help will be provided to all needy, then it will make it easy to gather information because people will come forward to give that information. Once we have gathered all the information, then we could decide who needs urgent help, and how much?

The experience of the West shows us, that the most vulnerable and poor are single parent families headed by a female. The next are disabled and elderly people with no support from their immediate families. If we aim to get just the bottom 3% of the poor out of poverty each year, then soon we would have eradicated the extreme

---

[36] Means testing is an investigation tool with which the government determines the income (means) of an individual or family to see if they qualify for government help or not.

poverty. We need to bring everyone above *Poverty Line*[37] first, and then concentrate on increasing the incomes of the poor who are just above poverty line, and so on. It makes a big difference how we define poverty line. There are rough and ready measures of poverty, such as, *International Poverty Line*. For example, people living on less than $1.25 (PPP[38]) a day are considered living in Extreme Poverty, and those living below $2 (PPP) a day are in Moderate Poverty.   According to 2009 estimates, in Pakistan 22.6% of population lives on less than $1 day, and 60.3% live on less than $2 a day. This is rampant poverty! Inflation has wiped out the middle class from Pakistan. There are now either the poor or the rich! I think that we the citizens, must have our own definition of poverty and a method of calculating it. We cannot rely on the government because they will always tell us that everything is hunky dory, but the reality would be much different. I hope the economists from our universities would create some Think Tanks to do parallel economic calculations to the government, so we could get nearer to truth. But for our discussions, we will use the international poverty line measurements and government figures.

As we analyse the Means Testing data, we would be clear as to which group of people are extremely poor and need help first. But without such data at hand we do know some trends. For example, we know that almost three-quarters of the poor live in rural areas. The vast majority of these poor are the serfs working for landlords. Serfs do not usually get money for their labour. Instead they are given land to live on and grains etc. They are rarely given money for their labour and if they did get any money then it would be extremely small amounts. This would compel borrowing money from their landlords for buying other items of households or for weddings etc. In such a system, the serfs will never be able to pay back their small

---

[37] Poverty line is the minimum level of income to buy necessities of life in a given country.

[38] PPP stands for Purchasing Power Parity

loans because they do not get any money for their labour. So they become enslaved further to their landlords for life. Here I am going to digress to discuss a very important issue, perhaps still present in our culture. I do not know the term used for such practice in Pakistan, but it is known as 'Droit du Seigneur' in French, and 'Ius Primae Noctis' in Latin, which could be roughly translated in English as 'Right of the Lord'. This was a putative legal right allowing the lord of a medieval estate to take the virginity of his serfs' maiden daughters. There have been mentions of such practices carried out by the Euro-Americans [39] to their Afro-American slaves. In his painting of 1874, Vasily Polenov depicts an old man bringing his young daughters to his feudal lord. The picture says it all! But I could tell you a true story closer to home.

In late 80's, I lived in Lahore for several months, studying computer languages. But I briefly stayed in outskirts of Lahore, some 30 miles away, in a town where an old lady living next door, used to visit us now and then. She must have been in her 70's. One day during conversation, not so openly, she mentioned the practice of *Right of the Lord* in a village where she used to live as a child. As she was telling me this, her tears were rolling down her wrinkled cheeks. I still remember the looks in her eyes, as if saying 'You are the future of this nation – do something to stop this heinous practice.' I was a young student then without any power to change anything - I lowered my head in defeat and shame. I did not have the courage to ask, where she came from.

It is the duty of the government to ensure all of its population is free and treated with dignity. It is not difficult for the government to free these people, but most of the powerful politicians have great many serf attached to them. In such situations, the media must create awareness in public who would exert pressure on the government to help the most vulnerable serfs. The easiest way to free them is by

---

[39] Euro-Americans are the white Americans, while Afro-Americans are the black Americans.

government making it a legal requirement that everyone, including serfs must be paid with cash for their services. The cash payment to most vulnerable people must be made into their bank accounts to ensure that the landlords do not get away with not paying and creating false records of cash payments.

The next group of poor are the people of religious minority, Hindus, Christians, Sikhs and other small minorities. Perhaps the things have changed now but when I was in primary school in Gawalmandi, Rawalpindi, I happened to visit the house of one of my Christian class fellow. I felt poverty there even as a child. I later observed that most of the people who sweep the roads, or do other dirty jobs are actually Christians. The questions of discrimination came to my mind but I could not understand the reasons then. I did not have direct contact with Pakistani Hindus or Sikhs but I learnt over the years that our Hindu brothers and sisters suffer extreme poverty. I am not certain but I get the feeling that our Sikh brothers and sisters are not treated badly. In a country which was created in the name of Islam, we must never have such discriminations for our non-Muslim brothers and sisters. We must treat them with dignity and as our equal because they are the citizens of Pakistan. Let us be clear that, we Pakistani Muslims do not have more rights than our non-Muslim Pakistani brothers and sisters!

Women of course, are the most disadvantaged and poor, but for our discussion, we cannot treat them individually, because they are part of poor families, unless they are widowed or divorced. The next group of poor people are the people of lower caste. Many of them are Muslims but they tend not to own much land. Even though this group as a whole may be poor, but it is not treated in the same way in every region. I come from a village where there were a few people of lower caste, who worked for the Awan families in the village. But they were all treated good. But people of the lower caste are not treated in this way everywhere. They could suffer discriminations and poverty in other parts of Pakistan. There must be other small groups of people who suffer from discrimination and poverty and need our attention. As you can see from our discussion that we need to adopt different strategies for every group because their needs are different.

Let us now consider the largest group of poor people, the rural poor. I think there may be a small measurement discrepancy here. All the rural poor that we may have counted as poor, may not be actually poor. Let me explain why?

The way to measure poverty is determined by the amount of money people spend. It is possible that some rural people may be cash poor, but asset rich. I mean, they may not have much cash, but they may have a lot of land and cattle. But the way poverty is measured, these people may also be considered poor. I know from experience, that landlord farmers ensure that they have enough grains and rice for the year, and they sell the rest. They have animals for milk, butter, eggs, and meat. They may also have small fields dedicated to growing vegetables. Further, they do not pay rent, because most would own their homes. Since these people are self-sufficient, they may spend very little money for other items which they do not get from their farms. So from the consumption point of view, they will be classed poor, because they spend very little money on food, housing, and clothing. Having said that, it does not mean there is no poverty in rural areas. If the figures show three-quarters of poor live in rural areas then it may just be half of the poor living in rural areas, rather than none at all. We would leave this for the economists to figure out. But we now need to consider how we could help them to raise their living standards.

The biggest reason for poverty is the lack of education, professional skills, and lack of job opportunities. Education and professional skills are discussed elsewhere so we need to think how we could create job opportunities for rural poor? First thing we can do is to provide them with financial and technical assistance in creating cottage industries, such as, bee keeping for honey, animal farming for milk, cheese, and meat etc. Here we should first help women who are heading their families due to being widowed, divorced, or illness of their husbands because these will be the most vulnerable poor populations. Also, from recent experiments in Pakistan where women received small loans to set up in business, showed a near 100% success rates. Our women are hardworking and determined. They are much more caring of their families, unlike us men! So by helping this group of women, we would have helped many families.

The planning commission needs to come up with a greater number of cottage industries that could be successfully promoted in rural areas of Pakistan. The financial assistance must be interest-free loans. The assistance should never be grants, because if anyone gets money for free, then they do not tend to care about it, which would cause failures. But if they know that they need to pay back the loan, then they are more likely to perform better. The technical assistance must be comprehensive and not just a few pages of instructions on how to run small business. The planning commission must hire the experts within each industry, whose job should be to train some people in each region on every aspect of cottage industries, from setting up business, day-to-day running, to marketing etc. Then these trained people should train the prospective entrepreneurs and guide them at every stage.

There are two reasons the cottage industry within rural setting would be worthwhile. Firstly, if these poor move out of their village for jobs then they will incur extra costs in housing and other facilities, which will reduce any benefits they would have gained by moving to cities. Secondly, the politicians do not like the movement of people from the rural areas to cities, because they create increased demand on resources, and are a potential threat to peace when a large population is concentrated in a small area. Further, in Pakistan, the constituency politics depends on a larger rural vote bank that put them in power. Any reduction in this vote bank will also reduce their chances of coming to power again.

However, there are only so many cottage industries that the rural areas could support, depending on the population. So not every poor could be helped with just setting her up with some cottage industry. We need to come up with other solutions. The solution I have in mind will, not only eradicate poverty but also help in resolving the issue of separatism in Baluchistan. There is a large amount of land in Baluchistan and there is a large population in Punjab, which means that Punjab would have greater share of poor people. If we send a large number of Punjabi poor and settle them in Baluchistan, by creating new villages, towns, and cities in strategically important locations, then we would have eradicated poverty for these people, and they would also help suppress the separatist movement by becoming Baluch native residents themselves. We must create comprehensive plans about what that economy will produce beforehand, so this operation becomes a lasting success. Apart from the free rural poor, the serfs must also be sent there because they will be able to easily survive there. But we must take steps to free the serfs from the landlords by creating legislations if needed, and eliminating all obligations on the serfs because they have laboured for so long.

These migrated people must be required to learn Baluchi language, and adopt Baluch culture and names. If we send enough poor Punjabis there then it will create enough loyal population to help suppress local separatist movements there. But the Punjabis are not good at living as a strong cohesive community. That is why they are thrown out of Karachi and Baluchistan as and when the locals wanted. On the other hand, Pakhtuns living in Karachi and Baluchistan are never thrown out because they live as a cohesive group. So it is utmost important to organise them as a group. Any such movement of people into Baluchistan will trigger hatred and acts of violence against these people. We must train and arm them to defend themselves against such acts. However, before we send non-Baluch population there, we should ensure that all the poor Baluchs have been sent to the new villages, towns, and cities. It is important to provide land and jobs to our Baluch brothers and sisters before we send any Punjabis there.

I know some people will criticise me by saying that I am proposing internal colonies. But our constitution allows free movement of people in any place within Pakistan, and if there is more land in Baluchistan then the government has to give land there to help eradicate poverty. One important thing to note is that we should never grant land outright to these migrants but transfer ownership slowly over many years, for example, 10 to 15 years. A 5% ownership as they move in, and then perhaps, 5% every year. This would ensure their loyalty, and they would unlikely to abandon the land for quick profit, or because of other risks.

Apart from sending people to Baluchistan, we need to send people to other areas within each province for growing strategic crops, such as, growing tea, coffee, and rubber etc if possible. I believe that studies have already been done to determine, if tea could be grown in Pakistan, and several areas in Punjab have been identified as suitable for tea growing. Since we spend a lot of our foreign exchange reserve on importing tea, this will remove that dependency and become a new source of wealth for the poor. If 3% of population is brought out of extreme poverty every year, then in a few years, we would have significantly reduced poverty.

Another way that we could help reduce poverty is by providing financial incentives to businesses that employ people in extreme poverty. There has to be a mechanism to identify the most disadvantaged people. For example, when population is means tested, they should be given a unique reference number. So when the employers employ such people, they could easily check this number with the officials that they are employing a person who is classified as someone in extreme poverty, so he could collect his reward from the government. A cash incentive to employer, of perhaps four months wages of the person they employed, will encourage many investors to employ poor people, because they are getting four months of worker's wages being paid by the government. But there must be some conditions attached to these payments such as, they should have employed the worker for at least a year, they should have trained him in his job and provided further training. So he could advance in his field of work, and that they will not fire this worker soon after they have received a payment from the government. This approach is good for all three concerned. It is good for the employer because he gets a worker for a year, but only pays him for eight months. This incentive is large enough that many businesses will be looking for poor workers to put them into work. However, we need to ensure that they do not fire the workers already there to get new cheaper workers. If this happens then it will take a certain group of poor out of poverty, but creates new poor who lost their jobs. Secondly, it is good for the government because it was going to spend a lot of money in getting people out of poverty through training programmes and still may not be successful, at least for many years. But this way, poor people immediately get jobs and the government only has to put in four months of their wages. This way the success is guaranteed because the government pays only for the results. This is especially good because if someone has gained a job and held it for at least a year, then he would have gained necessary skills to stay in a job and improve his financial status. Lastly, the worker obviously benefits because he is out of poverty and lives with dignity. There will be some who would criticise this approach because the government gives the money to factory owners and investors who are already rich. But, can they provide a better solution?

Apart from the simple solutions I suggested, we need to look at other issues that the poor face in Pakistan. Because of their low income and high inflation in Pakistan, the poor cannot buy nutritious food such as, meat, milk, and fruits. A significant number of people are living on just bread and water. So they would have severe

deficiencies of vitamins and proteins. I have discussed and proposed
national health policy in the second volume of this book, but here I
need to stress that we should identify people who are severely
deficient in important vitamins, proteins, and minerals, and provide
them food vouchers and food supplements for the short-term. But in
the long-term we need to bring these people out of extreme poverty
because only then we would have resolved the issues of their health.
While we are actively trying to help our poor we also need to look at
permanent solutions of access to fruit and meat for the entire
population. I suggest that we do two things. Declare fruits and fish
as public goods[40] and also educate our people towards alternative
sources of food. I have discussed in detail how we could provide
fruits and meat to entire population in the next section. So here, I
will briefly discuss how we could move our people into using
alternative sources of food because they could be more affordable.

In Pakistan, our staple diet consists of a handful of foods, such as,
wheat, vegetables, chicken, lamb, and beef. We of course consume
other food products but to a lesser degree, such as; rice, maize, and
fish etc. If we look at the world food production, then maize is
produced more than the wheat, so it is consumed more. People
around the world use many foods as their staple diet, but we are just
stuck with the usual wheat, a few vegetables, and meat from
chicken, lamb, and cow. We have many cows and goats in Pakistan
but we never drink their milk. We do not eat duck eggs. But if we
started using the cow and goat milk and eating duck eggs then a lot
of poor people will be able to get necessary foods. The ten most
staple products around the world are maize (corn), wheat, rice,
potatoes, cassava, soybeans, sweet potatoes, sorghum, yams, and

---

[40] Public good is a commodity or service which is provided to all people
without profit and no one can be excluded from it. If one consumes the
public good then it does not reduce its availability for others. For
example, national defence is provided by the military without profit. No
one can be excluded from it even if they wanted to. By providing
security to one person does not reduce it for others.

plantain. People around the world eat these foods daily but we ignore them even when they could be cheaper alternatives to the foods that we are used to. By adopting alternative staple diet would help our population feed themselves in the times of such high inflation and rampant poverty. We need to send our nutrition experts and chefs around the world to learn about these foods and then teach the population about alternative cheaper and tasty food available for us to grow and consume. With regards to meat consumption we prefer to eat chickens, lamb, and cows. We do not eat ducks, turkeys, ostrich, or camels etc. We do not consume much fish apart from people living in coastal regions. All of these could provide necessary proteins at low costs. I am now going to suggest a few methods that could provide more than enough fruits for entire population for free, and meat for either free or at very low costs.

Fruit & Fish for All

If the government adopts my suggestions discussed here then we would have created a heaven on earth for our people. Others will admire us and follow our example in their countries. What I am suggesting is that we declare fruits, nuts, and fish as public goods. So every man, woman, or child can consume them free of charge no matter if they are rich or poor. Would it not be good if there is plenty of fruit of every type near to where you live, and you could pick the fruit of your choice from any tree, all free? Would it not be good that every Pakistani could get meat free or at a very low cost so people could be healthy and not deficient in necessary proteins due to inflation and poverty?

There are about 200 million people in Pakistan and if we plant just 2 million fruit and nut trees then we would have one plant for every 100 people. I am not sure about the yields of different fruit trees and plants to decide how many fruit trees we will need for entire nation. Agriculturists and economists need to calculate how many trees we will need. But for our discussion here, let us assume there should be one fruit tree for every 50 people. This would mean we need to plant about 4 million fruit and nut plants and trees. This is not a difficult or expensive task. But before we discuss how we do it, we need to bear in mind that there are other important and lasting benefits to us from planting so many trees. For example, the environment will become cleaner with so many extra trees which will promote good health for all citizens. The extra trees are much more likely to increase our rainfall, which will be good for our harvests. The extra trees could also reduce the intense heat of our summers. The biggest side benefit which is closer to my heart is that, it will increase wildlife in our country. Many animals and birds will come to live in Pakistan because more trees could support more wildlife. A strategic planting of trees could also reduce the effects of floods, such as, erosion of soil etc. There are many more benefits from extra trees to list here.

Let us now discuss how we could achieve our goal. First thing that we need to do is make a list of trees that will flourish in each of our regions. Let me tell you that when the imperial powers of Europe started planting cash crops in their colonies, it destroyed the local soil there because the soil could not support those crops. So we need to ensure that by planting fruit trees we do not damage our soil. We should plant those trees which are not only suitable for respective soil, but they should also enhance it. And we should select the best types within the range of fruit trees to plant. Once the list of trees to plant in each respective area had been established, and then we need to decide on how many trees and plants to plant in each area. We then should decide which trees to plant first, because each tree has a different harvesting time. Some climbing/vine fruit plants produce fruit within a few months, but there are other plants and trees, which will take longer before producing any fruits. Some may take a year but others may take several years. At this stage of planning, we could publish this list so the plant nurseries around the country could prepare the nursery plants needed for our plans. If we do not plan, then it could cause disharmony and discontent among people. This is because if there are only limited amount of fruits available then everyone would want to have fruits but there will not be enough to go round. I may be wrong with my assumptions of disharmony and discontent: perhaps others could guide me on what to do to ensure there is no disharmony and discontent when there is only a limited amount of fruit available? But my preference would be that we plant fruit and nut trees in such a way that there is plenty of fruit available, all at the same time for everyone.

Once these decisions have been made, we could then recruit teams of volunteers who will work with our forestry department. There are perhaps more than a million public servants in our country that we could utilise to do public work. Further, our military is always happy to lend their hands for public works, so we could ask their help if needed. Apart from temporary volunteers, we need permanent volunteers who will look after our trees once planted. We should issue uniforms to our volunteers and pay token wages to permanent volunteers. In recognition of their service, we should award them for their performance. A system of accounting for every tree has to be devised so each regional forestry departments can ensure that no tree has been ignored and left to die, or no one cuts any tree illegally. When all the preliminary steps have been taken then we should start planting trees.

Let us now discuss how we could provide access to meat for every Pakistani for free or at a very low cost. We first need to calculate if we have enough fish available for our population if everyone consumed it. I guess if there is not enough fish available, then at least 50% of the needed fish is available in our rivers and seas. In any case, we need to increase our capacity and increase the number of fish available in our waters. The easiest way to achieve is to declare the fish in the first 10 miles of our seas a public good. This would prevent commercial fishermen from fishing there. This act alone should increase our capacity enormously, but this would also mean the cost of fish will be a little high. This is because fish needs to be caught and transported to the rest of the country, as a large population lives away from our coasts.

However, we also have many rivers, canals, ponds etc in Pakistan but they have been polluted by people and businesses. So fish cannot be farmed in such waters. People throw their household waste directly into our rivers, which is the fault of the local governments because they do not provide water treatment plants. Businesses throw their chemical waste directly into our rivers, because it is the cheapest method and there are no health and safety law implementation. By the way, the businesses not only pollute our rivers and seas, they also pollute our aquifers [41] by releasing chemicals into the fields, which eventually sink to our aquifers polluting our drinking water from the wells. Businesses do not just stop there. I remember travelling to Lahore by bus many years ago, and I could not breathe when the bus stopped in a town on the way outside a chemical factory. I am sure the whole population in that town would be suffering from a range of illnesses, but perhaps no one can speak out because the factory would have been owned by a powerful elite. I hope the situation has changed now.

So the first thing we need to do is to create and implement a *Clean Water Act* under which it would be illegal to pollute our waters. The local governments, businesses, and people could be prosecuted under this law for polluting our waters, or for not implementing the *Clean Water Act*. The best way to achieve this is to hand over all the powers and responsibilities of water supply and its removal through sewerage, and keeping the water clean, to WAPDA[42]. The WAPDA should be converted into a POC, as detailed in the next section, so

---

[41] An aquifer is an underground layer of water bearing rock or other material such as gravel, sand or silt, from which we extract our well water.

[42] WAPDA stands for Water and Power Development Authority.

the public owns it. It can then charge customers for supply of clean and removal of waste water. It would provide the same services to all businesses, and charge them accordingly. WAPDA will be the sole authority to prosecute any breaches of *Clean Water Act*, to ensure that no business or individual releases any chemicals to our waters. However, the local government has the responsibility in their areas to create by-laws derived from Clean Water Act, and then implement them. It would be the responsibility of WAPDA to install water treatment plants everywhere. While discussing this, I need to digress a little, and discuss the designs of our toilets, which may be the source of foul smell and diseases.

What I have seen in rural areas is that people install toilets in their homes with a concrete storage tank, which has two chambers. It is a sort of Septic Tank[43]. People think that it is all that is required for a toilet system to work efficiently. But the tank eventually is filled up with human waste, which overflows and creates constant foul smell and bacteria causing many diseases. Most people do not realise that these tanks need emptying regularly. Also the water eventually seeps through the concrete chambers into ground and into aquifers because these chambers are made from sand and cement, which do not have special water proof materials. This polluted water which has sunk to aquifers, makes it way to our table from the wells we draw our drinking water from. Unfortunately, in my estimate there are about 60-70% of the houses using this type of system, where there is no public sewage connection. If I am right in my estimation, then it is a very big public health issue. This must contribute to at least 40% to 50% of the diseases suffered by our population.

However, if we are serious about public health, then this is one of the largest factor causing diseases and it should be addressed urgently. I know that, to provide sewage facility to entire population

---

[43] Septic Tank is one of the main components of Septic Sewage Systems, which is a sort of small scale sewage treatment plant, used in areas where there is no connection to main sewage system.

requires a lot of money. Even if we did have the money it will still need many years before everyone gets this facility. So there is an urgent and important need for effective *Independent Sewage Systems*, which are cheap and effective. They also reduce the risk of disease from polluting water from badly designed current toilets. I will briefly suggest a temporary solution, but the government needs to identify the cities and areas that can be easily connected to the sewage systems, and then go ahead providing them with the sewage facility through WAPDA. The sewage systems must not be under local government's control, but the WAPDA should be given a monopoly for this, so it could centrally plan sewage facilities for entire country.

The houses that cannot be connected with a sewage system cheaply and quickly, and those who have toilets with badly designed septic tanks, should be given grants to install new septic tanks and *On Site Sewage Systems* (OSS). Apart from the septic tanks we need to treat the waste water coming out of our toilets and homes before we release it into the ground. But how do we do that economically?

The best way to do this is that, the WAPDA finds the best Septic Tanks and OSS from around the world, and then buys that technology, or make its own septic tanks and OSS. The government could encourage people to buy their own systems and provide financial help to those who cannot afford them, depending on their incomes. People could either install individual OSS or a slightly bigger onsite sewage system for a few houses in the street. We need to require people to replace their old concrete septic tanks with the new durable readymade tanks so our aquifers are not polluted and we could have clean drinking water. But we cannot just open up the concrete septic tanks and let all the shit out, because it will create a public health problem and foul smell. There is an easy way to do this by using special bacteria, enzymes, and worms who feed on human waste. They will eat up all the sludge gathered into these tanks. Only then we could safely replace the old septic tanks with more advanced and durable tanks. A method has to be developed to drill an adequate sized hole in the septic tank to drop the special bacteria, enzymes, or worms in it. This hole should have to be closed properly, or a foul smell will escape into air. Another, thing to watch out is that, these organisms in septic tanks also produce methane gas, which if builds up, could cause fire hazard. Some kind of system has to be developed to avoid such risks. If these proposals are implemented then we would have ensured our water in aquifers, canals, ponds, rivers, and seas remain clean and safe. After this digression, let us now turn to our topic of discussion, of cleaning our waters and farming fish in them.

The household and industrial waste which is already in our rivers and canals needs to be cleaned. But before we could start a cleaning process, we need to make sure that no new waste is added to our water. There are many techniques in filtering and cleaning water systems, such as rivers, but it could be left to experts to decide, which systems to employ for our purpose. WAPDA could do the research and adopt techniques and systems it thinks are suitable and then start cleaning our waters. Once the waters are cleaned, then our fish will return in large numbers. But we should actively farm the fish in our water systems so we could produce a large number for everyone to consume. We must be selective in the types of fish we farm, and not introduce the type of fish which normally does not live in our waters, because it will disturb the ecosystems of our rivers. Once we have large enough number of fish available then we need to distribute it to our people around the country?

There are three possible ways we could achieve this. Firstly, we allow anyone to go to any brook, canal, river, or sea and catch what they need. This is very close to the definition of a public good. But this would mean many people who live far away from any canals and rivers will not be able to get fish for their consumption. For example, someone living in Thar Desert cannot go out fishing, so they are naturally excluded from the public good even though no one is stopping them from going to the river. The Second method could be to issue licenses to registered volunteers who would catch fish on a larger scale, and then distribute to whoever wants it. This arrangement is likely to breakdown very soon, because there are little incentives and the cost of catching and distributing fish would have been born by these volunteers. The third method would be to allow professional fishing corporations to catch and provide fish at a very small profit, such as, no more than 3%. This could work very well if we only allow the POCs, explained in next section, to operate such businesses. This way any profit made, will return to people. Further, the POC is owned by entire population, so they will not overburden themselves with expensive fish, so the price will remain low. You may argue that why should such POCs make any profit because it is dealing with a public good? I would say to you that, yes, it is a public good, but if there are no profits, then these companies would eventually go out of business and we will lose an important source of cheap nutrition. Further, all the profit made does not go to any individual, but it would go back to whole population who own the POC. Also, if there are no profits, then there will be no improvements in distribution or other innovations. Innovations and improvements will eventually bring the cost down for the public, and these cannot be achieved from non-profit organisations.

Lastly, we need to bear in mind that the cost of storage, delivery, and distribution will be different for each area but we must keep the prices same, no matter where they are distributed. For example, the net cost of distribution to someone living on the coast is very low, than someone living a few hundred miles away, because we would need to keep the fish in cold storage during the entire process of catching, storing, delivering, and selling it. If we did not keep the same price no matter where the fish is delivered then, it will become expensive for some, while it would be cheaper for others, which would not be fair. The way to price the fish uniformly is by taking into account the cost of whole operation throughout the country, and then dividing it by the number of units for sale in an entire year. This may have to be estimated at first, but the actual costs will become available after a few months of operation.

POCs and Poverty Reduction

According to some recent estimates, more than 60% of Pakistani population is living below poverty line. The inflation is out of control, which has pushed middle class into poverty. So there are either very poor or very rich people, in Pakistan, because the middle class is vanishing fast. Those below poverty line cannot feed and clothe themselves and their children. They are also left without any health or education facilities. As I mentioned before, the first thing we need to do is to reduce inflation because it will increase the buying power of people, and many will come out of poverty just by reducing inflation. Apart from this we need other tools to reduce poverty and provide people regular incomes so they could buy life's necessities. I think there is an excellent opportunity now for every Pakistani to prosper, which only became possible because of the last government's negligence and incompetence. Let me explain.

We have many large state owned corporations that are making losses amounting to hundreds of billions of rupees every year, for which the government picks up the bill. For example, the three big loss making corporations are PIA, Railway, and Steel Mill. There are many other state owned corporations which are either making a loss or just getting by. The reason these corporation are making losses is very simple that no one cares. Instead, the government keeps its party workers happy by giving them employment into these corporations, causing over employment, which leads that company to make financial losses. The government likes to privatise these corporations for two basic reasons.

Firstly, to sell them at rock bottom prices to their friends and family, and secondly to get rid of the government's obligations to pay them funds every year to keep these corporations afloat. You may have noticed that any state corporation which was making loss before, instantly started making profits when it was privatised. There is no magic formula for turning a loss making firm into profits by privatising. All they do is to get rid of extra people and ensure the rest are working properly. When a corporation is privatised then it is owned by just one person or a few shareholders, who all have interest in making that company profitable. That is all.

But in the state owned corporation no one actually owns the corporation, so no one cares about making profit. If the above steps are taken in the state corporation, then they would also become profitable. But when large corporations, such as, PIA, Railway, or Steel Mill are privatised, and the new owners make thousands of people redundant, then the government will be in trouble from social unrest from these newly unemployed people. The opposition party, who gave these people jobs when they were in power, would also oppose privatisation fiercely. Further, judging from the Supreme Court's previous actions, it is likely that any attempts to privatise the state corporations would be challenged. This puts the new government in a no-win situation. But I do have some proposals which will not only solve the government's dilemma, but it will also win them more votes in the next elections.

I suggest that we should convert these state owned corporations into special type of corporations, called *Publically Owned Corporations* (POCs). There are PLCs or Public Limited Companies in the world but they are not truly publically owned. This is because they could always be converted back to Private Limited Companies. But the POCs I am suggesting will always remain a publically owned company, and no individual or government will ever be allowed to take it over, and it must be an unlimited company, so everyone can own it by investing at any time. We need to provide a constitutional cover, and all of the POCs must receive Presidential Charter. I suggest that the government must own 20% of the shares, but it must not have any power to interfere in the company. Government will only have the power to monitor the company by calling the CEO in front of parliamentary committee for major issues. The remaining 80% of the company must be owned by the public. Everyone will get just one vote no matter how many shares it owns. Since, there will be no limit to the number of shares the POC can issue; an unlimited amount of investment will flow into it. This would create opportunities for exponential growth to become the world's largest corporations. Among other rules, the company cannot be taken over by any lender but there must be a limit on the amount the company could borrow.

The POC will be a profit making corporation so it must pay dividends[44] regularly to its owners. Imagine if the PIA is owned by public, then huge amount of money will flow into it, which could be used to buy new planes and new routes, to make it more profitable. The government could also make rules for pension investments that at least a certain amount of pension fund must be invested into POCs, bringing more continuous investment into the publically owned corporations. Any money that is received by the government from selling state corporations to public must not be used for anything else, but this fund should be used for two things. Use one third of this fund to buy shares for the very poor people according to a predetermined formula, instead of giving them handouts. As I explained in previous section that to reduce poverty we ought to grant people land and interest-free loans. But those who are not helped by such schemes should be given shares in POCs to help them for the long-term. However, they must not be allowed to sell their shares for at least ten years, so they could receive regular dividends from them to help them a little, and to let them appreciate the values of these shares. The other two thirds of the money received should be put aside in a fund to help these newly created

---

[44] Dividend is the distribution of profits of a company to its shareholders.

POCs when needed. For example, the government could buy new technology or management using this fund to help newly created POCs to grow. These POCs should be able to get low-cost loans for expansion from this fund. Or this fund could also be used to create new POCs as the need arises. For example, the government could create a new POC with the help of Army to research and develop new defence technologies. For example, the Radar technology is very old. Further, there is a National Security risk from spy satellites, so we could develop technology to prevent these spy satellites from gathering information about our military and civil assets. There could be many other things that could be done with this fund to help our country.

If the above proposals are implemented then it will create more jobs, which will make people prosperous. The biggest challenge for the government of laying off thousands of workers from state run corporations would shift to people, because they now own these corporations. This way, if any laid off workers protest, then they would be protesting against entire population. So the protestors cannot obviously win. This would save government a big headache.

All utilities should be converted into POCs because these are the things that people need everyday, so they must be in the hands of public. Further, the corporations that were privatised many years ago should be bought back under *Compulsory Purchase Order* and converted into POCs as well. I have the special concern about our telecommunication company sold to foreigners who have not even paid for the company yet, but reaping profits from it. It is a daytime robbery! But my real concern is not that foreigners are earning profits from our company but it is a matter of National Security. Communications networks are part of the national security, how could we hand them over to foreigners? Our communications are not secure if foreigners own our telecommunication companies. We have no control on our communication currently. Are we going to compromise our national security? So it is utmost important that we take full control of our telecommunications, landlines or mobile communications.

If the government followed these proposals and allowed its citizens to own and profit from state corporations, then public will be much happy with the government. But thousands of poor people who received free shares in these POCs will be doubly happy and the government will win many votes this way. Benefits for the government do not end here. This way, they do not need to pay hundreds of billions in subsidies to keep the loss making state corporations going, but now it will also receive continuous profits by owning 20% of shares in these POCs. This will further help government reduce its taxes, winning more votes for the government. So converting existing state corporations into POCs is a win-win situation for the government and public.

Alcohol for Oil Programme

The most advanced nations of the world are using a lot of petroleum, and it is the fundamental driving force behind their economic and technological success. If you take the oil out of their economy, then everything will halt to a standstill. We had seen a glimpse of this when Saudi Arabia put an oil embargo on USA in 1973. But what implication it had for Saudi Arabia and the rest of the world following their embargo is another story. People in the West have greater freedom due to oil because they could live in the suburbs and travel to work in the cities, or for leisure at will. The number of motor cars in the West far exceeds than those in the rest of the world, because they have access to cheap oil. Is it possible that Pakistanis could enjoy the economic success and freedom that comes from the greater use of oil?

Of course! But we must be innovative and have the courage to implement difficult solutions. I am proposing an *Alcohol for Oil Programme* which could achieve above goal. You would ask, what is Alcohol for Oil Programme? An Alcohol for Oil Programme will be an economic programme in which we will produce and sell just enough alcohol to the rest of the world, to earn enough foreign exchange reserve to buy all the petroleum we need. We will sell no more or less. You may argue that it is not going to work in Pakistan because the religious leaders will oppose it, and they may run campaigns against such a programme. But I would disagree with you, because I believe that we could convince our religious leaders. Let me explain how?

Alcohol is Haram (forbidden) in Islam, so it is banned in Pakistan, but we know that almost everyone has easy access to alcohol if they wanted to. Unfortunately, many rich, middle class, and young Muslims drink alcohol in Pakistan. No religious leader is happy about this situation. So if I could guarantee them that no Muslim in Pakistan will be able to buy alcohol, then they will be much happier and will most likely to approve Alcohol for Oil Programme. I will show you how we could make good on our guarantee later, but let me put some more arguments in favour of this programme, which will satisfy most people. For example, we could argue 'Let the infidels get blind drunk to their destruction.' Or a more sobering argument could be that without oil, food and other commodities will become expensive, and people will not be able to use their motor vehicles for travel or commute. In fact the whole economy will suffer. So it is important to get cheap oil, and the Alcohol of Oil Programme is the best solution, because we are not giving away anything precious to buy oil. But currently, we are selling our cotton, wheat, and rice etc to buy oil. We could further argue that we will guarantee that we will not export alcohol to any Muslim country with one exception. There is at least one Muslim country, which is becoming Amsterdam of East, where prostitutes from around the world and alcohol are freely available. They call themselves Muslims but behave like infidels in the name of modernity and economic success. Unfortunately, our politicians and rich go there often for unexplained reasons. I have no sympathy for this country, and if we exported alcohol to them, then I am sure God will forgive us!

I am optimistic that our religious leaders are much more mature and will not oppose this programme if we made good on our guarantees. They are unlikely to approve it for obvious reasons but they may turn their blind eye, if we ensured that we would take alcohol away from Pakistani Muslims. Let us now consider three main things; who to sell alcohol to, what to produce, and how to ensure Pakistani Muslims will not have access to alcohol.

I think for us, there are four major markets for selling alcohol; India, China, North America, and Europe. Although the alcohol consumption is higher in some countries, but we must look for where we would be able to get highest prices, while the cost of distribution is lower. India is the second largest population in the world and people drink alcohol there abundantly. But the prices of drinks tend to be lower according to the disposable income of ordinary people. It is a fast growing economy and as the income levels increase their alcohol consumption is likely to increase as well, a trend found worldwide. India could be a good market due to lower distribution costs because its major cities are just a few hundred kilometres away from our major cities. But the prices we are likely to achieve from this market will be lower, and it would be a volatile market due to hostility between the two countries. Any tension between the two countries will halt the sale. We should never depend on this market especially when they know we are running an alcohol for oil programme. They will almost likely to sabotage it. So our alcohol sale to India must not be more than 10%, even when they are buying in higher quantities. This could just be a trick to make us dependent on them buying.

China is the most populated country in the world and is the second largest economy. Their income levels have increased dramatically over the last few decades. Chinese also tend to import a lot of alcohol due to increased demand, which in turn is driven by the increased income. China has been a long time friend of Pakistan and will prove a stable, large market for our alcohol. The distribution costs will also be lower due to our proximity to China and the distances will become even less when the train services between the two countries will start. We will be able to earn good amount of foreign reserve from alcohol sale to China.

Europe perhaps is the largest producer and consumer of alcohol. The competition there will be tougher, and the cost of marketing and distribution higher. But we must penetrate this market because this will likely be the most stable market with higher foreign exchange reserves. The consumers here are the most fussy and difficult to please, so we must hire the experts from Europe for our breweries. To break into this market, we will also need to hire expensive celebrities to promote our brands. But it will be well worth it. Because if we could please Europeans with our alcohol, then it will not be difficult to break into any other market.

USA is also a large market for alcohol sale and equally competitive. The so called *Free Market Prophets* are also the biggest hypocrites because they operate protectionism for their own industries. It will be much more difficult to get into American market than that of Europe, not because of competition but because of their protectionist policies. They achieve this end through World Trade organisation (WTO), which is another of USA concubines. The proof of this fact is in the USA winning the most trade disputes than any other nation. Despite these disadvantages, we must try to break into this market and finally take the bigger chunk of their alcohol market because we are likely to get higher revenues from this market.

Now let us turn to how to produce alcohol and what to produce? The best practice would be to produce the alcohol for each market according to their tastes. People in India will have a different taste and preferences than Chinese, who will be different than the Europeans and so on. We need to spend a good amount of money on researching each market and then producing beers, wines, spirits etc according to their tastes. We should hire experts from those countries where we want to sell. Our aims should be to become world leaders in alcohol production, which is only possible if we are methodical and not go for quick profits. Instead we should build brands for long-term revenue generation. But who would produce alcohol?

Most Muslims would not want an income which comes from prohibited items, so a POC will not be a viable option. But there are thousands of entrepreneurs in Pakistan who do not care where the money comes from, as long as they could make large profits for less effort. The government must ensure that it puts certain conditions for alcohol producers so a smooth growth in this market could be achieved. Two important conditions should be that, all of these firms will participate in government guided production, and they will put in mechanisms which will ensure that no sale of alcohol could fall into Muslims' hands. It would be counterproductive to have domestic competition in this market. Instead, the firms should compete against international producers. Too many small corporations will not be profitable or able to compete against three international giants in this field. So we should aim to limit the number of corporations so that these could become large corporations, which could benefit from economies of scale. POCs could be created if there was interest from enough numbers. New entrants in this business should not be prohibited, but if they can show that they will be able to make profits, then allow them to set up their businesses. The government should guide these corporations just like the Japanese did with their industries. It should offer research and development grants and loans on merit, so they could grow and not waste grants.

Finally, let us discuss how we could guarantee our religious leaders that, no Pakistani Muslim will be able to buy or consume alcohol in Pakistan, or at least ensure the government will do its best to ensure this. To ensure this we must create some new laws. For example, we could make laws which state 'The sale and consumption of alcohol is prohibited to any Muslim in Pakistan. The seller and buyer, who are found guilty, will have 50% of their assets confiscated at first offense, 75% at second, and 100% at third offence. There would be a 5 year jail sentence at subsequent offenses. No one will be spared despite their political, financial, or social influence. Any corporation found guilty of such offenses will have the corporation's and its CEO's assets confiscated, and jail sentence according to the same formula as an individual.' Financial penalties work best to prevent crimes and costs less than a jail sentence. Further, the government gains more revenue this way. We now need a simple plan to implement this policy.

If the government had implemented my proposals on monetary policies to make our economy a cashless system, where electronic payment method is used extensively, then it would become much easier to implement our alcohol sale policy. Firstly, we should issue licenses to buy alcohol, without which no brewery would be able to sell alcohol. We have a significant number of non-Muslim populations who should be allowed to drink indoors. Further, we also have non-Muslim visitors who may wish to drink, so we need to cater for these eventualities as well. Licenses could be issued to hotels and individuals, but there must be stringent measures so only non-Muslims could buy alcohol. Perhaps, a local councillor and police department needs to verify each application.

Secondly, the alcohol should not be available in the shops, but could only be ordered from a single source of purchase so that sales could be monitored. All the breweries should participate in creating a small sales outlet for their alcoholic products for domestic consumers. This would have an added benefit for these corporations that they would have delegated their responsibility to others, and could be saved from prosecution if any breaches occur. But they remain responsible for any alcohol theft from their corporations which could end in Muslims' hands. This single source of alcohol sale could monitor how much an individual or business is buying, to see if there is an abuse of law. When something is prohibited then it gets expensive and more profitable for those who have that product. So selling alcohol illegally will become profitable and attractive. To curb this, the district health officers (DHO) should be given power and responsibility to carry out raids, and prosecute any breaches of alcohol sale policy. He should have the power to seek police help in tackling any policy breach. The respective DHO should also have the power to inspect the records of selling and buying companies, and that of buying individuals.

Other precautions may include labelling each can or bottle of alcohol with a unique serial number for accounting purposes. Hotels and other businesses who sell alcohol to non-Muslims must be required to keep full records to who they sold the alcohol to. It must be compulsory to sell alcohol only electronically and no cash payments be allowed. This way, the hotels will be prevented from sale to Muslims. The record a hotel should keep must have the full names and addresses of buyers, their passport or ID copies stored in electronic format. They need to keep the alcohol in a locked cabinet/fridge where only authorised personnel have access. They should keep the full inventory of how much is bought, sold, and what is left in stock, so that the local DHO can inspect it at any time. This way any discrepancies would be highlighted instantly, and offenders punished. In case the hotel staffs have accidents and alcohol is spilt, then they have duty to inform local DHO instantly, or call a central contact number. So an official could visit the site to confirm the loss, and adjust inventory accordingly. A loss reference number and authorisation must be obtained by the hotel before cleaning the affected area. If the DHO decides not to visit the site, then the hotel is required to take pictures and make live videos of spill and cleanup operation so it could be verified at a later date. Another way the alcohol could get to Muslims is through non-

Muslims selling their alcohol. The selling company must forward records of all buyers and quantities to local DHO fortnightly, so that he could detect any likely resale and catch any offenders from more than usual purchases.

Once the initial steps have been taken, then we could go ahead with production and sale to earn just enough foreign exchange reserves to buy our needed petroleum for our industry and public use. Petroleum is a finite commodity and will end sooner or later, but the West is using it without any worry, then why should we care? We should not let the problem of lack of foreign exchange reserve come in the way of our economic growth, and individual's gratification that comes from their greater use of petroleum.

Water

More than 60% of our national income (GDP) comes from agriculture, which in turn depends on water. Further, one-sixth of our electricity depends on flow of water into our dams. Both the agriculture and electricity are parts of our National Security Policy, because they provide *Food Security* and *Energy Security* respectively. Unfortunately, the last few governments have not ensured our national security policy, which has put our food and energy security at risk. However, the new government seems to be serious about national security but we will have to wait and see? However, there is consensus among experts that we would have to do something, to ensure we have constant and adequate access to water. If the water is not available, then Pakistan will turn in to a desert: drought, famine, and death would follow.

We curse India for stopping our water by building dams upstream, but what have we done to store the vast amounts of rain water that is wasted every year, on which India has no control? Of course we need to tell India not to breach any agreements between us, or it will cause war between us, since it would have threatened our national security. India needs to know that God is on our side, because when, if we are to strategically bomb their dams, then the water will only flow down to us! But let us hope we do not need to resort to war over water. We ought to consider the water a gift from God, which should unite us all in Asia, because half of the world's population that lives in Asia, depends on water for its survival. I strongly believe the three superpowers in Asia; China, India, and Pakistan should have a permanent *Council on Water Access*, with single agenda to ensure water supply to everyone who lives in Asia, including those in other small Asian countries. The three superpowers of Asia house billions of poor people, to whom we owe a duty of care, whether they are Chinese, Indians, or Pakistanis.

Under this council, we could make new agreements to ensure the maximum amount of land would be made fertile by supply of water despite where it is located. The three superpowers should not put only their interest first, but they should treat all other weaker nations equally, at least when access to water is concerned, because human life depends on it. Where possible, we must not divert any natural flow of water, but it would only be diverted when it provides benefits to more people, without affecting the people who used to receive this water. We could also devise *Inter-State Flood Prevention Teams* to save thousands of lives, which are lost every year unnecessarily. If the cool heads of these three superpowers sit down together, then they could ensure the food security not just for Asia, but for the entire world!

But before we discuss our responsibilities in the short-term of storing the rain water, I need to discuss a few other things. It is alright to talk with India and China about ensuring equal water supply to all, but we need to look closer to home first, where unequal distribution of water is a major problem. We also need to look at how we could ensure continuous monsoon rainfall, because that may alter in future, due to things happening thousands of miles away.

I remember watching an interview on Pakistani TV a few months ago where an old farmer was interviewed because he had been protesting in Islamabad for a long time. He was not a poor farmer but was made poor by the powerful elites in Sindh, who had political connections. He told the interviewer that the other powerful landowners stopped his water supply for many years, and now his land has become infertile and barren, and he has become helpless and poor, because his only income was from agriculture. He told that the reason he was treated this way, was because these powerful elites wanted his land, and now it is barren and worthless. He was urging the government to help him to grant him equal share of water. We don't know how many other people suffer from these issues? I have lived in a farming village, and I know that one of the major sources of conflicts is water supply, which could also lead to murders. We need to sort out our own house first before talking to others.

Let us now discuss why I am concerned about the security of monsoon rainfall in future? To understand this we need to digress a little. Three quarters of our planet is water but still the water is not distributed equally between countries. Some countries get a lot of world's water, such as Amazon, while other parts of the world get very little, Africa for example. Pakistan has two sources of water; from rivers flowing mainly from Tibet, and monsoon rainwater. We will talk about Tibetan link in a bit, but the monsoon rain that falls here in Pakistan comes from the Arabian and Indian seas. The air above these seas is laden with water and it keeps more or less the same temperature of about 18 °C. This creates a high pressure. But if we consider the South Asia (parts of China, India, and Pakistan etc) as one big landmass then it heats up during summer much quickly due to its composition. This creates a low pressure, which is filled by the high pressure of Arabian and Indian seas, so it brings with it the moist air which rises due to mountain ranges on the way. But when it rises, it cools down and cannot keep water in clouds, which fall as monsoon rain. But some experts point out that Southeast-Asian Rainforests may also play a role in our monsoon. I am not sure about this connection but if it is so, then we need to be worried because this rainforest is being destroyed. If it affects our ecosystem, then we need to get together and come to an agreement with the countries that make up the Southeast Asian rainforest to preserve it. We could offer them incentives so they re-grow their rainforests, which is easier to do.

Now let us turn to Tibet, which is an ecosystem in itself, and is responsible for many rivers in China, India and Pakistan. If anything happens to Tibetan plateau then our rivers will dry out, causing droughts and large scale population reduction, or migration out. So it is important to preserve the Tibetan Ecosystem. China has political disputes with India over Tibet, so China will never allow India in any talk about Tibet. But we have very warm relations with China. So we need to ensure that China is doing everything it can to ensure the stability of Tibetan plateau. If it needs any assistance from us, then we should do everything that we could do, because it is the question of half of the world population's survival.

Finally, we need to store the huge amounts of water that we get every year from our rivers and monsoon rain, so we could provide it to farmers when they need it. Unfortunately, we lose millions of litters of water every year which could have been used in agriculture to help our economy. We could build many storage facilities cheaply if we use natural areas that may allow storage. Our aims should be to store most of this water on high grounds, upstream, so we do not need to use energy to redistribute it for agriculture. We need to learn to use nature to our advantage.

Bringing Law and Order

The law and order in Mongolian Empire was so strict that it was famous that, *a **virgin** maid with a **pot of gold** on her head, could walk from one end of the Mongol Empire to the other - with both intact.* If during the reign of Genghis Khan, a virgin maid with pot of gold on her head, could walk hundreds of miles and still kept her virginity and pot of gold intact, then there must have been absolute peace and tranquillity in Mongolian realm. But how did they get this kind of peace and tranquillity? Only through an absolute writ of the state. Everyone knew that they would be punished ruthlessly and instantly if they tried to steal that maid's gold or virginity! It was the fear of the state that kept the population in check.

We could find historic evidence to support the above view. For example, Niccolo Machiavelli mentions how Cesare Borgia, son of Pope Alexander VI, brought about peace in Romagna, which was full of robbery, quarrels, and every kind of violence. He appointed Ramiro D'Orco, a swift and cruel man, as governor. Ramiro quickly brought peace to Romagna but let us not discuss his fate. The point is that, the peace could only be won through cruelty and shear violence, as proposed by British political philosopher Thomas Hobbes in his book Leviathan. He wrote this book in the immediate aftermath of English Civil War, and described lawlessness and life then as solitary, brutish, and short. To bring about peace, he proposed 'a common Power to keep everyone in awe.' He further said 'Covenants, without Swords, are but Words,' meaning that the

social contracts or laws must be backed with Swords. Keeping the
above in mind, let us discuss the law and order situation in Pakistan,
what the history could teach us, and the kind of peace we want in
Pakistan.

Pakistan is one of the most dangerous places on earth in current
times, but a few decades ago it was a peaceful place to live in. As
far as I can remember, this peace was slowly broken with the start of
Soviet-Afghan War which started in 1979, and lasted for about nine
years. Kalashnikovs and Heroin started pouring into Pakistan,
creating thousands of addicts and criminals. In this backdrop, the
late president Zia ul Haq supported an ethnic group in Karachi to
reduce the power of his political rivals PPP[45] and JeI[46]. Fortunately
for late Zia, but unfortunately for Pakistan, this new group was able
to remove both the PPP and JeI's influence from Karachi and
surrounding areas, but it started creating a state within state of its
own, which persists to this day. They started killing and terrorising
people of other ethnicities, such as Punjabis and Pakhtuns, to
complete their control of the largest city of Pakistan. This group was
extremely gruesome in their terror tactics according to locals who
witnessed their cruelty. Such cruelty is not native to any of the pre-
existing populations of Pakistan, but came with some of the
migrating people. For example, members of this group would drill
holes in their victim's knees; burn timber yards and throw victims in
the fire alive; kill and chop body parts and put them in large sacks
for victim's family to collect; and gruesome of all was to remove
victim's skin, while they were still alive and trembling with fear and
shock! Their terror did not stop only to people of other ethnicities,
but they kept in check the people of their own ethnicity who would
oppose them politically or otherwise. This group then moved onto
other crimes to fund their operations. They used extortion regularly

---

[45] PPP stands for one of the largest political party, Pakistan Peoples
Party.
[46] JeI stands for Jamaat-e-Islami, a religious-political party.

to get money from traders, industrialists, and rich people, which is known as Bhata Mafia. They were also involved in kidnapping for ransom, which is a new trend. In recent times, this group has transformed itself to some degree, and moved into mainstream political system. Unfortunately, other players have also moved into Karachi's crime scene. For example, other political parties, and Pakistani Talibans (TTP), who came with the IDPs when they were displaced. The dynamics of crimes has changed dramatically since the arrival of TTP in Karachi, because they have emerged as the most powerful criminals displacing all other criminals into the second or third positions. That is why almost all the political parties that previously held power in Karachi demand military operation, so the Talibans could be moved out of the scene, and they could restore their power again.

While Karachi is burning, the other areas of Pakistan are not safe either. The largest victims of US-Afghan War are our Pakhtuns in FATA[47] and Khyber Pakhtunkhawa province. Thousands have lost their lives, uncountable number had been injured, and millions have become homeless in their own country, and are still waiting to return home. Their plight does not end here, but they are pushed from all sides. On one side by American drone attacks, on the other side by TTP who have killed almost 700 tribal leaders to establish their writ in FATA, and by FCR[48] from top. To add insult to injury, most of our Pakhtuns are poor and struggle to make ends meet.

Like Sindh and FATA, Baluchistan and Punjab are not safe either. There is insurgency going on in Baluchistan mainly supported by India, and allegedly by USA as well. At one point, an American congressman moved a bill to grant Baluch people right to self-

---

[47] FATA stands for Federally Administrated Tribal Areas.
[48] FCR stands for Frontier Crimes Regulation, and it is a special set of regulations applicable only to FATA, where they do not have a right to appeal, legal representation, or right to present reasoned evidence.

determination, which is a clear sign of their support for separatist movement in Baluchistan, and their interference in our internal affairs. If Americans believe in self-determination then why so many Blacks are rotting in their jails and Red-Indians restricted to small areas to live lives of poverty and misery? Their extreme prejudice against all those who are not Europeans can be seen from their categorisation of Blacks and Native Americans as Afro-Americans and Red Indians respectively. They call all Europeans as just 'Americans' as if no one else is American apart from them. But they should be correctly called Euro-Americans, because that is what they are, and how they classify other Americans.

Punjab being the largest of all provinces in population terms has more crimes as well. Murders and rapes are rife in Punjab as well as other crimes. There are two major reasons for crimes throughout the country; ineffective policing and extremely low conviction rates. Police will remain ineffective as long as the police are subservient to politicians due to the way their recruitment, promotions, and transfers work. But the conviction rates are lower because the witnesses and judges are afraid of criminals. Unfortunately, this is not a new trend, but the witnesses are always killed by powerful criminals, so no one would ever testify against them. But now the judges have been threatened by the criminals to avoid punishments. The reason for such practices is that the state has lost its writ, because the people who have been running the government did not protect state's employees. More than 250 police officers were targeted, hunted, and killed in Karachi by those against whom a police operation was launched by the federal government more than two decades ago. No police officer ever tried to catch cop-killers even though they know the killers, only because they are subservient to their political masters. If police and judges are not safe, then how a witness can feel safe? The root cause of all the issues mentioned above is that the state not having its writ in its domain. We need to ask ourselves if we want a peace and tranquillity similar to that of

Mongolian Empire or not? If yes, then we will have to have *a common Power which will keep everyone in awe*! But our discussion about law and order must begin with the National Security, because this will ensure the writ of the state within its borders and beyond.

National Security

Pakistan has National Security Council (NSC) but ironically no definition of National Security. If we don't know what is our national security then how could we defend it? When defining national security, the Pakistani politicians and military tend to focus on defence against foreign military attacks. Or when thinking about national security from internal threats, then we limit ourselves to terrorists' attacks.   They tend to miss many other important aspects of national security, such as, economic, self-determination and freedom from outside influence etc. I think there is a strong need for a clear and comprehensive definition of national security, which will guide our policies. I am going to make a start to define the national security, but it needs the inputs of intelligent people rather than me. However, we also do need to insert some ambiguities so it could be evolved as the new dangers arise. I am not going to re-invent the wheel, so I am going to borrow some ideas from other state's national security policies, and then add some ideas to tackle the unique security challenges we face in Pakistan. I quite like the definition of Harold Brown, because it is clear and measurable but I will modify it somewhat as below;

National security is the ability;

\ To preserve the nation's physical integrity, territory and control its borders.

\ To use counterintelligence services, secret police, or armed forces to protect the nation from internal threats.

\ To use intelligence services to detect and defeat, or avoid threats and espionage.

\ To use diplomacy to rally allies and isolate threats.

\ To maintain effective armed forces.

\ To implement civil defence and emergency preparedness measures.

\ To ensure the resilience and redundancy of critical infrastructure.

\ To preserve its nature, institution, and governance from disruption and influence from outside.

\ To follow independent economic & public policies according to the beliefs of its people.

\ To preserve its currency value, promote its use as a reserve currency, and defend it against misuse.

\ To keep economic relations with the rest of the world on reasonable terms.

\ To use economic power to facilitate or compel cooperation.

\ To make and implement security policies for unknown threats when they arise.

The above National Security definition is not complete and has a lot of room for improvement. It could be modified as the government sees fit.

Terrorism

At the time of writing, Pakistan had lost about 60,000 of its citizens including more than 5,000 security and military personnel's since the America's war in Afghanistan, which started in 2001. It is ironic that the country that started this war only lost 2,161 soldiers to date, while we, who supported them, lost almost 30 times more people.

Even then Americans accuse Pakistan for duplicity! But they ignore the duplicity they adopt at every turn. They killed 26 of our soldiers on purpose, at Salala. They kill our innocent citizens with drones; their CIA operatives kill innocent people in broad daylight and then claim diplomatic immunity! Their duplicity it not limited to just these events but almost all Pakistani analysts claim that Americans are behind the terrorist organisation TTP, who have attacked and killed thousands of Pakistanis. Some of the evidence they give for their claims is that these terrorists have highly sophisticated equipment, such as, night vision goggles, latest communication devices, and satellite images, not just from Google, accurately identifying where our most sensitive and critical assets are. It was revealed that not even the high ranking Pakistani military personnel knew where our Orion and AWACS planes were. Orion is an anti-submarine and maritime surveillance aircraft, while the AWACS performs air command and control, and battle management functions. These two types of aircrafts were destroyed in our hangers by these terrorists despite extreme secrecy. India certainly would not have known of our sensitive assets when our own high ranking military officers didn't know about them. They could have only been discovered by sophisticated means only available to Americans, who handed out this information to terrorists, claim most Pakistani analysts. Another reason for Americans being behind these attacks is that neither AWACS nor Orion planes posed any threat to TTP, then why would they destroy them? If anything, they should have destroyed the F-16s because they were used in military operations against them. The analysts claim that only the Americans have threats from our AWACS and Orion because they have submarines in our waters, which need to be protected. Even though Americans did supply us the Orion planes they do not wish us to have any such sophisticated technologies anymore.

I don't know the truth of these claims but there is weight in their arguments. In discussing how to tackle terrorism in Pakistan, we need to believe that this nexus between Americans and TTP exits, whether or not it actually does. Further, before we could devise an effective policy and plan to defeat the terrorists, we need to define all the nexuses TTP has with other organisations or countries, so we could cut off their support to weaken them before launching an assault. Let us now categorise the terrorists.

We have three main terrorists groups in Pakistan, Tehrik-i-Taliban Pakistan (TTP), Lashkar-e-Jhangvi (LeJ), and the Baluch separatists, who call themselves the Baluchistan Liberation Army (BLA). There are subgroups of these terrorists groups and also other small terrorist groups, but the most effective ones are the TTP, LeJ, and BLA. However, BLA is limited to its attacks within Baluchistan, and technically they are insurgents and not terrorists. While the LeJ is concerned mainly with targeting Shia minority, but the TTP is much effective and has attacked the high value targets throughout Pakistan. TTP and LeJ are not affiliated to BLA, but they have collaborated occasionally. Let us discuss them individually because they all require a different approach to deal with them.

According to Imran Khan and other religious leaders, the TTP originated in FATA in response to drone attacks by Americans. According to them, Pakhtuns, the tribal people of Pakistan who live on the North-West frontier region, do everything to avenge their dead. When the drone attacks kill a high value American target in FATA, it kills many innocent children, women, and men as well. To this injustice, the ordinary people pick up weapons and seek revenge. Some of them go to join the *Afghan Talibans* who are fighting Americans, so they could take their revenge there. But most of them attack Pakistan and its citizens, perhaps because they are easy prey. These terrorists argue that the drone attacks are carried out with Pakistan's permission, so by attacking Pakistani citizens and sensitive installations, they could avenge their dead. The leaders of the four political parties believe in these arguments, and they have called for an end to drone strikes. One of the leaders had even led an anti-Drone rally to North-West frontiers. This is where Pakistan has lost and the TTP has won, in dividing political parties and public opinion about them. I admit that those TTP leaders dressed in rags are much more intelligent than our sages and experts, because they have successfully divided Pakistani nation. But I fear that they will eventually put Pakistan on the War Path with USA, which will not be an outcome the world would want. Because if Pakistan and USA had a war, then all of American troops in Asia, which would be more than 100,000, are in clear range of Pakistani nuclear missiles, and I know that Pakistan will not have a choice but to use them, because we have less conventional war machinery than USA and cannot win with the conventional war. If this happens then a Third World War will begin! Let us hope this does not happen. But let us get back to why the leaders of political parties support TTP? I do not understand, why would people be so charged about so few innocent lives lost in Drone strikes, but they remain silent, aloof, and cold about more than 40,000 innocent deaths of Pakistanis at the hands of TTP?

Anyway, the TTP had been extremely effective in rallying support among politicians, journalists, religious scholars, and ordinary public to do their bidding. For example, at the time of writing there is a talk of negotiating with TTP, and almost all parties seem to go for negotiations. I do not think that negotiation will work simply because TTP is clear about a continued war with Pakistan even if America has removed its forces from Afghanistan, because they want to bring their version of Sharia in Pakistan. Negotiations is a useful strategy for TTP to try to remove our armed forces from FATA, so they could widen their control and then gain more territory, which comes from more territory and fighters. Unfortunately, our politicians are being played by TTP to remove our forces from FATA, and I fear it may be too late when our politicians would have realised that they had done TTP's bidding. But let us hope that they get wiser after talks with TTP. Anyway, it was TTP that was affected by drone strikes the most. Drone strikes eliminated the top two layers of TTP, so it was in the best interest of TTP to ask to stop drone strikes, and they have successfully managed to unite the whole nation to protest against such attacks. This also raises another important question. If Americans are supporting TTP, then why are they killing them through drone attacks? It is a paradox that we need to bear in mind while thinking of such a complex nexus. The paradoxical relationships do exist. For example, in America, *Nation of Islam*, an Afro-American movement opposed to integration of blacks and whites, joined forces with *Ku Klux Clan* that had executed many blacks, to further their agenda to oppose Martin Luther King's integration stance. Therefore, it is possible for Americans to be against TTP because they provide fighters for Afghan Talibans, but they may support TTP to attack Pakistan, so Pakistan stops the support of Afghan Talibans?

To understand the dynamics of terrorism in Pakistan, we need go back to *Russian-Afghan War* that started in 1979. At the time of this war, America was obsessed with communism and was locked in a cold war with Russia. The level of their obsession could be seen from McCarthy's List. Some three decades previously, he accused there were communists in the US State department. As the BBC put it, 'the senator Joe McCarthy launched an anti-red crusade.' At that time in history, Americans had an excuse to launch a war against any country that seemed to support communism, instead of directly attacking Russians, because they were sure to suffer un-repairable loss themselves. But for the last decade or so, Americans are fighting against Muslims. There was never any threat to world from communism then, and there is no threat to world from Muslims now. It is just an excuse to wage wars against weaker states, so America could control the most important resources in the world to keep its hegemony. By having their military bases in Afghanistan, USA can directly control all the natural resources of Central Asia! I think when the Americans are done with Muslims and their resources, then, if they found anything valuable in Africa, they will launch wars against them. They may give excuse that Africans are causing natural disasters in America, because all the storms in USA usually originate in Africa!

Getting back to why and how the dynamics of terrorism changed in Pakistan can be traced back to Russian-Afghan War, when America supported Afghan Mujahedeen. To participate in this war, Muslims came from all over the world, and USA not only turned a blind eye to them, but also provided them weapons and training. However, when the war was over, Americans went back but the Muslims, mainly from Arab and Central Asian countries, stayed behind, and settled either in Afghanistan or FATA. Please note that the majority population of Afghanistan, FATA, and Khyber Pakhtunkhawa are essentially the same race, Pakhtuns. They have the same customs and language, but most are very religious and conservative Muslims. When Muslims from around the world came to help Afghans to fight Russians, then it revived a tradition in Muslim history, going back to time of Hazrat Muhammad [PBUH], when the oppressed Muslims of Mecca migrated to Medina. People of Medina embraced the Meccans as their brothers, and shared everything with them equally. They even divorced their wives so the Meccans could marry them. Since the people of our FATA and Afghanistan are very religious, they married their daughters and sisters with the Muslims who came to help fight Russians. Most foreigners who married local women stayed behind. This is the finer point I would like you to bear in mind to understand the dynamics of terrorism in Pakistan.

Our Pakhtuns of FATA are patriots and have never attacked Pakistan. However, they are angry with the state about drone attacks and its support for NATO forces. They are also angry with the military operations in FATA. Despite this, they would not kill innocent Pakistanis who they know are their Muslim brothers and sisters. The real culprits are the foreigners who are settled in FATA and other regions. One of the proofs of this is obvious from the cutting the heads of our soldiers after killing them. The cutting of heads is specific to Central Asians or Arabs. Further, these foreign fighters have no devotion to Pakistan, while our Pakhtuns are patriotic Pakistanis. Even though the leadership of TTP may be Pakhtuns, but they are greatly influenced by these foreigners. We do know that many foreigners were killed or driven out to Afghanistan when a conflict developed between the local Jihadists and the foreigners, but these were mainly Uzbeks. The other foreigners, who married local girls, remain in FATA.

I think that these foreigners persuade our Pakhtuns by offering several arguments. At one level, they may have argued that Muslims are forbidden to help others who fight with Muslims. So by Pakistan agreeing to provide NATO a supply route, Pakistan had breached this rule. They may argue that this act alone takes the Pakistanis out of sphere of Islam. So fighting with Pakistanis is just as fighting with infidels. They may have offered arguments to console Pakhtuns that they will not be punished on the Judgement Day[49] if they killed Pakistanis, because they are no longer Muslims. While this argument may be powerful, it does not provide a constant drive. So they may have given them dreams of taking over Pakistan, a nuclear power, and installing real Islamic Sharia Laws[50] just like they did in Afghanistan. If they take over Pakistan, then they would start a Third World War. By the way, I think it is not impossible to take over Pakistan because their call for Sharia and Caliphate is gaining widespread support in Pakistan. Several officers from our armed forces had been influenced by the TTP and they had acted against the Pakistani state. For example, an officer was involved in an assassination attempt against former president Musharraf. There may have been inside job in attacks on our *Army General Head*

---

[49] Judgement Day is when the world ends and the final judgement begins.

[50] Sharia Laws are the code of law derived from Holy Quran and from the teachings and example of Hazrat Muhammed(PBUH).

Quarters, *Mehran Naval Base* and *Kamra Air Base*. Our police, bureaucracy and ordinary citizens also have sympathies for TTP's call. Police sympathy could be seen from their low resistance to a recent jailbreak where they freed about 248 prisoners. Some claim that police had colluded with the TTP. If this is true then TTP ideology is gaining a hold in our security forces, which is extremely dangerous. If TTP is able to gain enough support within the upper ranks of armed forces, which are more prone than the soldiers, then the possibility of TTP taking over Pakistan may become a reality. This may seem farfetched, but we have examples of our main political parties trying to please TTP before our last general elections out of fear of attacks. Ordinary people are deceived into the dreams of an era of early Islamic world. I have been shocked so many times by the comments of otherwise intelligent and sober people justifying the killings of many innocent Pakistanis by TTP, because they believe these sacrifices are necessary to achieve bigger goals of bringing Sharia and Caliphate in Pakistan! Such comments are alarming, and we must have a strategy to reveres these beliefs and views.

I am saying the above because these are the arguments we hear from TTP and its spokespersons, whether they are in the guise of politicians, religious scholars, or journalists. TTP knows that if they used the political process to come to power, then they will not win many votes. So they argue that the democracy is un-Islamic and Pakistan is practicing a system of government that is imported from the world of infidels. Obviously, *the grapes are sour*! Above arguments and beliefs are the driving force behind TTP, or it is their *Centre of Gravity*, as the Clausewitzians put it. If we could defeat TTP at the level of their beliefs then we would have achieved 80% of victory against terrorists without firing a shot.

The TTP also has connection with the Afghan Talibans led by Mullah Omar, because they accept him the *Leader of the Faithful* (Ameer-ul-Momeneen). Mullah Omar does not condone TTPs attacks on Pakistan, but he does not actively order them to stop either. This is a clever bargaining tactic to ensure continued support from Pakistan to help his cause. Pakistan does not see Mullah Omar as a problem but see him as an asset for obvious reasons. Pakistan never had any threat across border during Mullah Omar's reign. We share a very long border with Afghanistan, spanning thousands of miles, known as *Western Border*, and we never had to deploy our army on that border. In fact, we never had any military doctrine about our Western Border. Americans may call this duplicity, but we will have to live with Afghans when the Americans would have flown six thousand miles away. If we antagonise Afghan Talibans who we once had cordial relations with, then we will end up with a constant war with Afghanistan. This is because only the Pakhtuns could lead Afghanistan as they are the majority population and even ordinary Pakhtuns will not accept the minority government of Northern Alliance supported by Americans and Indians.

Mullah Omar is a Pakhtun leader who enjoys the allegiance of almost all Pakhtun population on both sides of the border. And now when the Americans are negotiating with Talibans, we are not out of our minds to start a war with them that is not necessary. We do not have enough armed force to fight simultaneously on Eastern and Western borders spanning some 5,000 miles, with Afghanistan and India. However, to tackle terrorism, we must break TTP's link with Afghan Talibans by pushing Mullah Omar, not to support or protect them on his side of border. We need to seal our Western border with landmines, or at least seal the strategic locations, because this is the easiest solution to contain terrorism. This will allow us to relieve our armed forces that have been deployed there for a long time. No soldier remains active in a war situation for too long, but he is usually relieved of his duties after six months to a year and not called back on to active line of duty for at least a year or so. But our soldiers are exhausted with years of active duty. We need to rest them so they could be refreshed physically and mentally. Also we must not engage a large number of our troops on the Western border because it is not a good strategy. Our forces will be divided and immobile this way. We should seal the borders with landmines to our side of *Durand Line*. Afghanistan will likely to object to it, but we need to ensure them that it is only a temporary measure until there is peace both in Afghanistan and Pakistan, then we will remove landmines. Sealing our Western border with landmines may also antagonise Afghan Talibans, because it may reduce their mobility, but we need to assure them that it is to protect our borders and not to reduce their mobility. I think America is likely to support this action and China will welcome it as well. But the question is how to lay landmines on a twenty-five hundred mile long border?

I am sure we could buy landmines that could be sown by aircrafts, which will make it quick and easy to cover the entire length of our border. But we must protect the communities on both sides of the border from landmines, and ensure that there is least inconvenience for them by laying landmines manually all along the settled communities. These landmines should be further protected with barbed wire so no one can trigger them by mistake. For settled communities, we should try to lay the landmines as far away as possible from the population. Other permanent markers should be placed to let the locals know of the dangers. Then we should ensure that locals are educated on both side of the border about these landmines. Our aim should be to have Zero casualty from landmines of the local people, or we will turn them against us. Accidents will happen and we need to ensure that we quickly control the situation as it arises. We need to ensure access points for both communities to go by their daily lives because these people are related to each other so we should be sensitive to their needs and not cut them off. We should issue fee free visas in the form of ID Cards with biometric data so we could identify the locals from terrorists. We should have all the equipment necessary for border control but not have the databases of such data on site, or it will put many lives at risk.

Instead, we could send and receive data over secured mobile networks for checking people's identity by scanning their IDs.

When laying the landmines, we need to let run those terrorists who want to run, because it will only help us by reducing the number of people to deal with at this stage. Also by pushing them against the wall, we put them on Death Ground[51] and they will fight with double the courage. Our aim should be to defeat terrorists with the least amount of force, and casualties to our side.

TTP also has a nexus with LeJ when their goals converge, that is, to kill Shia Muslims. TTP's main targets are not the Shia minority but when they cannot find a high value target, then they attack Shia population. It is important to understand here that TTP and LeJ both follow Deobandi school of thought, which is one of the two major Sunni sects found in Pakistan, India, and Bangladesh. Deobandi Muslims are also very close in belief with Arab Muslims. The extremist Deobandi believe that Shias are heretics, and killing them is not a sin. Some of them argue that the Shias do not accept the first three Chalifs who came to power after the death of Hazrat Muhammad[(PBUH)]. Because the Shias argued that the leadership should have stayed within the family of prophet, which would have been Hazrat Ali[(RA)], being the son-in-law of Holy Prophet Muhammad[(PBUH)]. But he was passed over Caliphate for three times before he was finally selected as Caliph. They further argue that the Shias curse one of the wives of prophet, Hazrat Ayesha[(RA)], perhaps because the arguments broke out between Hazrat Ali[(RA)] and Hazrat Ayesha[(RA)] for Hazrat Ali[(RA)] not putting enough efforts to find and punish the murderers of Caliph Usman[(RA)] (Ottoman). This further led to split between Hazrat Ali[(RA)] and Hazrat Ayesha[(RA)] who fought

---

[51] In the *Art of War* by Sun Tzu, he mentions of *Death Ground*, which is a situation where the soldiers are unable to escape war theatre. So they would have to fight to survive, or die fighting. He argues that when the soldier is put on death ground then he fights with double the courage and could snatch victory from defeat.

a war with each other but after Hazrat Ali[(RA)] defeating Hazrat Ayesha's[(RA)] forces, the situation was diffused. There are these and a few other accusations that Deobandi make against shias, which I also heard as a child.

For example, I heard that Shias believe that the current Quran is not complete because some of the verses which were written on tree leaves were actually eaten by a goat. We, as children also heard that we should not eat the food given out by shias in the month of Muharram, because they spit in it before giving it to Sunni Muslims. I don't know how much truth is in these arguments, but when I asked some of my Shia colleagues recently, they utterly deny all these allegations, and also challenged me to visit their prayer centre to examine the Quran, which they claim is identical to what the Sunni Muslims have. I had never made good on their challenge, because I do not have any reasons to doubt their claims. Please note that the LeJ was an offshoot of another terrorist organisation named Sipah-e-Sahaba (SSP), meaning the *Soldiers of Companions* [of Muhammad[(PBUH)].] The Companions usually refer to the first four Caliphs, including Hazrat Ali[(RA)]. This group was intensely against Shia Muslims for the reasons I cited above. This background was necessary to understand the nexus between LeJ and TTP.

Recently, I learnt of another interesting and important fact about TTP, which military has not disclosed yet for some reason. Many of the TTP fighters which were killed or captured during operations in Swat valley were not actually Pakistanis, Arabs, or Central Asians, but they were Indian fighters disguised as Talibans. This came as a shock to me when I first learnt about it. This news came to me through a friend, whose very close relative was involved in operations in Swat and was a middle ranking officer. They realised that some of the captured or dead TTP fighters were not Muslims, but they knew Quran and were fully versed in Islamic studies. They wore beard and portrayed themselves as Muslims. Breakthrough came when on inspection; officers found that none of them was circumcised. I told my friend that he had been the victim of military propaganda. These people could have been from Central Asia that were under Russian rule for so long that they may not have followed Muslim practice of circumcision. He protested at this saying, what would his close relative gain from propaganda to him? Further, the Central Asian features are very different than Indians and can be distinguished instantly. Well, if this is true, then the India had been putting a lot of resources in training these fighters in Islamic studies as well as military training. This reminded me of a scene from a Chinese film, *IP Man*, where Japanese intelligence exported Child Intelligence Operatives (Childint) during Sino-Japanese War. These children were portrayed as helpless young children abandoned by poor families, and were left outside rich people's homes in the dark of the night. The rich would feel sorry and adopt them. The Japanese intelligence idea was to create enemies from within, who are unrecognisable by the locals as foreigners. Perhaps, India had learnt from Japanese? But we ought to tell the India in clear and direct terms that no such intrusion will be tolerated anymore and this would be an act of war!

 The last nexus of TTP I want to discuss is what they have with criminals, especially in Karachi, which is the major source of their funding. They kidnap the rich, and then demand ransom for their release. If they do not get the ransom money then they do not hesitate to kill the hostages because it ensures future compliance by other victim's families. They had been so successful that they kidnapped ex-Prime Minister and Governor's sons. Their whereabouts is still unknown. This nexus, which is the major source of their funding is the most important for the terrorist to keep. If we starve them of cash, then their ability to operate will reduce to near zero. I have provided proposals in previous chapters on how we could use monetary controls and electronic money to defeat all types of crimes and corruption.

Our inability to tackle the terrorists is not due to our marshal inability or lack of resolve, but the terrorists enjoy widespread moral public support, even within our security services including armed forces and police. In this situation, any operation against terrorists will not be successful. We must break this public support for terrorists before launching any operation, but why does public like them?

Among other, there are two reasons. The terrorists say that they will bring in Sharia Law and Caliphate to Pakistan, and they will provide instant justice. Sharia law and Caliphate appeals to many because they believe that the reason for Muslims' downfall and current problems is our increasing distance from Islamic principles. Further, since the relaxation of laws by Musharraf, the Western culture has taken hold in Pakistani society. The things of particular concern to most people is the semi-pornographic television programmes and films shown on our mainstream media, and increasing prostitution for fun and money in our society. In a recent television interview, Sohail Ahmed, a stage & TV actor and comedian, displayed his concern and disgust about what he had seen on the stage, where a woman was dancing in her birthday suit[52], soon after Musharraf relaxed the rules. These things are neither part of our religion nor our culture. Many people want an end to this cultural invasion, so they morally support the terrorists because they believe that terrorists will restore an Islamic way of life in Pakistan.

The second main reason the public provides moral support to terrorists is because no one can get justice in Pakistan. The strong and wealthy can do what they please, and the poor victim will never get justice, or perhaps even be punished for asking for justice. Crimes are rife in Pakistan, and people do not feel safe for their lives, property and dignity. The top courts may be effective even sending the incumbent Prime Minister home for not following court

---

[52] Birthday Suit is the suit in which a child is born on the day of her birth, that is, bare skin. It is just another term for nakedness.

order, but the lower courts are suffering from corruption and bribery. Further, the courts allow Stay Orders[53] for years instead of resolving the cases. I remember of two killings in our village when I was only four or five years old, and now I am an adult but I don't think that the cases have still been resolved. People can spend their lifetimes seeking justice in Pakistan, but it is a rare thing, like diamonds! To gain moral support from public, the terrorists hold parallel courts in Karachi and FATA where they have control, and decide on cases there and then. They carry out punishment on the spot, all in a day. More and more people are turning to terrorists for justice. These are the systemic state failures which need resolving in order to break public support for terrorists. The major concern for me is their parallel courts in Karachi. FATA is not a major concern because our courts do not have jurisdiction there anyway, because people decide their disputes through their tribal council called *Jirga*.

Unfortunately, the public support for terrorists is not limited just to ordinary people, but the security personnel including military, and mainstream political parties also have soft corner for them for the same reasons the public offers them moral support. Four mainstream political parties, including two religious parties, openly demanded to negotiate with the terrorists instead of military action before last general elections. In turn, terrorists demanded the guarantees of the three parties before they could come to negotiating table. This was a clever tactic by the terrorists to divide the political parties because there was a talk of military action against terrorists then. Terrorists were successful because the political parties could not reach a consensus about military action or negations. Now one of the party that was all for negotiations, is in power in centre, while the other two parties are in power in one of the provinces. These two parties now seem to have come to a realisation that negotiation is not an

---

[53] A Stay Order is an order issued by a court stopping court proceedings until a further, specified event takes place.

answer. However, the two religious parties are unlikely to support any military action.

But for the military to take any action in mainland Pakistan, they need to declare *Martial Law* in that area for one important legal reason, which many ordinary people do not appreciate. Martial Law is imposed so the military has absolute power without fear of soldiers or officers being prosecuted. Under Martial Law, the Civil Laws or Civil Rights are suspended. On the other hand, in ordinary times, if a police officer kills a person during police operation, then he could be prosecuted for homicide[54]. Military personnel cannot be tried for any mistakes or excesses while performing their duties. This is the reason our military does not wish to carry out any operation against its own citizens unless it has full public and political support. It is not difficult to defeat the terrorists, but we must consider carefully all factors mentioned above, and then devise a plan and carry it through to the very end. We could follow the step-by-step plan below.

While our military is preparing for an operation, which takes several months, we need to do many things simultaneously to ensure operational success. So the military have to do the least work. It is possible that the terrorists may give up even before operation begins. So it is important that we make an unwavering solid decision about how far we will go? This is because the political parties and governments have inbuilt weaknesses and they usually give up half way through an operation. For example, they might decide to give up when the terrorists ask for negotiations. Giving up half way is usually a suicide, because the terrorists usually buy time to regroup and re-supply by entering negotiations. If we stopped half-way then we would have weakened our position, and lost all the gains we would have made. Let me give you an example which is very similar to our likely situation.

---

[54] Killing of one human being by another is called *Homicide* in legal circles.

Chiang Kai-Shek came to power in 1924 but soon after communism in China rose to its great heights under the leadership of Mao Tse Tung. Mao was a terrorist from the point of view of the government. He gathered a huge force and threatened to take over Chiang's government. But Chiang's forces, assisted by Americans, forced Mao to retreat his forces on a long trail lasting more than 6,000 miles. This trail later became known as *Long March,* a term which our politicians use loosely. During this retreat Mao lost thousands of his soldiers, and his force was reduced to only a few thousands. Chiang could have eliminated Mao's entire force, but he believed that Mao is too weak to be a threat to his government. Chiang was also distracted by the Japanese attacking China, so he left Mao and his small force alone. However, this gave Mao time to rebuild his force. He eventually took over the government and drove Chiang out of China, into Taiwan. So the moral of the story is that we should make solid decisions, and set measureable goals. And then do not stop until those goals are achieved even if we have the whole world against us. But if we left things half way, then our fate may not be much different than Chiang's.

Our starting point should be to make a public declaration, such as 'Today, we declare that we will avenge the deaths of every of our military, police, and civilian. We will find and kill the culprits no matter where they run, or hide. Let us make it clear to all that we will not rest until we have handed out justice to the last living terrorist. You have just three days from now to lay down your arms, and hand yourself over to us. We would be lenient to those who cooperate with us, but there will be no mercy for those who resist. We may pardon those who assist us in catching the terrorists. We demand that you hand over all the foreigners living among you, and then we may consider negotiating with you.'

This declaration alone will send a shiver down the spines of the terrorists. The demand for handing over foreigners is to eliminate the cruellest of the elements, and to divide them. If they hand over the foreigners then it is a bonus, because we could gather all the necessary intelligence from the captured. It is most likely that they will not hand over anyone but it must be tried. If this doesn't work then we should infiltrate our intelligence operatives or create double agents from TTP to start a war among TTP foreign element and locals which is the easiest to do. There are many ways to achieve this objective. Once this happens then it becomes easier for us to deal with the winners because they would be much weaker. Our aim should be to divide them into two groups at first, and once they are weakened, then divide them further. Once they fight with each other, they would most likely to lose public support because they would have caused collateral damage in the process.

Assuming we have sealed our border with landmines leaving some space for them to escape, and cut all the weapon supplies, the next step is to secure all of our critical infrastructures and communications networks, so the terrorist do not try to damage them to slow us down. We must first starve the terrorists in FATA or Karachi of electricity, petroleum, and telecommunications to limit their command and control. For Karachi, we could use fluoride or other substances in their water supply to reduce their physical ability. In the case of FATA, we should reduce the food supply just enough so the Taliban would have to capture it from the locals, creating a tension between locals and TTP. We need to empower our FATA residents with necessary weapons to protect themselves against Talibans. We must starve TTP of all these materials for the whole duration of the operation. Even if they have latest satellite technology, it would not work without electricity. All communication must be jammed. Only our propaganda materials through aeroplanes and through radio waves should reach the TTP and local public. We could drop pocket radio sets with special types of batteries which could not be used in other devices. Perhaps, a small solar cell is included for continuous operation of radio.

For Karachi, we should starve terrorist of cash, housing, and communication. I have already discussed in previous chapters how we could starve them of cash. Therefore, we need to ensure that we break their communication networks, so they could not operate effectively. This is not difficult to do by requiring everyone to register their mobile phone SIMs within 36 hours or it would be blocked from the network automatically. Notifying of lost or stolen mobile phones and SIMs must be made obligatory. Any breaches should carry a Rs.100,000 fine and a three year jail sentence to ensure compliance. This law is required in case the terrorist rob ordinary citizens of their mobile phones to communicate with their comrades. In such situations, the state does need to know if the terrorists are still able to communicate. Heavy fines and punishment will ensure the citizens inform the law enforcing authorities of loss of their mobile phones. Any landlines already installed, which may have been used by terrorists, should be cut from the network, and only restored when authorities are fully satisfied that terrorists are not using them. Some of the terrorist may also be using satellite phones, we need to detect and catch them or make them ineffective. Better still listen to their communication to gather intelligence.

In the case of Karachi, we must ensure that the terrorists do not have a place to live. We can do this by making it unlawful to rent out any house, shop, or any other type of house without registering it with the local council first. Owners must be required to have the ID cards of all tenants with their clear thumb impressions and photographs. This should include women and children. However, we ought to guarantee landlords that there will be no extra tax liability for renting out houses for accommodation: the rules for commercial property already exist. In any case, registration with the local council is only required so our security forces can detect terrorists living there. Tax office should not have access to these records, or people will not comply. However, we need to impose high enough fines and jail sentences to ensure compliance. For example, failure to comply with registration requirement will incur a fixed fine of 50% value of the property and 10 years jail sentence. Further, if a terrorist is found in their property then it would invoke Treason Act, and the owner of the house or shop will be prosecuted for aiding and assisting a terrorist to launch an attack on the state. There is no maximum fine for such offences: it could also carry a death sentence. Owners must also be required to notify of any suspicion about their tenants. Here we need to be aware of the fact that Karachi attracts hundreds of thousands of illegal workers from nearby countries, they may resort to illegal means to gain housing thwarting our efforts. We should announce that all the illegal immigrants will be granted five years work visa if they could prove they had been living and working in Pakistan for the last 3 years. Two bona fide Pakistanis should be able to verify their claim.

The next step is to break the biggest support of the terrorists, which comes from the foreign spies throughout the country in the guise of diplomats, or foreign local agents embedded in the NGOs. We have had a glimpse of such support in the cases of Raymond Davis and Shakil Afridi. Raymond Davis was a CIA contractor who shot dead two unarmed men in Lahore on January 27, 2011. Pictures of Pakistani military installations were also found on Davis. A four wheel drive vehicle that came to rescue Davis from American consulate in Lahore also killed a pedestrian when travelling on the wrong side of a one way street. Mark Mazzetti wrote in New York Times on April 9, 2013 that Obama claimed diplomatic immunity for Davis, but the government of Pakistan did not have power to release Davis, because of the problems of Federal government having no jurisdiction in Lahore, where these two men were killed. Davis was arrested by Lahore police, which was controlled by the Punjab province ruled by the archrivals of Zardari, who was in power in the centre. The matter was later resolved by the ISI on the request of American Ambassador Cameron Munter. ISI forced the poor families of victims to accept blood money, to forgive Davis for the killings, and drop all charges. Americans were also worried because it appeared that the Lahore High Court was about to decide not to grant diplomatic immunity to Davis, which would have set a precedent for any future cases, and it would make it difficult for Americans to operate there.

This article shows a dangerous picture of how many CIA agents were in Pakistan legally or on false identities at the time of Lahore killings, that the US Embassy did not have accurate records of their whereabouts. It further states that the new CIA chief wanted to recruit more Pakistani agents to work for the CIA, right under the nose of ISI. They wanted to expand electronic surveillance of ISI offices. Another thing that comes out of this article is the open admittance that the CIA has a station within American embassy in Pakistan. What does International Law say about this? Pakistan needs to demand closure of CIA station within US embassy and limit the number of visas to American diplomats. If it has to, it should cancel the visas. I think an easy formula could be arrived at for the ideal number of diplomats per embassy by taking two averages.

First average could be calculated by adding up the total number of diplomats present in Pakistan before Hussain Haqqani - the Pakistani ambassador to USA who helped issue thousands of visas to Americans - and then dividing this number by the total number of embassies. This number should dictate how many diplomats the USA should have in its embassy. We could also take a different approach. For example, we could look at how many US diplomats there were every year from 1947 until 2001, from the start of our diplomatic relations with the Americans to US-War in Afghanistan. We can calculate an average of this average to calculate the number of diplomats historically present in Pakistan since its diplomatic relations established. If there are more diplomats than this number, which is most likely, then Pakistan must demand a clarification of increased number of diplomats and their role in Pakistan. We need to tell the US ambassador that we are cancelling the visas of your extra staff and let us know which ones to cancel. If they don't give any list then just cancel the ones we think are suspected CIA operatives.

Another thing that I noticed about US Embassy in Islamabad, which I did not like, was the presence of their soldiers on top of their building in full uniforms. This is an insult to Pakistan. Do the Americans think we cannot protect their diplomats? Or are they showing their superiority by displaying their soldiers on top of their Embassy? Anyway, I did not like to see foreign soldiers on my soil. It is not a security threat but just an annoyance, and I think that we should also annoy the Americans by sending and installing our soldiers in our embassy in USA. They cannot refuse our soldiers because these things are reciprocal. If they refuse our soldiers then we could refuse theirs.

Let us get back to our topic. While Davis worked directly for the CIA in Pakistan, Shakil Afridi, a local doctor was working indirectly for the CIA. He was the American agent that led the American SEALs to violate Pakistani airspace and murder Osama Bin Laden. Americans claim that they killed and buried Laden's body in the sea, but we don't know how much truth is in it, because it seemed that the operation was designed to help Obama win the next election, which he did. We will only know the truth when this information is declassified. Anyhow, Afridi worked for the CIA and ran a fake vaccination campaign in order to confirm the identity of Laden. He was sentenced for 33 years by Pakistani courts not for CIA links, but for something else. USA demanded the release of Afridi and granted him Congressional Gold Medal and a US Naturalised citizen status. They have cut down an aid to Pakistan for $33 millions, $1 million for every year that Afridi serves in jail. These are the only two cases that came to light and we do not know how many CIA and RAW agents are operating in Pakistan directly or indirectly and embedded into NGOs? To establish government's writ throughout Pakistan and defeat terrorism, it needs to clean up its land of any foreign agents in any shape or form. This could easily be done in two steps.

Firstly, we need to ban all the NGOs working in Pakistan, and launch an investigation into the financial affairs of all the top management of these NGOs, to determine if they have any links to foreign institutions or governments. All the NGOs that are found guilty of being agents should be prosecuted under Article 6 (treason) of the constitution and these NGOs are banned permanently. These facts must be well publicised, so the public could see what these NGOs are doing. The other NGOs that come out clean, we need to make changes to how they will operate before allowing them to work again. For example, all the top management of all NGOs must get security clearance from federal government. There has to be a federal regulator for NGOs who would look at the financial affairs of the NGOs and their management regularly to detect any security risk to Pakistan.

To get rid of CIA, RAW and other intelligence agencies agents, we need to close down all the consulate offices throughout the country. We need to pass laws under the National Security Doctrine which also limits the movements of diplomats outside of Islamabad's diplomatic zone. All diplomats must get permission from foreign office to attend any meeting outside of diplomatic zone or to meet anyone. Any breach of these rules will mean the diplomats will lose their diplomatic immunity and treated as foreign spies. These changes will create a strong response from many countries, especially USA. But we need to declare that these measures are only temporary, and will be reviewed every year until the security situation gets better. We have a duty of care to all the diplomatic community in Pakistan to protect them, but in the current situation we are unable to do it effectively outside of diplomatic zone. They can make noises or protest that they will break diplomatic relations with Pakistan. Let them! Because these are our rules, whether they like it or lump it!

These changes will ensure that our security forces and agencies gain full control throughout Pakistan, and they will be much more effective without outside influence. Here I need to digress again and mention a few important facts from which we need to draw lessons, and make some permanent rules to avoid repetitions of such events. In a recent TV interview, the former Commander in Chief of our armed forces, Mirza Aslam Baig, said that, *when he saw American diplomats coming and going from the then Commander in Chief, Pervez Musharraf 's house, he knew that a military takeover was on the cards.* This tells us two important things, that all the current and former Commander-in-Chiefs live close to one another, and that foreign diplomats meet freely with our military commanders without the government knowing about those meetings. We must stop this, and put in place permanent laws, which prevent both the diplomats and our military officers to meet, without first getting government's permission. In this law, we must also include police chiefs and chiefs of all the bureaucracy.

The next step is to infiltrate TTP with our agents or turn their members into our agents to gain inside information. I don't think that it would be too difficult to infiltrate but if we are unable to, even then we should give a public impression that we have infiltrated by making subtle leaks in the press to unnerve TTP leadership. Once their leadership is unnerved, which is not difficult to achieve for us, they will become very weak, divided, and will make mistakes. We need to maintain this environment until we have defeated them all, in detail.

The next most important thing that we should have achieved before launching military operation is to remove TTP and other terrorists' public support. In fact, the public, especially of FATA should be prepared so much that they would urge us to go after TTP and other terrorists at all costs. We need to maintain this environment for a long time even after we have defeated the terrorists completely. If we failed to achieve such an environment then we must not go ahead

with military operation, because it will turn in to a protracted
conflict. The danger is that we may turn our FATA people against us
like we did in the last operation and then federation will be in a
danger of collapse. Here I strongly recommend that we bring slow
but steady changes to Frontier Crimes Regulation (FCR) to bring it
in line with the mainland Pakistan's Constitution. The reason is that
FCR is a method of extreme suppression of our FATA people. So as
long as the FCR remains in operation, our FATA people will remain
angry with Pakistan. FCR must be another reason that the FATA is
supporting TTP. If we want the support of our people then we will
have to bring FATA out of colonial suppression and into main
stream Pakistan.

If we made changes to FCR then it may not be difficult to eliminate
terrorists' public support. All we have to do is to remind our people
of heinous acts of these terrorists against our country and people. I
am against a propaganda campaign to our own people because it is
only for enemies. Our people must be told the truth no matter what
are the consequences. Here, I have to admit that the TTP and other
terrorists have shown some intelligence in selecting their targets so
not to antagonise the public at large. They selected their targets
carefully, for example, they selected the security forces, and other
minorities such as, Shia, Christians, Ahmedis, and Hindus. They
have generally tried to avoid complete indiscriminate attacks to
avoid losing public support. When the Sunnis see the terrorists
killing innocent unarmed Shias, we feel sorry for the victims, but
never have an intense hate against the perpetrators. This is because
Sunnis are also divided in to two major camps, Deobandis and
Barelvis. Deobandis generally tend to have less sympathy for our
Shias but not all Deobandis are alike. Further, the TTP, LeJ, and
other terrorists belong to Deobandi school of thought. On the other
hand, Barelvis tend to have more sympathies for Shias, but the

minorities are still an out-group[55] for the majority of public. So until, the TTP or LeJ does not target the Barelvis specifically, who are the largest Sunni group in Pakistan, we would not see a popular demand for a military operation against TTP or LeJ.

On the other hand, the BLA targets Punjabis working in Baluchistan. In almost all of these cases, terrorists checked the identities of their victims before killing them. We need to unnerve and frustrate the terrorists so they are less discriminating in their selection of targets, so a large majority of public would turn against them.

We could make it obligatory for the usual victims to change their names temporarily and issue them weapons to carry and use against terrorists. For example, the *Hazara community* and Punjabi workers in Baluchistan are usually targeted when travelling on buses. We need to order all the Hazara community to change their names temporarily so they are unrecognisable as Shias. We need to issue them new ID cards and other documents urgently free of charge, and later not charge any fees when they ask for new ID bearing their original names. Similarly, the Punjabi workers should be ordered to adopt usual Baluch names so they are unrecognisable as Punjabis. Similarly, issue them new IDs free of charge now and later. These measures will not prevent terrorists from targeting these groups but it will make it difficult for them to identify their targets. This would give enough time to Hazara and Punjabi people to kill the terrorists who may be checking their identities.

To break the public support for terrorists, we first need to have the power to prevent airing of any interview or programme, or printing of any material that supports the terrorist' viewpoint directly or implicitly. We also need to apply the same criteria to Internet and

---

[55] An in-group is a social group to which a person psychologically identifies as being a member. By contrast, an out-group is a social group to which an individual does not identify. So for Barelvis, Shia and other Sunnis will be out-groups, despite them having some sympathies for them.

social media and prevent any such materials to be viewed by any Pakistani. We could borrow expertise from China: how to control electronic media, because they have been doing it successfully for some time now. We could design our own social media applications to mimic Twitter, Youtube, and Facebook etc, for which we would have complete control. China has created their own versions of these applications, some even with better features, such as, QQ. By creating our own applications, we will improve our technical capabilities and Pakistani corporations will earn advertising revenue instead of foreign companies.

Once we have removed all the pro-terrorist materials from public life, then we could move on to cultivating public support for military action against terrorists. We need to cultivate this support from all around the country, but we will have to pay more attention to two important areas where the terrorists come from and hide, FATA and Khyber Pakhtunkhawa province. Unless these people are on our side, it would be a suicide to go against terrorists. We need to cultivate this support by using several methods and sources. For example, we could create documentaries showing public the videos and picture of the victims. Show the interviews of victim's families including children, who are much more likely to be in distress and emotional. These measures would create public empathy for these victims, their families and children. We need to continue this as long as it is needed.

Further, we could ensure there is enough public debate on TV and print media about terrorism to gain more support for military action. We could get Muslim scholars to debate on the issue of "one Muslim killing another". This debate will most likely put terrorist in the wrong from the religious point of view, which will turn people against terrorist at the higher level, that is, at the level of their faith. This is the most potent weapon, not just to get the public on our side, but also to sow the seeds of doubt in the terrorists' minds. While listening to finer points of these debates from renowned religious scholars, the terrorists will start to doubt their own beliefs on killing Muslims of Pakistan, whether in uniforms or civilians. The scholars need to show them a way to salvation so they give up terrorism and cooperate with the State of Pakistan. In the past, we have seen that anyone who spoke against the terrorists, were killed and the state did not protect them. This time we must be much more responsible and ensure the safety of all those who speak against terrorism, including religious scholars, TV show hosts, political analysts, and politicians etc. We need to guarantee the safety of these people and their families as long as it is required, which should be assessed by our intelligence agencies regularly. We need to have an automatic constitutional cover to protect these people because they are risking their lives to ensure the safety of the rest of the population.

We further need to remind the people of FATA how the terrorists killed more than 700 of their elders to take over the leadership. It was not only a great loss for the tribal communities but also for whole of Pakistan because an ancient tradition was destroyed. They must avenge their elders and re-establish their way of life again by overpowering the terrorists even though some of them may be their own brothers. We need to empower the descendants of the elders killed, any other suitable heirs, or other emerging leadership. We need to ensure that we help people of FATA financially and ensure a long last thriving economy for our tribal brothers and sisters. We should not do these things temporarily for our tribal families just so we could serve our purpose for now. This would be deceiving our own people, and would be fatal for our federation. We should be utmost honest and sincere with our tribal brothers and sisters. The same goes for our Khyber Pakhtunkhawa families because they both have suffered more than any other Pakistani since the Russian and later American invasion of Afghanistan!

Another source of terrorists' recruitment ground that we have ignored are the hundreds of religious seminaries. Since Zia era, there had been a large drive towards opening and running new religious seminaries. Most of the children who study in these schools come from very poor families who cannot afford to send their children to private schools, because the state schools had become useless in providing satisfactory education. These religious schools filled that gap. Most of the religious schools are providing social services of education and boarding for poor children, but a handful are the breeding grounds for terrorism. Another problem we have is that there is no central regulator for these schools. So how the child turns out when graduated, is all dependent on the benevolence and the beliefs of the person running the school, who is usually also the teacher. These teachers are not rich themselves but they rely heavily on public donations for which there is no shortage in Pakistan, despite country being very poor. I believe that these schools are now nominally regulated, but I doubt the effectiveness of such control. Perhaps, we are regulating these schools just to keep Americans happy.

These schools should be the starting point for our intelligence gathering, because we could build up a database of all those who studied there for the last four decades when these schools were first opened. We could then trace these students and figure out who is involved in terrorism? We could perhaps ask the families of terrorists to appear on TV requesting their sons and brothers to lay down their arms. This would break their morale, or divide them. Perhaps, some would defect. Nothing would be lost with this exercise, but we would have gained greatly from it. After covering all these steps we are now ready to launch a military operation. I do not need to go into more details because our military is the professional force and one of the best in the world: it knows what to do. But before we launch a military operation, we need to ponder on a very important question that Imran Khan posed, but most people ignore it. He asks what will we do if the military operation is not successful? Unfortunately, no one has answered Imran's this important question. Perhaps, they think that a military operation is always successful. Here I empathise with Imran in his concerns. We must have carefully considered our options if Imran's scenario present itself after military operation. I can only see one answer to his question, an all out war with the TTP! But I am not an elected leader like Imran, so only him and other political leaders who have public mandate could decide on this issue.

Let us now turn our attention to BLA. We have to deal with BLA in a different way because they are not purely terrorists, but they are a separatist movement partly supported by India. The events that led them to demand independence from Pakistan are fairly complicated, but we can see a systematic failure of our state to attend to their concerns. Further, our response to their demands was perhaps disproportional, which created further discontent among our Baluch brothers. We may perhaps be repeating the same scenario in Baluchistan as that of East Pakistan?

Some analysts claim that a dark economy has developed in Baluchistan because of long standing military control there. Some military officers are benefiting greatly from this dark economy, so they do not wish the situation to resolve there. These analysts claim that kidnapping for ransom and smuggling is rife in Baluchistan, and it is done with the blessing of military, for which they receive their share from criminals. I don't know how much truth is in these claims, but we do need to keep our eyes open. It is not difficult to resolve the issue of BLA insurgency, but we must understand the reasons for their discontent before we could move on to any possible solutions.

Baluchistan is a tribal society with a population of only about 8 million, which is roughly 5% of total population of Pakistan. But it is the largest of all the provinces in term of landmass. Baluchistan has natural resources including gas, copper, and gold. The royalties are paid to the tribal leaders known as Sardars. This arrangement keeps the population poor while the Sardars keep getting rich. I suspect that some of these Sardars may have been playing on poor population's sentiments, that the central government is stealing our resources, so they could negotiate higher royalties for their personal profits. However, the poor population is mostly illiterate and perhaps unable to understand the dynamics of the whole situation that they are being used. Whatever are the dynamics of these people picking up the weapons against state, the bottom line is that these people remain poor and disadvantaged. If we addressed this issue fully, then we would have resolved the issue of BLA insurgency without much bloodshed.

But our response to their attacks was to quash them with military force, without resolving the underlying issues. Almost all the Baluchistan is under the control of military even though the provincial government is functioning. I can understand that the emotions run high when the military see their comrades butchered by the BLA, but we must not respond similarly, because we are the *State* and not rogue militants. One of the main reasons that we have been unable to control insurgency in Baluchistan is that our agencies are using tactics, which are usually reserved for enemies, that is, torture. It seems that the military commanders believe BLA is a small group so we could subjugate them with terror and force easily. But they are mistaken, because when we torture and kill these separatists and throw their bodies on the streets - then it does terrorise them, but it does not subjugate them. This is because they have outside support and are not helpless. Instead, they become more determined than before, to launch revenge attacks. This creates a vicious circle of each group responding to the brutality of the other. Let me tell you that the torture against our own people is not only morally unacceptable, but it also creates a permanent and intense hate against the perpetrators and the state.

Similarly, our intelligence agencies are picking up the insurgents and holding them for a long time. Families do not know of the fates of their loved ones, so they seek justice from Supreme Court, which had been dealing with the ISI with a heavy hand. I did not like the discrimination that the Supreme Court had shown towards ISI recently. Let me explain.

There were two cases in Supreme Court, back to back. First case was the Contempt of Court against the Prime Minister Raja Pervez Ashraf, and the second was Missing Persons Case against ISI. In the Contempt of Court hearing, the court sensed that the judges will be insulted by the lawyers representing the government, judging from their temper in the previous hearing. So the Supreme Court allowed hearing that case in private chambers, away from any TV cameras. However, when the ISI requested a private hearing, away from the cameras, then the Supreme Court refused point blank. So ISI did not pursue their defence. I cannot understand why the court would not allow a private meeting to ISI who will be sharing State Secrets with the Supreme Court, while allowing a private hearing for contempt of court hearing, which had greater public interest? Well - I rest my case!

Let us now discuss how we could resolve BLA insurgency? The new government of Prime Minister Nawaz Sharif had taken a positive step by allowing the nationalists to form their government in Baluchistan, even when he could have formed his provincial government there because he held majority votes. This is the first step in the right direction but it is not enough on its own. We will need to have a comprehensive plan to successfully resolve this issue. The first thing we must do is to stop lifting and holding people for indefinite periods without letting the families know of their whereabouts. The second thing we need to do is to stop torture of the people who we hold, because torture has no benefits. Valuable information could be extracted without resorting to torture. If we know that someone has the important information we need, but he is unwilling to give it to us, then the easiest method to extract information is through psychological means, to show him the torture cell. Sit him in the torture position, and let him feel what it would be like to be tortured. Perhaps, animal blood on torture equipment will soften him. Show him an animated film on a large screen of torture being carried out on someone, and then let his imagination run wild. Most people will share the information at this stage or even before. But if someone is stubborn, then have someone ready to perform torture, but he should take a long time in setting the torture apparatus while the victim is in the torture position. As the torture is just to be applied, someone should interrupt, requiring the person torturing to go out to attend something else. This would relieve the insurgent temporarily, and break his will. Repeat this process often enough and all the information will be had without actual torture. But if still the prisoner does not give any information then probably does not have anything to share.

Instead of holding insurgents for indefinite periods, there is an easy solution of Electronic Tagging. In the West, electronic tagging is widely used for prisoners when they are released from prisons to ensure they remain in their homes during certain times. These devices are linked to a landline or mobile networks to track the offender with its GPS location. We could buy these systems from Europe or North America, but if our agencies believe that these are unsuitable for insurgents then we could develop our own tagging system with a few modifications.

For example, the tag could be made from hardened steel with all the electronic monitoring capability, which cannot be cut off. However, if we want to really terrorise the suspected insurgents, then we could make hardened steel tags which will fit the neck, instead of ankle. There could be small amount of explosives on the inside of tag, and the inside of tag body could be perforated like a hand grenade to allow detonation of tag, capable of killing the person wearing it. These tags could be detonated when someone tries to temper with it, or they could be remotely set off by the control units. Many more features could be built in them. For example, automatic detonation when it is out of range in case someone tries to cross the border and runaway. Or it could be detonated when someone is dead and has no pulse so the enemies cannot figure out the technology. If these types of tags are used then we would not need to keep anyone for more than a few hours. Suspects could be picked up, investigated, and if the investigator thinks that the suspect is likely to be dangerous then put a neck tag on him and release him within a few hours without any torture. The real torture would be hanging around his neck. He will be constantly in fear, and eventually may give up insurgency, or become a double agent. The problem of missing person will be solved with this method.

Once we have successfully removed the issues of torture and missing persons, then the BLA would have lost reasons to carry out insurgency. This would weaken BLA and there will not be any new recruits for BLA to continue its resistance. But we should not stop here but show our Baluch brothers that we are serious about addressing their concerns and offer them opportunities to grow economically, and provide them education and health facilities. However, to win their hearts and minds, we could offer a few scapegoats.

We first should change the military command in Baluchistan with able and politically sensitive officers. We then need to find a few scapegoats to assure the Baluch public that we have punished the perpetrators of violence, and these things will never be repeated again. Secondly, as I mentioned previously, we need to offer land to the poor Baluchs to build their houses, farms, and businesses. Then create jobs for them where they will live. I am not going to repeat the details of how we could achieve this because it is already mentioned in another section of this book. However, we should be strategic about selection of lands for our Baluch families so that insurgency is not repeated in future. For example, they could be located away from border regions, closer to mainland, and locate poor people from other three provinces in the border regions. While we are empowering our poor countrymen, we also need to check the

power, influence, and wealth of the Sardars there for a peaceful
Baluchistan.

Bhata Mafia & Kidnapping

Bhata Mafia and Kidnapping for ransom was a localised problem of
Karachi a few years ago, but it has now spread to whole of the
country, partly due to media attention and partly because it is the
most effective way to rob money. Historically, only the local gangs,
who had the support of political parties, used to use extortion,
known in Pakistan as Bhata, against traders and small businesses.
These gangs divided their areas of operation and had a sort of
unspoken and unwritten agreement not to trespass each other's
patches. The amounts the traders used to pay as Bhata were not too
high, and it had become part of civic life in Karachi. But for the last
few years, when a lot of *Internally Displaced Persons* migrated to
Karachi, many terrorists came with them because they were of the
same race and spoke the same language, Pashto and no one noticed.
Terrorists need money for their operations, so they did not limit
themselves to Karachi to make money from kidnapping rich people
to get large sums of money in ransom, but they expanded their
operation to the rest of the country. This funds their terrorist
activities, but a lot of work is required in kidnapping someone. For
example, they have to research who to kidnap, find out where they
live and work, how much money they have, and much other
background work was needed before kidnapping someone. They
need people, weapons, and vehicles to carry out kidnapping and then
collecting ransom money. There is always a risk of losing their
operatives if the other parties are armed, or if the police intervened.
It is a costly operation in terms of time, money, and personnel. But
then they stumbled across Bhata, which is less risky, less time
consuming, less costly but is the source of regular income. I think
that media is partly responsible for spreading Bhata throughout the

country. They talked about Bhata in their TV talk shows regularly giving details of how it worked, going into details which many people outside of Karachi did not know about. They told public that it was the easiest and most effective way to make money. I am not against reporting crimes but harping about the same thing day in day out, and then giving out details of how the criminals commit crimes is not necessary or required for good journalism.

Anyhow, the terrorists, the new entrants in to Bhata business, improvised their methods. It is no problem now to go into details about how it works because now every child in Pakistan knows about it. The old timers, used to go round businesses and give them a piece of paper (known as Purchy or Chit) with their business details and amount of money they needed to pay. I think that they use duplicate books or something similar for accounting purposes, so they could track who has not paid them, so they could go round teaching them a lesson, by beating or even killing them. This method ensures compliance by the rest of the traders. However, the terrorists who are familiar with new technology, send text messages instead of giving them a piece of paper for how much, when and who these traders should pay. There may be many methods used to collect Bhata, but one thing is clear that it is the easiest and most effective way from criminals to collect money from traders and others.

Let us now discuss how to eliminate Bhata Mafia and Kidnapping for Ransom? It is extremely easy to get rid of Bhata and kidnapping once we understand the underlying dynamics that keeps it going. Currency notes, that is, our money is the only thing that keeps theses crimes going. So if we remove the cash, the currency notes, from our economy then these crimes will vanish. I have explained this in detail in previous chapters, but here I will briefly mention how to tackle Bhata and kidnapping for ransom using monetary controls. All we have to do is to force everyone to use electronic money, that is, to tell everyone to use their bank cards for buying everything. Restrict all adults to carrying no more than Rs.500 per month through their bank accounts. Next, everyone should be required permission from a federal department to transfer large sums of money. That is, if anyone needs to buy something of the value of more than Rs.10,000 then he would need authorisation from a special federal crime prevention branch. These measures will ensure that the criminals will not be able to get any money from Bhata or kidnapping because they will require a bank account. If there are many transactions into criminals' bank accounts, then it could be easily detected and their bank accounts frozen. Anyone paying Bhata or ransom could let the state know and they could catch the culprits. But for this method to work, the government will have to set up an efficient department which will have banking, police, and intelligence agencies working together to monitor and figure out which transactions are suspicious and should be stopped. But the government must ensure that this branch does not become a hindrance to our economy by creating another bureaucratic hurdle in normal business operations. This department has the risk of becoming corrupt due to it having the sole authority for all large money transactions. There has to be an oversight on this department for it to be a useful office.

Unfortunately, there will be some killings of our citizens initially by the criminals because they may yet not believe that the victim has no power to pay them money even when he may be billionaire due to restriction on large payments. But soon they will learn and the bhata and kidnapping for ransom will vanish from Pakistan, as long as these systems are in operation.

Murder Victims

More than 60,000 people were martyred or murdered in Pakistan since America's War in Afghanistan. Of these, more than 6,000 Security personnel, and uncountable ordinary citizens were martyred by American drone attacks, their friendly fire, and by terrorists who are reportedly supported by USA, India, and other countries. By far the largest numbers of people were murdered in Karachi because of political parties' turf war and Bhata Mafia. On average more than ten people are murdered everyday in Karachi. Other regions of Pakistan are not safe from killings but their dynamics are quite different, and they are not as systematic as in Karachi.

You may be wondering why there are so many killings, and will we ever prevent them? There are many reasons for these killings, but the solution is only one. The state will have to re-establish its writ in every inch of its territory to end these unnecessary killings. Pakistani state will need to declare explicitly and implicitly that the distributer of extreme violence is the sole domain of Pakistani state. You may be shocked by my assertion, but it is an accepted fact that only the state has the monopoly to distribute violence. There is logic in it, because if only the state has the right to violence, then no one else will be able to act violently against others. This will create a peaceful and orderly society. If the state ensures that it is the only distributor of violence within its boundaries, then the terrorists and criminals can never kill others!

The above argument is also used by the women's rights organisations that if ordinary men distribute violence against women, then the state had lost its dominance of violence. They argue that violent men actually challenge state's authority, and the state must take back that authority by punishing those men and by re-establishing its dominance over violence. It is of course a powerful argument, and I endorse it wholeheartedly.

There are several reasons that the Pakistani state does not have its writ within its borders. Firstly, the institution of police has been destroyed and they are made servants to elected members of parliament. Policeman is the weakest person in the state of Pakistan. His fate depends on politicians being pleased with him. If the police do not do the will of the parliamentarians, then they are demoted, transferred into dangerous areas, or even killed by the gangsters employed by the politicians. When they are dead, then their families and children are left helpless with no one to support them financially or morally. There is nothing their fellow police officers could do to help their colleagues or their families. In this backdrop, the police are de-motivated and have become apathetic. The system forces police officers to be subservient to politicians, who use them for subjugation of their constituents. Perhaps the politicians do not know that Pakistan became an independent state in 1947, and it is no longer under British Raj to use the police for the subjugation of local people?

The second reason the state does not have its writ is because it does not care about its security personnel. More than 5,000 soldiers and police officers were killed by the terrorists and gangsters, and the state had been unable or unwilling to catch or punish the culprits. If a state cannot protect and avenge its guardian's deaths, then the guardians will become de-motivated, apathetic, and helpless. The surviving families of those who sacrificed their lives to protect Pakistan have been broken and dispersed due to financial hardships they faced, never mind the justice they should have received.

Thirdly, there have been more than 50,000 killings in Pakistan linked to America's war in Afghanistan. There had been some local dynamics but largely these killings are related to this war. We have not sentenced a single criminal to death yet. This has made Pakistanis helpless but increased the morale of the terrorists and criminals.

Lastly, the courts have been afraid to sentence terrorists and criminals because they receive telephone calls to threaten them that terrorist know where they live, and which schools their children go to. Several judges have been killed in this way. In a court hearing, a terrorist boasted to having killed more than 100 people but the court let him free. This is the level of fear among judges. Again, the state has been unable to protect its organs and is dying a slow death!

The solution is simple but I am not sure if the politicians will implement it because their power will wane? Firstly, the police needs to be made independent of politicians as I mentioned in the next section. This will uplift their morale and performance. Secondly, the state needs to declare clearly and openly that it will avenge the deaths of all of its security personnel and citizens, no matter how long it takes. Look at how Israel adopted intelligence, and other means, legal and illegal, to punish the perpetrators of Jewish killings in Germany in Second World War. So even if we have to kidnap perpetrators from other countries to bring them to justice, we should not hesitate. There is no point in the trials of known killers - they should be shot at sight. But if we are unsure about some, then they should be caught and tried because we do not want the blood of innocent people on our hands.

As we are taking steps to provide justice to the families of victims of murders, we need to provide financial help for the families of all of the murder victims because they were made helpless. These families would have been broken and dispersed due to financial and social hardships. We must gather all the members of these families and unite them. The state must pay them a significant compensation, at least Rs.1,000,000 to each family, because it was unable to protect their loved one's lives. Then provide them financial and social help until the children are old enough to stand on their own feet. The widows must be given pensions for life.

Reforming Police

A four-member British delegation headed by Sir Richard Barrat, Her Majesty's Chief Inspector of Constabulary, visited Pakistan in January 1990. It concluded that the current system of policing in Pakistan was created many years ago under colonial rule, whose main purpose was *to maintain power by methods of suppression and control.*

According to Asian Human Rights Commission, in a 2001 overview, Dr Shoaib Suddle, former Inspector General Baluchistan, highlighted six constraints in policing in Pakistan. He argued that the police officers are increasingly recruited, trained, promoted and posted without regard to merit, and mainly in recognition of their subservience to people with influence and power.

Dr Shoaib Suddle and Sir Richard Barrat, both high ranking police officers, are saying the same thing, that our system of policing is a colonial one, whose purpose is to maintain power by methods of suppression and control. The only thing that has changed in the last sixty-six years is that the Pakistani politicians have become the new masters, who have replaced the old British masters But their purpose and method remains the same: to maintain power using suppression and control!

Most people curse the police officers for their brutality, unfair dealing, and the bribes they take. But I believe the police are actually the victims of the system, and are helpless. When the gangsters supported by politicians in Karachi, were killing more than two hundred fifty police officers who had taken part in an operation earlier, then the police as a group, could not do anything to protect themselves or their colleagues. They only hoped that they will be spared. Are they not the victims of the system?

The system has turned police into the servants of the politicians, who maintain their power using police force as if it was their private army. The police are helpless because the parliamentarians control the recruitment, promotion, or transfer of police officers. Until we free the police, and make them fully independent of parliamentarians, the police will remain subservient to politicians, and will suppress and control us with brutality on the orders of their political masters. By the way, the police are not the only victims of these politicians, but the system makes almost every bureaucrat subservient to these parliamentarians. Let me tell you of a story which I believe is true but I cannot verify it.

I met a retired police officer a few years ago who told me a story of how a local parliamentarian misused his power? This politician visited a girl's school and saw a young beautiful but a poor teacher there. On his return, he told the District Education Officer (DEO) to transfer her to the far corner of the district where there is no public transport, or very little. This young teacher was the only child of the family and had lost her father a few years earlier and had no one to support her. Her mother was ill and needed regular treatment and care. When she was told that she was transferred to a school far away from her home, she protested. Because she would need to spend many hours daily to travel, and she will have to leave her home before dawn and will not be home late in the evening due to travel times. A young woman far away from home is an easy prey. She also complained to the DEO that the travel will cost most of her wage, and she would have to leave her ill mother unattended for many hours a day. Could he not stop her transfer? On this, the DEO apologised for his powerlessness and replied - the only way to stop your transfer is if you could make the local parliamentarian happy. She guessed what he meant. You can imagine what would have happened to a poor, helpless young woman? Could it be a case of *Constructive Rape*[56]?

This is the kind of society we live in. I don't mean that every parliamentarian is that way, but they do have the power of a Prince in their constituency. When someone has so much power then it is likely to corrupt them, as Socrates said 'Power Corrupts.' If we want an orderly society, then we must take the power of a prince away from the parliamentarians. Unfortunately, they would not give it up voluntarily. I believe the Ex President Pervez Musharraf decided to make the police independent, but he was prevented by his political

---

[56] We could define *Constructive Rape* as when a woman has not been physically overpowered, but a powerful man creates circumstances for her where she has no choice but to engage in sexual intercourse with him. She feels that she has been raped albeit no physical force or threat.

allies for obvious reasons. No one gives up their power voluntarily, so we must demand that police be made independent, at least at next elections. We must push all the political parties to make this part of their manifesto. When police are independent, then they will behave much more humanely and respectfully towards public, because then they would not serve political masters, but they would serve public. Our police have the ability to solve crimes and catch even the most dangerous of criminals even now, but it is prevented from doing their job by their political masters. But it is not difficult to reform our police.

All we have to do is to put the power in the hands of public to check the police force. For an effective policing, cleaning our society of crimes and terrorism, we must put the power in the hands of one person, but the public must have the power to remove him if he does not perform. For example, we could elect an IG Police, through direct election every year. We must not elect him for more than one year at a time, so public has the full control over him. This means there will be only a single IG police and the rest will be his deputies. Once elected, he would have absolute power to do what he needs to do to bring and maintain law and order in the country. He will be free to appoint who he wants and remove who he does not like. He ought to appoint DIGs for each province, which in turn will have the power to select their teams and so on. Islamabad should have its own DIG due to its capital status. This system will protect its top officers and colleagues just like the army does, which will ensure the police will not succumb to any political pressure. Many would worry about so much power in the hands of one person. They would argue that the police are already suppressing public, what will they do once they have so much power? We need to relax, because public will control the man at the top, and if he runs a system that suppresses the public, then he would be automatically removed within a year, at which point the public will make it clear to prospective candidates to serve the public, and not become its master!

However, how do we ensure the IG police will be fully independent and has no political or other affiliations? To ensure his independence, the first thing that we should do is to ensure that no political party is allowed to support any of the candidates for the post of IG police. This way, the IG will not owe any obligation to any political party. Secondly, the state TV, PTV should give equal amount of air time to all the prospective IGs and whole of their campaign should be restricted to TV, radio, and Newspaper interviews and speeches. This way, no money would be required to run for such an important office and anyone with the ability could be elected. If any TV channel or newspaper had given air time or column space to one candidate, then that channel or newspaper must be obliged to give the same amount of airtime and column space to all the other candidates. The airtime and column space must be of the same quality and quantity. For example, if someone is given prime time on a TV channel, then all of them should be given the primetime. The whole point is that all the candidates have received equal opportunity to be selected and no one is disadvantaged.

If these suggestions are adopted then the police will emerge as an independent institution, which will bring law and order throughout the country. This will lead to economic conditions ready for economic growth. The weak will now have a strong institution to protect her. In the passing, I need to mention something important. I noticed that in UK, all deaths are required to be registered and post mortem is an automatic requirement in all deaths except when the patient had been in hospital of more than 26 days or so, or where his doctor has determined previously that he is ill with a terminal illness. We, as Muslims, get annoyed at UK authorities for such fuss, but I think there is wisdom in it. I have heard of many people who died in suspicious circumstances in Pakistan, and they were buried after a quick funeral prayer. I think that hundreds of unlawful deaths are going unnoticed by the police, and the justice is not given to the dead and their families. It is the duty of the Prime Minister to ensure that the justice has been provided to every of his subjects. He could ensure this by adopting new laws that require compulsory death reporting and post-mortem examination where the cause of death had not been determined. Any breach of such laws should carry punishment with a sentence and financial penalty to ensure compliance.

If the above police reforms are not adopted sooner, then we should at least make a temporary change. We should give federal police jurisdiction throughout the country in the cases of murders, rapes, and serious crimes committed by powerful elites. Let me explain my point with a recent example but there must be hundreds of such examples which do not come to light.

In a television talk show, *11th Hour*, hosted by Waseem Badami, which was aired on April 22, 2013, a young innocent daughter, of a man murdered by powerful politicians in Naudero, Sindh, appealed for help and justice. Police did not do anything because they were subservient to politicians under the current system. You can imagine the power of these politicians from the fact that no lawyer wanted to take their case against these politicians. How the weak and powerless will get any justice in Pakistan? The temporary solution is by giving jurisdiction to federal police to intervene in such cases on the request of the victims, or if it comes to their notice in any other way. We could require the provincial police to report all cases of murders, rapes, and serious crimes committed by powerful elites to federal police. But we would have to define what we mean by powerful elites.

Lastly, a lot of crimes go unreported because an F.I.R., *First Information Report*, is difficult to lodge with police. In many cases police does not even register an FIR of a poor or a weak person. In many cases people have to use the influence of a powerful relative or friend before the police registers an FIR. According to rules, an FIR must be registered when someone makes a verbal complaint, but the reality is much different. The government must ensure that police issue an FIR number instantly for all complaints by phone or by person. To check compliance, it could send officers disguised as victims of crimes to see if police is complying with FIR registration or not.

Reforming Courts

In 509 B.C. Monarchy was overthrown and Roman Republic was founded by *Lucius Junius Brutus*, known as '*Brutus*' after he assassinated the then king of Rome, *Tarquin the Proud*. Tarquin's son had raped a noblewoman *Lucretia*, but that was not the real reason for his assassination but that is another topic. However, the real justice came when Brutus condemned his own two sons to death for the crimes they had committed. He was present at the execution of his sons and had said that, I must put aside the love of my beloved sons for the sake of justice. If I have assassinated the King Taquin for his crimes, then I must execute my own sons for their crimes. Would we ever see Pakistani politicians, elites, and rulers punishing their own sons, or are we condemned with NROs[57]?

You could spend your lifetime looking for justice in Pakistan, but you may still not get it. You would be a handful of lucky ones who get justice in their lifetime. For many cases of murders, rapes, land disputes etc could take twenty to forty years, or even longer before a decision could be reached. The conviction rate for most crimes is about 7%. In other words, Pakistan is a criminal's heaven!

The reasons for such failures are many. For example, we have not employed enough judges in our courts, and the lower courts are suffering from corruption. Police takes bribes from the perpetrators so they do not prepare the cases properly leading to low conviction

---

[57] NRO stands for National Reconciliation Ordinance, which granted amnesty for all the crimes committed by politicians, dictators, and elites.

rates. Poor people cannot afford lawyers to represent them so they do not pursue justice. We have two parallel court systems of ordinary courts and Sharia court, so those convicted in normal courts are freed in Sharia court. Above all there is a tradition in Pakistan of threatening or killing the witnesses, so no one will give evidence in courts against criminals. Now it has become a norm not to give evidence against anyone, powerful or otherwise. The powerful do not stop only at threatening the witnesses, but they also threaten judges who do not give verdict against them out of fear for their and their family's safety. So how on earth could we resolve these monstrous issues?

It is not impossible to resolve these issues, but we would have to make simultaneous changes to the system. Firstly we need to increase our budget for courts for the next twenty years or so. We should give courts an extra Rs.20 billion a year at least to employ more judges and for their training, to create specialist judges for cases of murders, rapes, financial crimes, and corporation disputes. By having specialist judges for these four areas will help clear cases quickly and with least mistakes. Our aim should be to clear all the old cases in the next five years or so, because the justice delayed is justice denied. Further, by clearing all the cases quickly, will send a signal to criminals that their time is running out before the law will catch up to them. This will help establish the government's writ in its entire domain.

The next step is to create a Legal Aid system which provides legal assistance to everyone, so everybody, especially poor, has equal access to lawyers to represent them in courts. We should initially start it off with about Rs.5 billion fund a year for this purpose, which should be adjusted as needed. Even if we have to spend much more money to provide access to justice for all, we should still not hesitate, because then we would have fulfilled our moral and religious obligations of providing justice to our public. If run properly, then the legal aid fund will not need much more funding from the state after initial injection of cash. We will make the losing party pay all the court and legal costs for the winning party. So if our courts decide cases in less than a year, then we would have put the money back into the fund, which was paid out initially. Also the 50% of all fines in criminal cases should go to legal aid fund. We could borrow the rules for Legal Aid System from the countries that are running such a system, such as, UK. We could then modify it according to our unique needs. But the legal aid should be provided on means tested basis, and any financial help received must be repaid, even it may take someone several years. The loan, that is the legal assistance amount owed, must be interest free, but a maximum of 2% inflation element could be added when the value of money is reducing. The inflation element must never be more than 2% or it will discourage people from using legal aid.

The corruption from courts and police could easily be eliminated with the use of new laws for civil servants and monetary controls as I mentioned earlier in this book. The threats to judges and witnesses can be countered by moving such cases to federal police and federal courts, and an automatic doubling of sentences and fines for the perpetrators. But if the police is reformed as I mentioned previously, then we would not need to take such cases to federal courts or police, because the local police would have much more power to deal with the perpetrators and protect victims. To threaten witnesses and judges is an old social disease in Pakistani society, which must be eliminated completely with new legislations and continuous vigilance, if we want peace.

Apart from the issues I mentioned above, the cases of rapes need our attention the most, because of its high prevalence in Pakistan. According to a study by Human Rights Watch, there is a rape once every two hours, and a gang rape every eight hours. I am not sure about these statistics but if the problem is not this big, then it is not far off either. The rape of a woman or a child is the extreme form of violence where the victim has lost her dignity. But if she is raped by a gang, then there could be nothing heinous than that in the world! There is another added problem for the victim, because the society automatically thinks the victim was a willing perpetrator. Even other women, who should have supported the victim, also think the rape victim must have been willing or at least brought it on themselves. So the society thinks of the rape victim as dirty, and no one would marry such a woman. For these reasons, many, perhaps 95% of the rape cases would go unreported. This is extreme form of cruelty imposed on women - implicitly by the society. These attitudes are signs of an unjust society. Unfortunately, the women are the worst enemies of themselves. Almost all cruelty on women is usually perpetrated by other women. Of course, the rapes are carried out by men, but the victims are treated badly by other women following rapes. For example, usually other women, and not men, blame the victims for bringing it on themselves. It is usually other women, who mark the victims of rape as dirty. If the women do not support other women, then who will protect women?

We hear on TV talk shows that the victims that do get justice from our courts could be denied justice by the Sharia Court, because it has appellate authority over lower courts and higher courts in Hudood[58] cases. The defendant who lose their cases in mainstream courts, take their cases to Sharia Court, because it has strict laws regarding witnesses. So they get away with their crimes. If this is actually true then it is a serious miscarriage of justice, and it has the effect of as if we have institutionalised rape in our society!

Many analysts blame our Islamic scholars for not allowing DNA evidence as fulfilling the witness requirement, because it is just as good as four witnesses due to the science behind it. They argue that our scholars should participate in Ijma[59] to come to a consensus about DNA evidence. But most scholars distance themselves from

---

[58] Hudood cases include theft, fornication, adultery, apostasy, and consumption of alcohol and other intoxicants.

[59] Ijma is the consensus or agreement of scholars on religious issues.

Ijma on DNA. The real problem with our scholars in my opinion is that they suffer from intellectual paralysis, because of a philosophical problem known as Act-Omission Doctrine. Let me briefly explain this philosophical phenomenon, so we could understand why our religious scholars feel intellectual paralysis.

Suppose a terminally ill patient is in extreme agony and pain, and he asks the doctor to carry out euthanasia[60] to end his life. But the doctor refuses because he is fearful that he may be playing god by taking someone's life. However, we do not hesitate to kill a dog or a horse in the same situation. On the other hand, the same doctor may not hesitate to remove the life-support machine from a comma patient and let him die slowly. Why is this contradiction? In the first case, the doctor believes that by killing someone *actively* through euthanasia, he is playing god. But in the second case, by removing the life support machine, he has let the nature take its course and let the comma patient die a natural death. However, if we take a closer look at it, then it becomes obvious that carrying out euthanasia is no different than removing life-support machine, because the result in both cases is death of the patient. But the doctor feels guilty by *actively* killing someone, but he does not feel guilty by **omitting** life-support machine and let the patient die. This is why it is called Act-Omission Doctrine. Our religious scholars have the same dilemma as the doctor above. They believe that by deviating away from what is laid down in Quran and Sunnah, by allowing the DNA evidence as fulfilling the witness requirements, they would be playing god, and will be punished on the judgement day. However, if they did nothing then they would not be guilty of such a sin. But would they not be answerable to God for denying justice to all those women who were raped, by allowing the rapists to go free, when they knew deep down in their hearts that these criminals could be

---

[60] Euthanasia is the painless killing of a patient who is suffering from an incurable or painful disease. Terminal illness is any illness that ends in death, and there is no possibility of recovery.

found guilty if they allowed DNA evidence? Would the religious scholars be not guilty of not coming to a consensus through Ijma on DNA evidence when there is a need for it? I urge Islamic scholars to gather for Ijma on DNA because it is their responsibility to lead Ummah in the light of Quran and Sunnah. If they honestly, and faithfully taken part in Ijma and came to a conclusion, then they have nothing to fear because they made their decisions honestly and faithfully. So even if they made a mistake, then I am certain that God will forgive them because He knows what is in our hearts and minds! But if the scholars did not fulfil their responsibilities out of fear of making mistakes, and Ummah suffered as a result, then I am sure the scholars will not be forgiven on the Judgement Day for not acting!

Unfortunately our politicians also suffer from intellectual paralysis through Act-Omission Doctrine when the situation presents itself. For example, being the Chief Executive of the country, if the Prime Minister let the murders, rapes and other crimes go unpunished then he will also be responsible for not taking action. I strongly believe that on the Judgement Day, the PM will not be able to blame courts, police, and scholars for their inefficiency in bringing about justice, because he had the power and authority to put them right, and if he failed in his duty, then he is equally guilty. No one can be absolved of their responsibilities through omission!

If we seriously wish to reduce the cases of rapes and gang rapes in our society, then we could apply other penalties instead of the jail sentences. For example, for a proven rape case, we could apply four different punishments; castration, a fine of value up to 50% of offender's assets, cancellation of educational and professional certificates, and preventing offenders from obtaining a passport for the rest of their lives. Let me briefly explain how these punishments will effectively reduce the rape cases in Pakistan to almost zero.

When someone rapes an adult woman then we should apply castration by removing just one of his testicles, that is, half castration.   At his second offence, the remaining testicle will be removed, which will effectively turn him into a Eunuch. Then physically, he will be unable to carry out any further rape attacks. However, if a child is raped, that is someone under the age of 18, or it is a case of a gang rape, then a full castration, that is the removal of both testicles, should be applied to offenders at first offence.

By giving out fines of up to 50% of offender's wealth, will be a great deterrent to those who own significant amounts of wealth, but it will not do much for the poor perpetrators. In such cases, a heavy fine should be imposed which they are unable to pay off with their 20 years of income. If we have a cashless economy, then it will be a very effective punishment. A court order should be made which will allow the current and future employers to deduct fine from their wages. This would effectively make a slave out of him.

Cancelling the educational and professional certificates of the offenders pushes him instantly into poverty. For example, if a doctor rape a woman but his professional and educational certificates are cancelled, then he cannot practice as a doctor anymore. He will have to work in a factory, or in a physically labouring job. It is an excellent deterrent for the educated and professional, but not for an illiterate. But when we make it illegal for the offenders to hold a passport then we limit their movement, and any chances of an illiterate person to go to a rich country to earn a better living. We should also put all of such offenders on exit control list.

The above suggestions, if implemented, would have protected our women and created a safer world to live in for everyone. But we must not ignore any misuses of these strict laws. What would happen if a woman, after having sex voluntarily with a man, claims that she had been raped? The man would lose out enormously. To prevent such abuses, we could require the women to prove a rape by satisfying one criterion, that she had tried everything in her power to avoid being raped. For example, she had scratched or bit the offender and made noises for help. Further, there need to be signs on her body of force used by the offender. For such things to be effective, a countrywide awareness campaign must be launched. Further, if the women try their best to avoid being raped, then men will be deterred anyway. But under the current system, it is in the best interest of a woman to be quietly raped, and get out of her ordeal as soon as she can!

Apart from rape cases, there are many other heinous crimes, for which we need to come up with punishments that will deter even the hardest of criminals. Financial penalties are one of the best deterrents but are never used. The whole point of punishment is to deter others from committing crimes, the gratification that comes from punishing offenders is only a side benefit and not important. I hope to see a day when a virgin maid with a pot of gold on her head, could walk from Gwadar to Gilgit, with both intact!

Stopping Drone Attacks

Many foreign policy experts describe the relationship between Pakistan and USA as an *unhappy marriage*. A fictitious short story below will illustrate the nature of this relationship and its link to drones.

P'Khan was only a few years old when the mother Burtania put him in the lap of much older wife, Lady Liberty. Mother Burtania gave birth to Lady Liberty in 1774, while P'Khan was born to her in 1947. P'Khan was a gorgeous child and Mother Burtania did not want to let him go, but she had to succumb to the desires of her much stronger daughter Liberty. Mother protested to Liberty that P'Khan was in a way her half-brother, and she did not want them to have incestuous relationship. But Liberty reminded her that she had Frank blood in her, so the relationship was not strictly incestuous. Liberty reminded Mother that she was too old and weak to look after so many children. She promised her that she will take good care of

P'Khan, because he needs the care of a strong and rich woman, because he was orphaned when he was only a year old.

Ever since their marriage, Liberty had been grooming the baby bridegroom P'Khan to do her bidding. She had always been domineering and demanding, but not always faithful. But P'Khan was powerless as he was a Gharjamai[61].

In the last few decades, as P'Khan was growing and reached puberty, he developed a Nuke. Like other adolescents, he was high with hormones, particularly Uranium. He was playing around like any other teenager, and sometimes developing intimate relations with other girls. In the process, he spread his seeds to Lyba, Korry, and Irene. But Lady Liberty was angry about his actions and demanded explanation. P'Khan replied innocently 'I never protested about your promiscuity with those Drones[62], then why can't I have fun'? But she repeated the Melian dialogue[63] to him 'The strong do as they can, and the weak suffer what they must.' Saying that, she ordered her bodyguards to take P'Khan to operating theatre to cut off his Nuke.

Now that the Lady Liberty has had her own way, and P'Khan is on the operating table, we don't really know the fate of poor P'Khan? Would she order the doctors to remove his Nuke, or will she spare him? I don't know about his fate, but why would she need P'Khan's nuke when she has so many Drones buzzing around to please her?

I hope you found the above short story interesting and informative. So Let us turn to drone attacks and how they could be stopped without confrontation with the USA? We do have the capability to

---

[61] Across the Asian sub-continent, the term Gharjamai refers to a live-in son-in-law. The term literally means *househusband* where he is financially dependent on his wife's family.

[62] Drone is a male honeybee that is stingless, performs no work, and produces no honey. Its only function is to mate with the queen bee.

[63] *Melian Dialogue* was a debate that took place between Athenians and people of Melos during their confrontation in 416-415 BC.

shoot down the drones, but it would not be wise to create confrontations with a much stronger superpower when our economy has taken a nose dive, and our forces are divided between Eastern and Western borders. It does not mean that we are powerless: we actually do have several options.

In the first instance, it is important to understand that the drone attacks are targeted strikes, which rely on credible and accurate information of targets. If we are able to disrupt the flow of this information, then we could dramatically reduce the drone attacks. Secondly and surest way to stop drone attacks is to convince the American public that these drone attacks are counter-productive, and kill more innocent children, women, and men than the actual terrorists. Lastly, if we can change the world opinion about these attacks then it will exert pressure on USA to stop them. Let us now discuss how we could implement these options in practice.

The drone attacks happen because the CIA gets information about the targets. If the CIA does not have this information then they will be unable to carry out any such attacks. So to stop these attacks we need to destroy the information networks CIA is using. They are likely to get their information from several sources, such as, satellite images, communication interception, and Humint (human intelligence) on the ground. Out of all the sources the Humint is most crucial, without which the target could not be identified and verified. USA does have its CIA operatives throughout Pakistan, but they are most likely to be using the local Pakistanis because they could easily mingle with the terrorists.

Firstly, we need to discourage people from providing such information to CIA by making use of Treason Law. We need to make it known to people that if anyone provides information to any outside agency, which leads to an attack on our soil, then such person will be caught and punished under Article 6 of the Constitution. We could put head money on these operatives to encourage the locals to cooperate with the state. If no one provided information on these culprits or no culprits were caught, even then they will be greatly discouraged to share information with the CIA. These two actions alone will reduce the drone attacks. But if USA decides to act without credible information then, it would be killing the innocent civilians, which will turn world opinion against USA.

Secondly, we need to manage all cellular, landline, and satellite communications. Perhaps, we should stop all cellular and landline communication for unlimited time in FATA except for our security staff. We may have to buy signal detectors and jammers to prevent any form of cellular, or satellite communication in that area including 25 miles radius into Afghanistan. The Afghanistan government might protest, but we will do whatever it takes to secure our country. We must get the very latest equipment despite its cost from Europe, China, or Russia who will all be willing to cooperate. Getting it from USA will be ineffective because they could render these devices useless if they wanted to, as they would have left inbuilt controls for them.

The next stage is to convince American public and the world that drone attacks are counter-productive and kill hundreds of civilian including women and children. In fact, it turns victim's family against Americans, which creates more terrorists. Here, Imran [64] Khan's view has greater weight that the tribal people always take revenge for their dead. Being a tribal person himself, he understands how these people think and behave to accurately predict the likely outcome. But many of us are the victims of American propaganda that USA wants to get rid of terrorist from around the world. This is exactly against the policy that America follows. Wherever America had been, it has always ensured it had left behind enough terrorists wounded, burning in revenge, who will later challenge USA. This way, USA will always have an excuse to interfere in other countries to keep its hegemony.

---

[64] Imran Khan is the cricketer turned politician who leads the third largest party PTI, in Pakistan.

So we need to understand that the drone attacks are actually part of American policy so that these people from Pakistan will attack American interests in future. So it will have an excuse to return and attack Pakistan. We need to foil their policy somehow without creating any confrontation. I have two proposals.

Firstly, we should create documentaries, interviews, and films based on facts, which show how the lives of the innocent victims and their families had been turned upside down. There must not be any propaganda, or the world will not believe us about anything in future. But it must have live interviews to capture the deep emotional trauma caused by the drone attacks. We then need to translate it into many languages so the most important parts of the world could understand the plight of these people. Then we should air it on every media around the world. This will certainly change American and world's view on drone attacks in Pakistan.

If having done all that, the drone strikes still do not stop, then we could adopt another method which will be effective, but it may also trigger some confrontation with the USA. I am not sure how the American establishment will respond, but it may cause a confrontation on diplomatic level, or may even lead to American attacks on our High Courts.

What I am proposing is very controversial. Our courts could prosecute American president in office at the time of drone attacks for murders and grievous bodily harm of all the victims. These cases should be televised live around the world, and cases should be stretched to a year or two to get and hold world attention. The courts should be perfectly impartial so they have credibility worldwide. The American president should be offered to attend the court in person or through his counsel, which he will surely refuse. A constant update and an order to attend the court should be sent to the American ambassador in Islamabad, who will not acknowledge or reply to these orders. But these things should be shown to the world that we have tried everything we could to give the accused party every chance to respond to the accusations against them, but they did not respond. We know that Americans will not respond because these have greater implications for them. But if we run a one-sided trial then it will not have much weight. The courts should then order the government to appoint a defending lawyer for American president because the government of Pakistan had been a non-NATO ally. The government should comply and appoint the very best defending lawyer to give the prosecutor a hard time to create credibility and interest in the case for world audience.

A daily televised court hearing will create world interest, and it will surprise the world that a weak nation's courts are putting the world's most powerful man on trial. However, I see several hurdles in going forward with this method.

Firstly, the government must never become a party to such trials or there will be a lot of diplomatic implications. It must act as a disinterested spectator. It should only comply with the court's orders and nothing more. Public should try to understand the difficulties for the government and must never push it to become a party. Instead, an NGO can be created with public fund to pay for the prosecution for each case. Public will be more than happy to contribute for such a cause, which provides justice to these victims.

The defending lawyer will certainly question the jurisdiction of the court and this will be a real hurdle. The FATA does not fall into the jurisdiction of Pakistani courts, and this is where most of the victims are. I am not a legal or constitutional expert, so the legal experts need to find a solution to the issue of jurisdiction. But I can offer a few proposals. Since the FATA is administrated by the Federal Government then by derivation the federal courts should be able to hear such cases and should have jurisdiction. If I am not right here, then the federal government can sign an agreement with the FATA leaders that gives the federal courts a jurisdiction in FATA. This jurisdiction must extend way back to 14th of August 1947. This jurisdiction going back to the birth of the country is a must if we want to include all the drone attacks. Otherwise we would only be able to try American president for future drone attacks. I am certain that if FATA's tribal leaders knew that they are signing the agreement for helping their own victims, then they will happily sign such an agreement. If that fails then a constitutional amendment could be made which recognises all FATA residents as domiciled in Islamabad.

The courts should hear these cases with utmost seriousness and provide justice to all victims and order the government of Pakistan to pay reasonable compensations to all victims with which they could to rebuild their lives. Pakistani government may or may not collect these payments from USA.

Other Important Issues

In this section of the book I will briefly discuss some of the most important issues which are actually part of the second volume of this book, but these issues need urgent attention, so they cannot wait until the second volume comes out. The biggest challenge that I see for Pakistan is that we have not yet become a cohesive nation after more than half a century. There are many reasons for it but I see the politics being the biggest reason. Our politics revolves around local issues, and it promotes segregation based on someone's clan, mother language, and religious sect. Pakistan has been unable to produce a leader who could have united every person of every clan, language, and religious affiliation.

Kashmir dispute is another issue that needs some new ideas to resolve it. We have fought at least two major wars over Kashmir with India, provided sham independence to people of Azad Jammu & Kashmir (AJK), and have resolutions in UNO to determine the fate of Kashmiris, but occupied-Kashmir remains in India's hands. They torture our Muslim brothers and rape our Muslim sisters, but we act like uninterested spectators. Perhaps, it is a time for a different approach on Kashmir.

As I mentioned earlier that our nation is divided on the basis of clans, language, and religious sect, but the religious divisions have been the most instrumental in internal terrorism. Since the American War of Afghanistan started, we have lost more than 60,000 civilians and security personnel due to terrorism directly linked to this war. We have terrorists among us who are killing Muslims, but they are also Muslims. The reason is that Muslims are divided, and each sect is trying to dominate the other. This terrorism in Pakistan is allegedly supported by several countries including India, USA, Afghanistan, and two Muslims countries which are using it as a proxy war between them. Each of the country has a different objective for their involvement, but all of their interests converge on supporting terrorist groups in Pakistan. We need to tackle this and try to broker a peace agreement between Saudi Arabia and Iran. We should also found a *World Muslim Council* to unite all Muslims as Ummah, and to address issues that keep us apart.

Our political system is a mess, we are a republic but all of the power is concentrated in democratic element of republic, and there are no checks and balances. A ceremonial state head is the commander-in-chief of the armed forces instead of the chief executive of the country. Health and education is delegated to provinces, which creates disharmony and different levels of facilities.

Our military and defence ministry needs some reforms to make them effective and to remove foreign influence on them. I am also proposing a new ministry, Ministry of Lies (MOLE), which will become extremely powerful foreign policy tool in the hands of a capable minister. Here I like to talk about fear many Pakistanis have about China moving away from Pakistan and getting closer to India. They also fear that an unfriendly Afghanistan will create war situation on our western border. Even though I am all for closer ties with China and a friendly Afghanistan, but I consider them *Crutches*, because we rely too much on China for economic and military assistance, and rely on Afghanistan not to cause troubles on Western border. We must not fear if China moves away from us, or Afghanistan becomes hostile to us, because this will take away our crutches and we will become stronger by standing on our own feet without any help. If we are fighting on our Eastern and Western fronts then we will improvise and become even stronger. Despite this, I would suggest that we enter into a *Loose Confederation* with Bangladesh and Afghanistan initially, where we will have free movement of people and free trade first, and then we will engage in other things. We should astonish the world by helping Afghanistan, a landlocked country, to have a Navy which uses our coasts. Of course, we will decide on this after being in a loose confederation for several years, and when the both countries have been united as one. After this, we should include Iran and other Muslim Central Asian countries in our confederation and so on.

Foreign culture and values have been imposed on us through foreign media because we had dismantled our cinema and film industry thinking that we will get rid of ills of society. But we did not think of people moving to Indian and American films for entertainment, and now our thinkers and religious leaders complain of widespread problem of pornography, prostitution, and loose morals because of foreign influence. If we want to avoid foreign cultural invasion in our society then we must have an effective film industry and cinema.

Further, we have not only millions of Afghan refugees in our country, but also have our own population which is made homeless for many years. We need to help Afghan refugees to return, but armed with the skills and knowledge to be able to contribute to their country's rebuilding efforts. Similarly, we must not ignore our IDPs, and should help them to return to their homes in safety and help them financially so they could rebuild their lives as soon as possible.

Finally, I will be briefly discussing about regulating media and making PBS independent. So they do not misinform public, but become useful tool for public decision making process. Let us now turn to our first topic.

Making of the Nation

Pakistan is a nation - but the Pakistanis are divided into many cultures, languages, religions, and sects. For example, culturally the Punjabis, Pakhtuns, Sindhis, and Baluch are very much different than each other, because each one of them has their own customs and norms. Urdu is the national language and 90% of the people can speak and understand it, but they can only understand the very basic Urdu, and when they speak, they speak it with a heavy native accent. Only the highly educated people could understand Urdu literature and poetry. Urdu was adopted to bring unity among Pakistanis who have different languages, cultures and customs. It was a good idea but it has not brought any unity. Instead, it created hate against Urdu speaking population in Karachi because the majority believes that Urdu was adopted so that a particular minority could dominate the bureaucracy and government. This is because, Urdu was required for all civil servants, and the newly migrated people had advantage over locals because Urdu was their native language. Sindhis particularly felt disadvantaged by Urdu, not only because they could not speak the new language, but because the first capital city of Pakistan, Karachi, had more migrated population than the whole of province's population put together. This meant that more jobs, especially government jobs would go to newly migrated people instead of the locals. These facts are important to know if we are to solve the violence in Karachi. It is not the terrorism or criminals that have made Karachi the most dangerous city in the world, but it is a war between the Muhajirs[65] and Sindhis, which continues to this day. So the Urdu language created more problems for the nation than it solved.

More than 95% of Pakistanis are Muslims, but they are divided into many different sects, such as, Sunnis, Shias, Salafis, Deobandis, Barelvis, and many more. These divisions among Pakistanis are so

---

[65] People, who migrate into a different place or country because they were persecuted for following Islam, are known as *Muhajirs*.

strong that they do not inter-marry into other cultures or religious sects, even though they are all Muslims. So there is a strong need for something that will bring them together to make them a nation.

I do not mean that we all just abandon our regional cultures and native languages. Instead, we need something that unites us all in such a way that nothing could separate us. I think there are two things that will unite us strongly with each other, a common language and inter-marriages.

We are all Muslims, apart from a small minority, but we do not intermarry. However, if we abandoned our prejudices against others and started marrying with the people of other sects, languages, and cultures within Pakistan, then it will create cohesion among us. This way we will be able to understand their cultures, customs and the problems they face, so to help each other. For example, our Baluchs complain that they are not treated well by the state, so by greater inter-marriages between Baluch and the rest will make their spouses and families understand the plight of Baluch people first hand, and they will support them to gain their rights.

Similarly, our Muhajirs complain that they are also not treated well, so they have united as one large group to emerge as a political power. But they are in a constant conflict with Sindhis, Pakhtuns, and to some extent with Punjabis. But greater integration and inter-marriages between Muhajirs and the rest of the population will ease the tension, and bring about greater harmony. However, our Muhajirs must stop calling themselves Muhajirs anymore, because it has been more than sixty years they had been in Pakistan, and they are perhaps into their third generation, but they still have not abandoned their past identity. They must break away from the past, and start to believe that they are the natives of this nation. By identifying themselves as Muhajirs, they are sub-conscientiously seeing themselves as *outsiders*. However, the Muhajirs living in Punjab do not feel the same way, because they adopted the host culture and language, and mingled with the locals well.

I think that it was a big mistake to put all of the incoming Muhajirs in one area at the time of independence, because they formed their own community, and isolated themselves from the rest of the country. There must have been a greater drive for integration and adopting local languages and culture. Unfortunately that did not happen in Karachi. We must be aware of these facts when we bring the Biharis from Bangladesh who supported West Pakistan. Unfortunately, the people who supported us in 1971, we have abandoned them to be treated badly by Bangladesh so far. They have appealed over and over for more than forty years, but we have not helped them. Their second generation has been born, and it is our duty to help them, and grant Pakistani citizenship before they even arrive here.

Apart from greater inter-marriages, the second most important thing for unity of our nation is a common language, which will be adopted by the whole nation wholeheartedly. I have already mentioned the problems with Urdu. Therefore, we need a language which will unite us on many levels. What better language than the language of the messenger of God, Hazrat Muhammad(PBUH) ? Arabic, is the language in which we pray every day, and read Quran. So if we adopted Arabic as our national language, then it will strengthen our pre-existing religious ties between the different cultures of Pakistan by being Muslims. This way, all of us will be linked religiously, spiritually, as well as nationally. But when I suggest adopting Arabic as our national language, then I do not mean to speak just the very basic language, because then we would have the same problems that we had with adopting Urdu. But we must adopt Arabic language with its culture, customs, and literature. Further, the Arabic that we adopt should be the Meccan dialect, because that was the dialect spoken by the Prophet, as he spent most of his life there from birth. We must learn it to a level that it would be difficult for someone to distinguish between us and a native Arab, when listening to us. Let us now discuss how we could implement it.

The first thing we should do is to announce Arabic to be our first national language, while keeping Urdu and English as second and third national languages respectively. However, we should not be hasty in implementing Arabic too quickly, because it may cause many problems. Instead, we should implement it slowly and in stages. Our first aim should be that everyone could speak, read, and write basic Arabic, and they continue to learn higher levels. Only then we should implement it as a pilot project in an area or department that would be least disrupting, so we could figure out problems and learn how to overcome them. Even when the pilot project is successful, we should still implement it in stages starting from non-critical areas first. But the question arises, how do we encourage everyone to learn Arabic?

I think that at least half of the population will welcome Arabic as national language and they will learn it quickly, but there will still be a significant number who may resist as they may think that we would be going back instead of advancing. This is because they may believe that the English is the way to go. I do agree with them to a degree that currently if anyone wishes to progress then they cannot do so without English, because that is the language of learning sciences, art, and technology. But Iraq was the place for learning for the world in not too distant a past. I am not asking to abandon English as yet, but it could be done with in fifty years or so, when we have advanced well enough. Hopefully this would convince most people to adopt Arabic. But to motivate them to learn and adopt Arabic quickly is to provide them with cash incentives. However, for better learning we should create several levels of fluency, perhaps, nine levels. This way, people could easily manage small amounts of study, and would see their progress within a few months, which will keep them interested.

To ensure that everyone speaks exactly the same dialect, we should hire Arab teachers native to Mecca, who would prepare video and audio language learning courses, as well as the classroom courses.

They should then teach the teachers, who would eventually deliver these language courses. We then should allocate a few billion rupees a year, for cash incentives, to pay out to those who pass the different levels of Arabic. To receive the cash rewards a person must have achieved at least 60% score in any level. The testing should be strict, but free. People could learn through video lectures which should be available on the Internet, on free DVDs, and on national TV. The payments on passing each level should be decided according to a set formula, which will create good incentives for people to learn. For example, we could pay Rs.3,000 to anyone who passes Level 1, and then keep increasing it by Rs.500 for each next level. So the cash reward for level 2 would be Rs.3,500 and so on. It may seem a large amount of money to be paid out for whole of the population, but we need to bear in mind that not everyone is going to go to the top levels. Further, the amount we will have to pay out would be spread over several years, especially for higher levels. We should be willing to pay any price for becoming a cohesive and strong nation!

For making a nation, we tend to ignore the role of women in nation building. God delegated creation to women, after he had created Adam and Eve. Women are the creator of the nation, yet we push them back when deciding the fate of our nation. Without women, neither you, nor I would exist! Unfortunately, it is not the men who keep women behind, but it is the women, who are responsible for their backseat role. They do not realise their power, and those who do realise their power, do not propagate it to other women. Women are their own worst enemy, which is the reason they are helpless and powerless. If the women realised that they have the power to change the nation within a single generation, then they would unite. It is easy to see the amount of power the women have in changing the fate of the nation from the role they play as mothers. I could have turned out to be a criminal, if my mother did not teach me the ethics, values, and norms of our religion and society. My beliefs and values, as an adult, were actually formed when I was a child. The beliefs and values that are formed in childhood are difficult to shake off. Childhood is the point in someone's life where the nation could be shaped at individual level, and the mothers are usually at the helm during this period of their children's lives. Once this point is realised, the next stage is to decide on what kind of society we want to have, and then plan on achieving it.

The starting point in deciding on the kind of nation we want is to list the ills of our current society, so we could eliminate them; and then listing the qualities that we want to promote. I could provide a starting point by listing them both here, but we need intellectuals, thinkers, philosophers, and many other professionals to create a consensus on the type of a society we would like. Then we need to give our women the task of changing our society to make it into a nation to be proud of. I will make a start by identifying and proposing some solution to some of the things that we ought to change.

The biggest ills of our society that I have observed are jealousy, unjustified anger, too judgemental of others, and false ego. The jealousy is responsible for many problems. For example, jealousy gives someone a feeling of lack of something that others have but they don't have, such as, money, beauty, job etc. Since jealousy is a negative feeling, it drives a person to bring others down to their level, instead of him trying to reach their level with his wit and hard work. When someone cannot have a beautiful woman then he throws acid on her face. When someone cannot have wealth, then he tries to collude with others to steal other people's wealth. Our religion teaches us gratitude, which could eliminate jealousy, but we are too ungrateful to understand the power of gratitude!

Like jealousy, the unjustified anger is also rife in our society. Parents hit their children at the slightest of mistakes; husband lashes out on his wife at minor things; and mother-in-law becomes aggressive and abusive to her daughter-in-law over nothing, or vice-versa. As far as I could understand, the driving force behind unjustified anger is the inability of someone to control their own circumstances. It is not the mistake of the child, wife, or daughter-in-law, which creates anger, but the person displaying anger is consumed in his or her own problems, which he or she cannot control. For example, if a parent is suffering financial difficulties, then he would lash out on his child even if the child has only asked him to buy him a book for his studies. A husband having trouble at work is going to take it out on his wife. A mother-in-law worried about her future, thinking who would look after her in old age if her son spends most of the money on his new family, becomes aggressive and abusive to her daughter-in-law to get her out of the picture. But love destroys unjustified anger, just like the light destroys darkness!

I have noticed that we Pakistanis are far too judgemental of others, and quick to criticise almost anything about anyone. When we are judgemental about someone's behaviour, social standing, or their facial features etc, then what we are actually doing, is to find our faults in others. For example, if a woman does not like the shape of her nose, then she will always tend to find fault with other women's noses. None of us is perfect; we all have small shortcomings in our physical bodies, behaviours, education, wealth, or job etc. A wholehearted acceptance of ourselves and others will eliminate our judgemental attitudes.

The problem of false ego or 'A*nna*' is rife throughout our society. We all want to be seen as important persons in society, and we want people to respect us. A great majority of us are poor, uneducated, and do not have important roles in society. To counter this, we boast about our links to important persons. I used to be guilty of this behaviour as well. The boasting goes like this; my uncle is commodore in Navy; another of my uncle is director at PTC; or my brother was a fighter pilot, even when he walked out before he even sat a foot in the cockpit. I would have been speechless if anyone asked me 'what are you then?' A student, who hardly passes his exams, and no accomplishments! When I speak with Pakistanis in UK, it amuses me and reminds of old times. It seems that almost all of them have control over ministers, or at least the DCOs (District Coordination Officer) of their districts. Some of them seems even to have links with the prime minister and president! I have never met a white British who had links even with the local councillor, never mind a minister. This side of false ego or self-esteem is not very dangerous but just a little fun.

But the dangerous side of false ego is when a brother or father kills his sister or daughter, because she had married a man they did not approve, or she had an affair with another man. There is legal punishment for a woman who has extra-marital affair or simply a love affair without wedlock. But the social punishment for these women is far too harsh and disproportional to the crime, the killing of that woman. This is known as honour killing, which is seen as acceptable by our society. Even the police seem not to take a notice of such killings. We have never heard of a father or brother killing his son or brother because he had an extra-marital affair or love affair? Is there a difference between a son and daughter committing the same crime? If we fear God, then we must not involve ourselves in such heinous crimes, which stem from false self-esteem or false honour. Apart from above four ills of our society that I mentioned above, there are other serious social diseases which we suffer from, such as, murders, rapes, and suicides etc. Women could shape the attitudes of society if they are guided as a group.

Lastly, I need to draw your attention to foreign influence in our lives which prevents us from becoming a nation. For example, men feel proud to wear a three-piece suit, but they feel like an illiterate Paindoo[66] when wearing Shalwar-Qameez[67]. Similarly, women feel proud of not wearing head covering, but they feel like peasant girls

---

[66] Paindoo is a Punjabi term for a rural uncultured person.
[67] Shalwar-Qameez is a usual Pakistani dress.

if they wore a Dopatta[68]. Further, women wear make-up and some also go for cosmetic surgeries to look like the film stars. Most of us feel proud to pepper our conversations with a few English words to seem educated, cultured, and important. All of these are influence of the West on our society. Let us discuss briefly, how the above things prevent us from becoming a nation and what we could do about them.

The reason for us not feeling proud of wearing Shalwar-Qameez perhaps is that it looks like rags, made up of thin cloth. Shalwar-Qameez does not compare with the Western suit in quality of cloth used and its fit to body. It just flaps about in the wind. Apart from this, the suit is an accepted dress of the wealthy, intellectual, and influential persons, giving it more power over local dresses. We could change this perception and design flaws by coming up with best designs and fits for a national dress. We could invite the designers from around the world to compete with one another in designing a Pakistani National Dress which has strong national elements. We could reward the winner with large cash prizes and give them a five year royalty fee for every dress prepared in Pakistan. The designs should have dresses for summer and winter. The male and female designs do not need to be much different apart from the head covering for women. Once we have dresses designed by the best designers of the world then it will have an automatic respect for it and people will feel proud to wear them, and we would have gotten rid of foreign influence on our daily lives. In the passing I like to mention what I observed, which amuses me. Women in sub-continent, whether Muslims or not, had been wearing Dopatta for hundreds of years, but they have never figured out how to keep it on head without letting it slip every few minutes. If we started counting, then we may perhaps find that a women wearing Dopatta has to pull it back every three minutes or so when it slips of her head.

---

[68] Dopatta is a see-through head covering that most Pakistani and Indian women use to cover their heads.

Further, we find that many educated women feel ashamed to wear head covering like Dopatta. They tend to believe that only the peasant or village girls wear Dopatta, but they forget that wearing Dopatta had been part of sub-continent's culture for thousands of years, and it is also part of our Islamic pardah requirement. Have we not observed that people tend to respect those women more who follow cultural and religious rites than those who do not?

Wearing make-up and cosmetic surgeries are other issues our women suffer, mainly because everyone else is doing it. But these practices have deep psychological implications. Let us first understand the reasons the make-up became so wide-spread. Make-up was mainly used by stage artists as far as the recorded history, but its use became regular since the arrival of cinema when the film stars started using it because without make-up they would not look good on screen. But as the older rich women learned about the make-up that it could make them look younger, they started wearing it as well. The corporations making the make-up products must have realised that they could make huge profits if they had convinced the majority of women to use it. They were successful, and now it is multi-billion dollar industry. Now from the young girl going to school, teacher, factory worker, to a female CEO, all wear make-up to feel good about themselves. This means that when they are not wearing make-up then they must feel bad about them?

The make-up industry had been successful in making women feel that they are not as beautiful as they should have been. So by using make-up they could fill that flaw. It is good for the make-up industry, but it is not good for those poor women who feel bad about themselves. Before the make-up was introduced, many women did not feel bad about their facial features, so they were psychologically healthy. But now many women suffer from this ill and they spend a lot of money and time preparing themselves, just so they could feel good. It is not good for them. The best solution is self-acceptance, of how God has made us, and be grateful to Him. The beauty of a

person is just not in her face, but it is only one element of
personality. A person's attitudes, beliefs, and behaviour give her the
real personality. What good is a beauty that could wash away easily?

Women wear high heel shoes to copy the Western women. I am
certain that they have not considered the reasons why the high heel
shoes were introduced, because if they knew about it then they may
not wear them. In about 10th century China the practice of *Foot
Binding* emerged in court dancers. Under this practice, when the girl
was about four or five years old, all of her toes except the big toe,
were broken and the feet were wrapped in binding cloth for years so
her feet would not grow larger than 4 inches. Therefore, as an adult,
her feet would not be able to support her body weight, so when she
would walk, she will be constantly shifting her weight on the other
foot, creating a *Wave Like Body Movement*. This style of walk
pleased kings and aristocrats. So the practice of foot binding got
hold in China. They later created high heel wooden shoes for
women, which created the same wave like body movement in
women walk. High heel shoes are the evolution of foot binding
practice, which is only to gratify the thirsty eyes of men. Similarly,
the Western miniskirts and low neck blouses which show parts of
women bodies are all designed to gratify men! These Western trends
could only be changed when the women of high status give them up,
because ordinary women just follow the women in power or of high
status.

One final foreign influence I like to discuss is that of English
language on our lives, attitudes, and self-esteem. English is only a
language but it has a different kind of significance in India and
Pakistan. People who speak English are seen as important and
intelligent. Speaking English is part of someone's status in Pakistan
and India. I think it stemmed from the time when British were ruling
India. English automatically gained respect because it was the
language of the conquerors. Further, all of the local people who
received privileges and power, spoke English because they had to

communicate with their English masters. That attitude of seeing *Masters* speaking English is still with us after gaining independence more than 60 years ago. So by deduction, anyone who speaks English must belong to the Master Class!

That is why you see educated people pepper their conversation with a few English words, but most of them cannot string together more than one or two sentences, and they have to revert to Urdu. Let me tell you a funny but true story related to this. Recently, I met someone who was a year junior than me in college in Pakistan. We were talking about college life, and during conversation he admitted to me that one day he was walking along with one of his friends near his house, he lived in cantonment area of our district where you see many wealthy people, and by chance two girls, perhaps from UK, were walking ahead of them, who were talking in English. They felt ashamed of not able to speak English. So they started reading aloud *Newton's Laws of Motion* to each other in English!

Resolving Kashmir Issue

Jammu & Kashmir, which I will refer to as Kashmir for ease of reference, was to be part of Pakistan at its birth in 1947, but the Indians occupied it illegally. Hence it is known as Indian-occupied Kashmir. The rest of Kashmir is allied with Pakistan and is known as Azad Kashmir (independent Kashmir). We have fought at least two major wars over it, and Kashmir is the major source of conflict between India and Pakistan. We will not rest until whole of Jammu & Kashmir becomes Pakistan, because it rightfully belongs to us, and we have shed so much blood for it.

Both, India and Pakistan are armed with nuclear weapons, and any war involving nuclear weapons would be a catastrophe. Millions will perish in such a battle. It is not difficult to capture Kashmir, but to hold it with force will require constant war with India, who will never accept its defeat because it considers itself a superpower. We ought to understand one important thing about war, that the victor never has the power to end the war, even though it has won it. The power to end the war is always in the hands of defeated nation. If we defeated India, but it still remains in war, then we would have no option but to use the same strategy as USA and drop a few atomic bombs on India, provided we had removed their second strike capability. That would bring un-measureable suffering to people of Asia.

For these reasons I disagree with those who wish to win Kashmir by force. If we are to have Kashmir, then it must be for eternity. We must not waste our blood and sweat for untenable cause. We would have to think of other solutions, and I have a few in my mind. But before we discuss other solutions we need to put our own house in order. We are confused about what we want from Kashmir. Do we want it to be an independent state that is friendly to Pakistan, or we want it to be part of Pakistan?

Why I say we are confused is because we have created a sham independent state of Kashmir, which has its own government, a President, Prime Minister, and a cabinet. But they are controlled by Pakistan. I think that we have done it so we could tell the UNO and rest of the world, that we want an independent state of Kashmir. We think this is the strategy which will free the Indian-occupied Kashmir. But it has been sixty-six years of these policies, and several resolutions were passed in UNO but Jammu & Kashmir is still occupied by India. Are our policies working?

Well, the UNO is the concubine of USA! She will do the will of her master-lover. Forgive me for a little digression, but people think of UNO as the divine institution, but she is nothing but a whore! UNO could only decide on Kashmir if America gives it a green light. But now America is in love-affair with India. Oh no! Nehru is at it again, but this time with Lady Liberty! So there is no hope of anything going in our favour for another hundred years. We need to forget UNO, and we should not keep the old policies on Kashmir to please her. For the Third World, UNO has served her purpose, that is, they gained worldwide recognition, so she must be disbanded now. Since her inception, she had been the American tool of domination. America uses UNO to hold every other country back while it fights a war with a weaker country. Under UNO rules, the decisions made by *Security Council*, which is dominated by USA, are binding on all member states. So no other country can intervene to help a country that is fighting with USA. It is like a street gangster having his accomplices pretending to stop a street fight, but they actually are holding the victim from defending or attacking the gangster. This way the street gangster could beat the hell out of his victim, without ever getting hurt. On a larger scale, America is the street gangster while UNO it accomplice!

The only reason we, and other countries joined UNO was to get recognised by many countries after being decolonised from European imperial domination. At that time, the most powerful nations of the world were members of UNO, so by joining UNO, we could instantly be recognised as a sovereign nation. But all the weaker states that are members of UNO, have been dominated by America. We and hundreds of other countries are recognised world over, so we do not need UNO anymore because we do not get any benefits from it. Instead, by being member of UNO we are accepting implicitly the domination of USA. We hear American presidents playing democracy champion and promising that they will export democracy in the entire world, even by regime change. Even if we ignore the morality and legality of regime change, the question arises, why the USA has not brought democracy to UNO in New York, right in the heart of America?

The reason is simple. If there was democracy in UNO then America would not be able to dominate the world, or wage its wars. So it wants to export democracy to rest of the world, but does not want it in its own backyard. I am sure most of you will know that the *General Assembly* of UNO is nothing but a debating club.

Representatives of all member states debate there and pass resolutions, but those resolutions are not binding on any member country. On the other hand, when the Security Council, which has about 20 members including America being the permanent member with veto power, passes a resolution then it is binding on all the member states. How ironic!

I would want Pakistan to cancel its UNO membership because we do not benefit in anyway, instead we pay them our fee for membership. However, by just coming out of UNO will isolate us if no other country abandons UNO. So it is better to convince all the Third World nations to cancel their memberships and make our own UNO which has equal rights for every state without any prejudice. There should be no veto powers for anyone in a new UNO. But I don't think that many countries will want to leave UNO due to their allegiance with one of the five veto power holders, and the little benefits they get from them. So the solution is to break it from inside. We should campaign for two changes in UNO, ending veto power and making every state the member of Security Council. This way the powerful nations' power will be reduced to that of a weaker nation and the world will have peace. There could be three possible results from this campaign. No change; UNO breaks and members leave due to double standards; or UNO accepts both demands. First outcome is most likely, but any of the second or third outcomes will be better for the world.

Now we know the least importance of UNO in our Kashmir dispute resolution, we could change our Kashmir policies that will be much more constructive and will lead to a desired result. We have fought at least two major wars over Kashmir and lost thousands of our soldiers and citizens. We continue to sacrifice more of our men, women, and children on Kashmir. What for? So it can become an independent state, which may or may not be friendly to Pakistan? Most Kashmiris want to be with Pakistan, but we have adopted a policy of appeasement towards them, so we could please the rest of the world. But this policy is firing back, and now a small significant minority is demanding that they would become an independent state, free from Pakistani control. If we did not handle this situation with wisdom and delicacy then we will have a major problem at our hands. We would have lost everything. Appeasement never works as we know from Munich Agreement, when UK, France, and Italy tried to appease Hitler by letting him annex the border areas of Czechoslovakia to Germany. Then he wanted more. A recent failed example of appeasement is UK devolving its power to its units, and allowing Scotland to have their own parliament some years ago. Now Scotland is demanding a complete cessation from UK and there is referendum to be held in 2014 to decide its fate. So we should learn from others. But we have not only adopted an appeasement policy on Kashmir but also for rest of our provinces, which is only going to bring ruin to our federation. A time will come when all of Kashmiris would want independence from Pakistan. I hope I am wrong.

To counter the damage of our policies of appeasements, we should make subtle changes to the form of the government in Kashmir first. We could award a higher status to Kashmir and FATA than other provinces to let them know that we value them higher. In china, they use the term SAR, Special Administrative Region, for two of their territories, Hong Kong and Macau, which were foreign dependencies. These two SARs have a high degree of autonomy and they are registered with UN under binding inter-state treaties. We need to borrow just a few ideas from this arrangement. We need to call our Kashmir and FATA, SAPs, Special Administrative Provinces. Both Kashmir and FATA do not have the same level of autonomy as Chinese SARs so we must not create problems for us by providing them more autonomy than they have now. We would allow them to have their own government but the top most ministers will not be Prime Minister, but it would be called *First Minister*.

There will not be any president but a federally appointed Khedive[69], which will have higher rank than an ordinary governor of any other province. This process will require backdoor diplomacy and constitutional amendments and should be handled quietly.

To resolve the issue of Kashmir, at this moment in time, I only see one solution because by winning it with war will require perpetual wars to hold it, which is not a permanent solution. We and India both know that the Kashmir should have been part of Pakistan. But they will not give it up so easily because they have also fought two major wars with us and lost many lives. Also, by giving up Kashmir, they would show a weakness, which they will never accept. The easiest and most workable solution is that we accept India's superiority in occupied-Kashmir and offer to buy it for a nominal price. By us buying Kashmir, and they selling it, India can save its face in the world. On the other hand, we would have saved Kashmiris from constant Indian brutality, and reunited the families on both sides of Kashmir. But the problem is how to convince India, that it is the best solution?

The only way to convince India is to make them realise what would happen if they did not agree to above deal. We could use several strategies to achieve this end. For example, we can do to India, what it is doing to our best friend China. China holds and controls Tibet, which was once an independent state. The leader of Tibet, Dalai Lama fled to India in 1959, and India had allowed them to have a *Tibetan Government in-Waiting* on its soil, which puts immense political pressure on China, and challenges its legitimacy of rule in Tibet. We could do the same to India and have a *Kashmiri Government in-Waiting*, in Islamabad for the occupied-Kashmir, with full working offices and responsibilities. We could also create *Governments in-waiting* for the princely states that had Muslim majority at the time of partition, and should have joined Pakistan,

---

[69] The term Khedive is an Ottoman Turkish title equivalent to English viceroy status.

but India forced them to cede with her. These tactics will put and keep political pressure on India.

Further, we could give asylum to all the separatist leaders of India, provide them moral support, and perhaps allow them to create *Governments in-waiting* in Islamabad. If we do that, then we must ensure that no one is able to support or launch a terrorist attack in India, while they are in asylum in Pakistan, because it is not right and it will also call for a war. Our support for these separatist leaders should be only the moral support to seek justice and self-determination, and nothing more. These steps will create great pressure on India from the rest of the world to stop violence against its own citizens, and perhaps India may have to award them independence. It is indeed a heavy price to pay for India for not resolving Kashmir issue.

Another thing which we should have done all along, but have failed miserably, is to show the world the brutality of Indian soldiers, their daily torture of unarmed and weak Kashmiris, continuous gang rapes of many Kashmiri women, and general misuse of their power against Kashmiri Muslims. We need to do this until Kashmir becomes part of Pakistan no matter how good our relations are with India. We should never compromise Kashmiri cause for any price or friendship. We could make documentaries; perhaps provide satellite or communication uplink for Kashmiris to send us videos of their plight, so we could show it to the world.

If we show our resolve and are able to convince India that we would not hesitate to take these steps, then it will start to think to negotiate a settlement with us on Kashmir. If we put our prejudices aside and see the whole issue impartially, then it is India that will benefit more from Kashmir resolution. This is because a war with Pakistan will halt its fast growing economy, and put it 100 years behind. What the war could do to us? We are already a divided nation with dead economy; we have nothing to lose from a war! A war perhaps could unite us, and make us stronger!

If India comes to negotiating table then we should not be too harsh on them, but should offer generous concessions. For example, we should allow a joint police force for next 25 years or so to ensure that the non-Muslim residents of Kashmir under Pakistan will not be disadvantaged in anyway. We will leave everything as it is, and ensure maximum autonomy with a few exceptions. For example, the Khedive (governor) of new Kashmir will be a Pakistani, but the public is allowed to choose their own First Minister. We may also allow the existing political leader to complete their terms in office, and allow any non-Muslim to run for higher office for the duration of our agreement. We will not alter any water systems to stop it flowing into India as long as both countries exist, unless both countries agree to a change. We will grant non-Muslims dual nationality status that was there at the time of handover of Indian-occupied Kashmir to Pakistan, but we do reserve the right to prosecute anyone who acts against the state of Pakistan. But if we did prosecute anyone then we will allow India into investigation and prosecution to ensure justice. The properties of people already living in new Kashmir will be protected for an unlimited time and no one will be forced to leave, directly or indirectly. I am sure with these generous terms India will agree to a handover of Jammu & Kashmir to Pakistan. However, if the India still does not hand over Kashmir then it should be prepared for perpetual wars with Pakistan!

World Muslim Council (WMC)

There are about 1.3 billion Muslims around the world and there are 57 countries in the world whose official religion is Islam. Unfortunately, there is infighting going on within the Muslim world mainly stemming from the hostilities between Saudi Arabia and Iran, where the former belongs to Sunni and latter to Shia Islam. The difference between Sunni and Shia Islam is very little, but there are hundreds of killings happening each year due their proxy wars in other Muslim countries. However, Islam calls all Muslims to unite, and forbids killing of a Muslim by another Muslim. But the killers get around this prohibition by declaring the other side heretic. The basic reason for conflict between these two sects is that one believes that his version of Islam is correct, so he wants to impose his version on the other. Apart from this conflict, there is infighting within Sunni Muslims, mainly between Deobandi and Barelvi. Deobandis are closer to Arabic versions of Islam, while Barelvis are closer to Sufism. Hostilities between these two groups are also fierce, to the extent that some would go to the extremes of believing others to heretics. So they do not hesitate in killing each other. In other words, it is a race for the one section of Muslims to dominate all others. I am unable to pinpoint the time when these hostilities between Sunnis and Shias started in recent past, but I think they may have been set off by Iran-Iraq war of 80s. The hostilities between Deobandis and Barelvis would have been set off by the arrival of Arabs in Pakistan and Afghanistan, to participate in Afghanistan's war against USSR. Unfortunately, most of the Arab rulers remain in power because of America's blessings. So America uses them against Iran, which is a threat to Israel, a client state of USA. So these wars continue and there is no sign of peace in sight. However, there is a possibility of peace, if Pakistan and a few other Muslim countries brokered a deal between Saudi Arabia and Iran, and have also setup a permanent *World Muslim Council* as the single authority for all Muslims, no matter which sect of Islam they belong to.

Many used to believe that *Organisation of Islamic Conference* (OIC) would be able to resolve conflicts among Muslims, but they were proved wrong. Unfortunately, OIC is nothing more than a place for gossip. I am proposing a World Muslim Council, which will aim to achieve three goals as explained below. Once these have been agreed by all parties, then the Muslims infighting will end, and a mutual harmony and respect will result.

I am proposing a council of all the Muslims of the world, which will be the supreme authority for the Muslims of every denomination. The council will have three separate elements, a Religious Council, Political Council, and a Higher Council. The religious council will have authority over all religious matters. For example, it will be the only authority to issue a Fatwa, and it will be the sole central authority to operate all mosques and religious schools in entire world, so there is a religious harmony among all sects of Islam. We could borrow the management system used by the Catholic Church and modify it according to our unique needs. The reason is that this system had been functioning for more than 2000 years successfully, so we should not try to reinvent the wheel.

The political council will be made up of foreign ministers of all Muslim countries, who will oversee the day to day political matters, such as, trade, economic cooperation, technical assistance etc and to resolve issue that come up. Apart from these, this council will have two other important jobs; to ensure that every Muslim is able to speak Arabic fluently despite their native language; and to ensure all Muslim countries agree to and sign a No-War Treaty, which will include a clause that no support will be given to others who may be fighting a war with another Muslim nation. The Higher Council will be made up of heads of states of Muslim countries, which will oversee the works of other two councils and provide guidance and support to them.

In countries like Pakistan and India, which has large Muslim populations, you naturally get more religious scholars. Further, the sub-continent has many local religions and traditions from which the scholars draw influence, which develops into differing views about Islamic practices. You could call them schools of thought, for example, Deobandi and Barelvi both are the names of places in India, where these traditions developed. Where these differing views on religious matters create progress, they also become sources of intense conflict. These conflicts can be so intense that they issue

Fatwa[70] against each other which cause their followers to kill each other. I think, this ability or power to issue Fatwa by any jurist is one of the fundamental reasons for conflicts within Muslims around world. The terrorist organisations like the TTP or LeJ would be powerless to launch terrorist attacks against their Muslim countrymen, if they did not have the backing of a Fatwa giving them moral support and legal religious authority to carry out such wicked attacks of terrorism. If we have a central Muslim authority, which has the World as its jurisdiction, with the sole power to interpret Islamic laws, and to issue a Fatwa, then most of internal conflicts in Muslims will end. But how is it possible to bring all the Muslims together to agree to such an authority?

It would be impossible to get a consensus among all the Muslims of the world at first sitting. What we would have to do first is to create an organisation that is sincere in its purpose, and which recognises the conflicting views among different sects of Muslim society. Its aim should never be to change everyone's beliefs and converge them on a single sect or belief. But its first aim should be to find the common beliefs and practices among all Muslims and then try to resolve the least controversial issues among different sects. For example, every Muslim, no matter what sect he belongs to, agrees on the oneness of God, Quran, and five pillars of Islam. This must be the starting point for our World Muslim Council because it needs no effort.

The next big issue is between Sunnis and Shias. As far as my knowledge goes, the fundamental reason for their conflict is not the different interpretations of Islam, but they differed on who should be the next Caliph after the death of Hazrat Muhammad[(PBUH)] ? The Sunnis believed that the most able person should succeed Hazrat Muhammad[(PBUH)] and they decided on Hazrat Abu Bakr[(RA)]. But on the other hand, the other group which came to be known as Shias,

---

[70] *Fatwa* is an Arabic word, which is a technical term for a legal judgment issued by a qualified jurist called *Mufti*.

argued that the successor must be from Hazrat Muhammad's[(PBUH)] family, and Hazrat Ali[(RA)] was the natural successor to Hazrat Muhammad[(PBUH)] , being prophet's son-in-law and cousin. This conflict among the two groups continued and increased and Hazrat Ali[(RA)] eventually became the fourth Caliph after the death of third Caliph Hazrat Usman[(RA)](Ottoman). However, the conflict became intense, and a war broke out between umm al-mu'minīn Ayesha[(RA)] and Hazrat Ali's[(RA)] forces. They both reconciled after 110 day of fighting, but that conflict is still with us, even though we cannot change history. There are a few minor differences between us Sunnis, and Shias, but the fundamental reason for conflict is what I described above. But you would have noticed that this conflict only arose after the death of Hazrat Muhammad[(PBUH)]. We cannot change history, and cannot change what happened between Sunnis and Shias just after the death of Hazrat Muhammad[(PBUH)]. We both should leave this to God, because only he knows, who was wrong and who was right. We should not try to decide who was at fault, because we have no authority to judge about the umm al-mu'minīn and the Companions. The best way to avoid conflicts is to ignore Islamic history after the death of Hazrat Muhammad[(PBUH)] and try to find guidance and answers in the history during the life of the holy prophet. Our prophet taught us to pray to one God, pay the prescribed alms, and follow other Islamic obligations. But we are engaged in proving ourselves right, and others wrong!

But while there is a conflict among Sunnis and Shias, there are further divisions and conflicts among different sects of Sunnis. The Sunnis are mainly divided into two major sects, Deobandis and Barelvis. Deobandis are closer to the three main Arabic sects of Hanbali, Salafi, and Shafis, while the Barelvi Sunnis have elements of Sufism, which the Deobandis object to because they argue that it may take them away from the idea of *Oneness of God*, the fundamental tenet of Islam. But the Barelvis claim that they never, for a moment, stray away from *Oneness of God*. As you can see from the brief analysis above, there is no difference in the fundamental beliefs among Muslims of any denominations. However, all of the conflicts are on peripheral issues, which should not be difficult to resolve. If we are unable to resolve these issues, then at least, tolerance of others' view should be developed. Let us now discuss how to organise the Religious Council.

The biggest challenge would be to get agreements among many sects of Islam? Let us first talk about the structure of Religious Council. I think that we could borrow the management and hierarchy structure from the Catholic Church, because it had been working successfully for the last two thousand years. We would modify such a system to suit our needs. This way, a central command would control all the dioceses around the world, without any day-to-day interventions. This would be possible because such a system will have structured management, training, recruitment, and promotion system for every Moazan, Imam, Khatib, Mullah, Ulama, Mufti, and Grand Mufti etc, who will all have a specific role. Here I need to mention that all the mosques, madrasas, and all other religious institutions will all fall under the authority of this council. But this would not mean they would all follow a single sect of Islam. Instead, the council will have representatives from all sects of Islam to set the Standards within each specific sect, which will promote cohesion and reduce enmity. If a school is of Shia denomination, mosque of Barelvi, and madrasa of Deobandi, then they all remain the same, but their management would receive training and nomination from the council to ensure it follows the standards set by the council. Further, the council will own all of these institutions by default, and will be responsible for running them, including housing and paying wages of all staff.

The Religious Council should be headed by a President with about twelve councillors, which should be the best scholars from around the world. Each Muslim country should select or appoint at least three best scholars, or there could be a formula for how many scholars could be appointed according to population. The president of the council should not have a long term in office, but it should be limited to four months, so each country could hold the presidential office in shortest time possible. Even then it would take 19 years before every country had held the presidential position. This way, no one will feel left out. We could also divide Muslim World into regions and rotate presidential position between regions first. For example, there are 21 Muslim countries in Sub-Saharan Africa, 19 in Middle East & North Africa, 9 in Europe & Central Asia, 6 in South & East Asia, and 2 in Latin America & Caribbean regions. We could perhaps, rotate presidential position in each region to keep everyone happy.

I think that Pakistan should be the founding country of WMC. A large area in a suitable location should be allocated for its head office. We should start negotiating with all the Muslim countries to join in. In the beginning many may not join, but it should not stop us from going forward. We will leave empty seats for heads of states and foreign ministers for the countries who have not joined initially, so that whenever they are ready to join, their places are available. We must not force anyone to join, and no one should be discouraged if they did not join at our first request. Initially, perhaps only four or five countries may join in, so we need to ensure that the basic structure is laid down in these countries and all of their mosques and religious schools follow the directions of the council. The council will provide training to all the teachers, mullahs, and scholars, according to their denominations. The Council will not dictate what will be the official sect for each mosque or religious school, but it will only ensure that a prescribed, accepted mode of training according to their sect is provided by the council. This will ensure that most, if not all of the material is removed from the syllabus which could cause conflict among different sects of Islam. Further, no person, other than a scholar nominated by the council, should be allowed to issue fatwa on any matter. These scholars must be required to send their Fatwa to a committee of the council for approval before issuing it. This will ensure the authority of the council.

A further change should be that all the donations collected by any religious school or mosques should be deposited in the council's bank account. In turn, it will be the responsibility of the council to provide wages and housing to all of the people in the service of mosques and schools. This financial element is very important for control, and to ensure the hegemony of the council. There are far too many smaller mosques, it may be a good idea to build larger mosques and reduce the numbers to create cohesion among Muslims.

Pakistan should pick up the bill for running the council for the first five years at least, and then all other member countries could contribute according to their ability to pay. However, Pakistan must pay the largest share as a host country for the council. We should eventually build regional head offices in all the five regions, so no one feels left out just because they were less important in terms of size and economy. To avoid such likely complaints, some of important high level meetings should be held in the regional head offices.

As we are working on the first goal, we should push for a single language, Arabic, for all the Muslims of the world. This will have many benefits. For example, we all pray and read Quran in Arabic, but many of us, the non-Arabic Muslims, could not understand what we are praying or reading. In this regard, we are no different than parrots. By adopting Arabic, we will come closer to Islam, because this way we would be able to understand what we are reading and praying. Further, if all the Muslims of the world speak Arabic, then it will promote communication, trade, and cohesion among Muslims, creating an Ummah.

However, before we could unite as an Ummah, we would have to resolve one of the issue sooner, rather than later, of how to get Sunnis and Shias agree to become part of the same Religious Council? This is because, unlike Sunnis, the Shias follow Ayatollah of Iran, as their supreme religious leader. If the council is to be the sole Muslim Authority then what happens to the office of Ayatollah? Our Shia brothers would be unwilling to give up their supreme leadership position and accept the Religious Council as the Supreme Muslim Authority. But I think an easy compromise could be reached between the council and Ayatollah, by the council allowing him to nominate one Shia councillor out of the twelve. In return, the Ayatollah will not issue any Fatwa, but provide his support for the council. However, if the Ayatollah wishes to retain his power of Fatwa, then it could be agreed that, he does not issue Fatwa regularly but only reserve this power for an occasional and important matter. Even then he should consult the council through his appointed councillor for council's view and support before issuing such a Fatwa.

However, the Sunnis may object to the authority and office of Ayatollah. This could also be easily resolved through a method that the USA used when dealing with some countries making territorial claims on Antarctica. USA being the superpower could engage in a war over territory of Antarctica and claim it all, but this territory has no uses for America yet, and a war with seven countries at the moment is not wise. So she resolved this by saying, we neither accept nor deny your claim of Antarctic territories. So this avoids war for the present but leaves an option open for USA to claim territory later. Similarly, the Sunnis could resolve their issue of authority of Ayatollah by neither accepting nor denying his authority; a neutral position, but without any negative implications as in the above example. When both the Sunnis and Shias join the council then much of Sunni-Shia conflict will end in Asia and Middle East, where it has become a headache for almost all the governments. A workable solution may develop among Saudi Arabia and Iran?

Finally, there should be a mutual treaty among Muslim countries of not engaging in war against other Muslims, and not supporting anyone in a war against a Muslim state. As I mentioned before that many Muslim countries are weak and poor and under the influence of Western superpowers, so they may not be able to sign such treaties. But it would be much easier for those countries that are far away from each other, to sign such treaties. Even though such treaties may not make any difference to the security of signing countries that are far away from each other, but these agreements will be significant for world politics.

Fixing Political System

Pakistan's full name is Islamic Republic of Pakistan, but it is run as a democracy instead of a republic, and many of its laws are un-Islamic. It has a non-executive president, but an all powerful Prime Minister. It is a federation with almost autonomous provinces. On one hand, it has Kashmir with its own president, prime minister, and cabinet, but still under the domain of Pakistan; while on the other hand, Pakistan has no jurisdiction in its tribal areas. In fact, Pakistan is not just a mishmash of different, conflicting institutions and systems, but it is also a hodgepodge!

A system like this is doomed to fail, or at least, it will not function properly. Let us see how we could bring some clarity and order to Pakistani political system. Firstly, we need to distinguish between a *Democracy* and a *Republic*. A true democracy is where the people rule themselves, like the ancient Athenians. Unlike modern world, the Athenians were free to indulge into government affairs, because they did not have to do anything themselves. This was because there were slaves to do all of their jobs. Such a system is not possible in today's world, so we have developed a type of democracy, where the public chooses its representatives who would rule on their behalf. So it is called a *Representative Democracy*. But the problem with representative democracy is that, in its extreme form it could turn into a *Mob Rule*. Under such a system, the majority could oppress the minorities, and we do have some examples of mob rule in Pakistan.

But to understand republics we need to understand two other types of governments, *Monarchy* and *Aristocracy*. In a monarchy, there is a king who has absolute power, but this type of rule could turn to *Tyranny*. We never had a true monarchy but the presidencies of Ayub, Zia, and Musharraf were a type of monarchies, and we know the disadvantages of such a rule. These tyrants tend to rule in their own interests, rather than those of public. The last form of government we need to discuss is aristocracy, where a few elites rule the country, but this form of government could also turn into *Oligarchy*. We did not really have any oligarchic rule in Pakistan, but our establishment could be defined as oligarchic. We have the upper house called *Senate*, which is a rough equivalent of aristocrats, but most of the senators in Pakistan are ordinary people without any aristocratic background. So it is a sham aristocracy. Now the question is why do the countries form themselves to be republics?

As I mentioned before that all the three major forms of governments, monarchy, aristocracy, and democracy over time tend to take their worst forms of tyranny, oligarchy, and mob rule, because these forms of government have inherent flaws. So political theorists tend to prefer a form of government which has all the three elements with certain check and balances to achieve a more stable government. The theorists did not just come up with this idea, but the republics evolved from these three forms of government, for example, Roman Republic. The reason political theorists prefer republics is because it is the most stable form of government to date. For example, Roman Republic lasted for more than 500 years.

Unlike our republic, in a real republic, the president will check the powers of senators and prime minister, while senators check the power of parliament, and they also check the powers of each other. But if the republic has independent courts, then they will check the power of all the three elements of republic in case of dispute. From this discussion we could conclude that for a good functioning of a republic, like Pakistan, we need a powerful and independent president, independent senators, and a prime minister with full executive powers. If we apply these criteria to the political system of Pakistan then we find many discrepancies. That is why the state is not functioning properly.

Let us now discuss specifically the issues in our form of government. Our prime minister is elected by the public who vote his party, so there is nothing wrong with the *Democracy* element of the republic. But our *President* and whole of the *Senate* is elected by the *Electoral College*[71], that is, they are elected by the elected parliamentarians of national and provincial assemblies. This is the major flaw in our political system because it concentrates all the power in the hands of prime minister. The Electoral College in Pakistan cannot vote independently because they all are obligated to party leader for giving them Party Tickets to contest elections. In other words, the prime minister actually elects the President and the entire Senate. If the president and all the senators are obliged to the prime minister, then how could they check the powers of the prime minister? In the current Pakistani political system, the prime minister has the power of a dictator but with the face of legitimacy, due to winning elections. Such a system is bound to fail. Here I like to mention of another interesting discrepancy of the political system. Interestingly, the president is the Commander-in-Chief of the armed forces, while he has no executive powers.

---

[71] *Electoral College* is a body of elected members of parliament that select other higher offices, such as, president and senators.

Let us now discuss how we could bring clarity and order to our political system. To have a functioning republic, where all of its elements have independent powers to check each other, all we have to do is to elect the president and the senators with direct non-partisan elections. If the president and senators win their seats through direct non-partisan elections, then they will not be obliged to the prime minister, and they will act independently. However, they must participate in elections on a non-partisan basis, because if they participated on a party basis, then they will be obliged to the party again, defeating the whole object of direct elections. Here I wish that the decedents of our founders, Allama Muhammad Iqbal[RA] and Muhammad Ali Jinnah[RA] (if they adopt Islam), raise themselves to a high standard to prepare for the job of the president, then there could not be a better thing. Unfortunately, Quaid-e-Azam's family has distanced themselves from Pakistan. So our hopes are with the family of Allama Iqbal's[RA] family. But they must rise above all political prejudices, be humble, and cultivate the qualities of their ancestor to lead our nation. For Quaid's family, we must always keep our doors open for them, and treat them as state guests whenever they visit Pakistan.

Let us now turn to the question of president being the commander-in-chief. This is a very bad idea, especially in the case of a war, because the president is not the chief executive but controls the armed forces. On the other hand, the chief executive, the prime minister, will not have direct control of his armed forces. This is a real mess! But under new rules, the president is just a ceremonial post with no powers. What is the point of having a president then? Let me explain my point with a true story.

When I was a child, our father, being a soldier, used to wake us up early in the morning, and would take us all for a walk after Fajar prayers. We used to walk round the Presidential Palace, which was not far away from where we lived. I believe it is now turned into *Fatima Jinnah Women University*. Anyway the president's residence was protected by soldiers in their posts on high walls, about two hundred yards or so apart. I did not know at that time that the late president, *Chaudhry Fazal Ilahi* was imprisoned there! I later heard some people wrote on the walls of Presidential Palace 'Free Chaudhry Fazal Ilahi!' He wasn't really in a prison but this of course meant that the president was a political hostage to prime minister. But I always wondered how did these people managed to write such a thing on the walls of Presidential Palace under the watchful eyes of those soldiers? But I think you have understood my point that, having a ceremonial president does not serve any purpose.

I think, the president should have the power to dissolve the government to keep the government in check. The politicians should have no fear from a president who was elected by the people in a direct election, where he promised the public that he will protect the federation. Having said that in favour of president, but he must not be the commander-in-chief, because he is not the executive. The commander-in-chief must be the prime minister, because he is the chief executive. Making war should be in the hands of prime minister, and not in the hands of any generals or president, because it is a very delicate matter, on which depends the whole nation's destiny. But in Pakistan, we know that the army chiefs do not like the prime ministers to be their commander. The reason is simple and solution is not too difficult either.

Historically, the military always saw the politicians to be corrupt, unintelligent, and incompetent. On the other hand, the military officers had reached the highest positions through their ability, competence, and courage. It is unacceptable for them to be commanded by someone who is less educated, less intelligent, and has no moral authority. Their observations and reservations are by and large true. For example, just in the last five years alone, one prime minister was accused of corruption in the case of Rental Power, and another prime minister's son was accused in ephedrine drugs case. Many ministers and parliamentarians were disqualified because of their fake educational degrees. We could list hundreds of such cases, which drastically reduces the moral authority of politicians. But this does not mean every politician is corrupt, incompetent and illiterate. What about those military officers who held very sensitive positions, but now work for foreign think tanks for a few dollars? Have they not compromised our national security? But I hope you have got my point that the military commanders think that the current politicians do not have moral authority to command them. But this issue could be easily resolved.

If we could create prime ministers who are competent, honest, and have moral authority, then the military will not have any problems in accepting them as their bosses. Currently, the military commanders do accept the legal authority of the prime minister, but deep down they do not accept their moral authority to command them, which is not good for the country. It would be much better if they accept the legal and moral authority of the prime minister, which could be achieved through educating and training our prime ministers in different areas. Let me explain which areas and how to.

It is ironic that the current system of the world requires a doctor or engineer to spend many years in education and training before they are allowed to practice their chosen profession. But anyone with no training in government, economics, or public policy is allowed to run the affairs of an entire nation! In USA and UK, we see many failed lawyers becoming successful politicians. This trend is catching up in Pakistan as well. Anyway, the best way to prepare our prime minister and other politicians for their jobs is though our universities preparing special training courses. These training courses will prepare our prime ministers and minsters in various areas. For example, the prime minster should be competent in economics, public policy, international relations, maintaining law and order, art of war, and being able to analyse and act on intelligence. In parallel to our universities, our military should prepare training courses in art of war, war theory, analysing and using intelligence especially for prime minister and defence minister. The prime mister should be fully trained by the university and military in all essential areas within six months of taking the office. The reason he should be trained by a university is so that he could see things from different perspectives and not just the military point of view. I would go a step further and say that, if the prime minister is physically fit, then he should be trained as a military commander to be able to command a small infantry unit. He should spend a few days a year with his men, bearing the same hostile conditions to understand the military affairs first hand. He should go on training in tanks, aircrafts, ships, and submarines with his men to gain insight of the capability of his army, which will be greatly useful for him later when deciding on war and strategy. He will also gain the respect of his soldiers and officers.

Here, I like to remind you that there is one area where most of the rulers have struggled throughout history and lost wars and destroyed their nations. It is the effective use of intelligence that many rulers failed in. So we must not make the same mistakes. Let me give you some examples.

Joseph Stalin, Churchill's *Uncle Joe*, did not believe or acted on the intelligence that the Germany would attack Russia. He thought that Germany would not attack Russia because it was Germany, who helped them come to power. Another failure on his part was that, he believed all of the planted intelligence, and executed almost all of his best generals for treason. He could not distinguish the real intelligence from planted, and lost his best generals. Worst of his mistakes was not to analyse the situation that, it was best time for Germany to attack Russia when his military was weak due to lack of experienced generals. Hitler could be another example, who himself was played by Churchill, by making him see threats everywhere, so he did not act on the advice of his generals and did not move his forces to the right places, which cost him the war.

Similarly, is it possible that the CIA did not know of *Twin Tower Attack* beforehand? Of course they knew, but they failed to analyse and act on their intelligence. Almost in all of above cases of state's failure in taking an action, is due to their inability to analyse the available intelligence, and then acting on it. So it is utmost important that our prime minister and defence minister be fully trained in analysing and using intelligence, so they are effective in making more informed decisions, instead of heavily relying on the intelligence agencies for their opinions.

As we have seen above that in almost all the cases of an attack or national security breach, the intelligence agencies usually have information, but they are still unable to avert attacks. This is because they are too lazy to uncover the truth. Instead, they send threat reports everyday to interior minister or prime minister to cover their backs. The problem with such a system is that if an interior minister or prime minister receives intelligence reports of possible threats every day, and nothing happens, then they do not pay attention to these reports anymore. Our intelligence agencies are behaving like *The Boy who Cried Wolf*! This way, the real threats are missed and prime minister or other ministers could not act on them. This system is very dangerous and should be improved. I think that if a prime minister receives three consecutive reports which do not materialise, he should call the intelligence chief to explain why these bogus reports were sent? Why his operatives did not try to gain more information? However, we need to handle this matter delicately because they may not send any information that may require your attention.

Finally, our new constitutional amendments have given absolute powers to party leaders, which is very dangerous. In the last government, the president had no executive power, but he ruled indirectly through his power of being the co-chairman of the party. The powers given to party chairman include cancelling the membership of any of his party member even if he is prime minister.

That is why, the last two prime ministers of the last government, followed the orders of their party co-chairman. Let us see if the new leader of a new party speaks against such absolute powers of party chairpersons? He has always spoken against *Family Limited Parties*, but will he let go of his own absolute power of being the chairman of his party? The easiest way to counter such absolute powers is to revoke that part of the constitutional amendment. But again we are at the mercy of politicians to check their own power, which is most unlikely.

In the passing I like to talk about the Governor Houses, which Imran Khan wants to raise to ground. I agree with him that the governors live in these grand palaces like the kings and they should not, but I disagree with his symbolism of demolishing them. This is because we could put these governor houses to strengthen our Federation. I am sure Imran will agree with me on this. Let me explain. Machiavelli in *The Prince* talks about how to hold a territory once conquered. The best two methods he argues are, either to send a colony there, or the prince should go and live in the new territory to hold it. Our provinces are like new principalities because they have many complaints from the Federal Government. We have a separatist movement going on in Baluchistan. The reason for such discontent is that our rulers are sitting in Islamabad and do not have firsthand knowledge of what is happening in other parts of the country. A ruler must be close to its people as Machiavelli says. So I suggest that the governor houses should be divided into three sections. The centre section for the President, the right hand side for Prime Minister, and the left section for the Governor. We should also have *Khedive Houses* in FATA and Kashmir similar to governor houses. Then the President and Prime Minister should go and live there alternately. I do not mean that they should go for a holiday, but they should run their offices from there during their stay. They could go to different provinces for a few weeks at a time. So this way they would have covered whole of the country in a year.

This will bring rulers closer to its people, and they will be able to identify any problems to nip them in the bud.

I have already talked about the unnecessary extra layer of provincial governments, so I will not repeat myself here, but I do need to discuss with you the problems we have created by delegating three important functions to provinces of policing, health, and education. I have already talked about reforming police and making it independent of provinces and central government. Let us discuss public health issues next.

Public Health Issues

I see no wisdom in delegating public health department to provinces. There will be a different health policy and spending in each of the provinces, which will cause a major issue in the case of an epidemic or pandemic outbreak? For example, we had the major outbreak of *Dengue Virus* in past, but the virus or bacteria do not stop at the provincial borders. By devolving power to provinces to set their own health policy would lead to different levels of healthcare for their respective populations. Under such systems, we will all be at risk of an uncoordinated response to an epidemic outbreak, which may cause deaths of thousands of people. But a federally controlled healthcare policy will not only have properly coordinated responses to such outbreaks, but it will also deliver a uniform healthcare to all of its population.

Public health is a complicated subject, and whole books could be written about it. So I will write in detail about how we could improve our healthcare system in another book, but here I will offer you some fundamental proposals.

We tend to think of health as a physical disease and ignore the mental health altogether. Humans are physical, as well as mental beings. So we need to look at health in a holistic manner to ensure physical and mental health at the same time. Let us first discuss mental health briefly.

Many people may disagree with me, but I would class jealousy, hate, and suicidal tendencies as mental diseases. Many Pakistanis suffer from these diseases, and if we classed them as epidemics, then we would not be far wrong. Jealously and hate are basic human emotions and we cannot eliminate them. But if we examine the cases of murders, acid throwing, and serious bodily harm, then we will clearly see the jealousy and hate played main roles in these crimes. So it is important that we deal with these emotions as mental diseases and treat them. The good news is that, just as the light destroys darkness; gratitude to God, and forgiveness for people destroys jealousy and hate.

On the other hand, the main causes of suicidal tendencies in our culture are the mixture of apathy and our films and dramas. When someone tries his best to change his circumstances, but the factors beyond his control would not allow him to change his situation, then he may develop suicidal tendencies. For example, if someone goes out to find work but cannot get the work because there is no work, but he has a family to feed, then he is in a state of apathy and would feel helpless. In Pakistan, this is the daily situation for more than 60% of the population, and this is the major underlying cause of suicides. Some people even sell their children and their organs to make ends meet. Women and young girls are forced into prostitution because of wide spread poverty and high inflation. Those, who are unwilling to live with these indignities, commit suicides. These are the external factors playing a major role in suicides in Pakistan, which are dangerously on the rise.   From a psychological perspective, when someone believes that no matter what he does, his circumstances will not change because there are forces outside of his control that have the power to control his destiny. For example, if he sees that the government's policies, nepotism, and corruption prevent him from getting a job or getting out of poverty then he will feel helpless and apathetic. When he sees things in this way, then we say he has an '*External Locus of Control*'. That is, he feels he is not in control but others or external factors control his destiny. These people are at risk of falling victim to suicides. But on the other hand, if someone in the same situation as the person mentioned above believes that he is able to change his circumstances despite external forces, then that person has '*Internal Locus of Control*'. That is, he believes that his destiny is in his control. People with internal locus of control tend to be more resilient to social and financial pressures. We could see that people in exactly the same situation behave differently. Further, people do not actually need to have a real control over external forces and their destinies, but a perception of having internal locus of control equally works.

Therefore, there is a strong need to cultivate an 'internal locus of control' in our people so they could cope with the pressures of their lives, even in the face of adversity. Our religion provides us a simple solution, of believing in an all powerful God who controls everything in this universe. A strong faith will be much more potent to combat suicides in our society.

However, we cannot ignore the roles of our films, and TV dramas on the rate of suicides in our society. Let me elaborate. I have not watched Pakistani films or television drama for many years so I cannot comment on them. But when I was in school and college in Pakistan, then I found that the films and TV programmes promoted Self-induced Injuries and Suicides. Breaking someone his legs in an accident, or someone killing himself for love, were seen as heroic acts. I am sure that if the psychologists carried out empirical analysis on the historical data of suicides, and the films and TV programmes played at that time then they will see a clear link. Our TV dramas and films are famous because they stir strong human emotions. That is why we have more facial shots in our films and dramas than actions. In our action films, a punch makes a whooshing sound, but in Hollywood movies, people don't make a single noise even when they are killed! The health minister should have the power to censor any films and TV drama that promotes self-injury or acts of violence against others.

Now let us turn to physical health. In UK, and the West, most of the very best doctors and surgeons are Pakistanis or Indians. On the other hand, Pakistan is left with some of the most incompetent doctors and surgeons. Of course, there are still some of the very best doctors in Pakistan, but they are only a few and far between. I believe the syllabus taught in our medical schools is perhaps the same as someone who studied medicine fifty years ago. That was the case when I was in college. There seems to be little change in the syllabus from the new research. I am not aware of any *Continued Professional Development (CPD)* programmes in Pakistan, which will ensure that the doctors are aware of changes in medical research and technology, so they could apply them for the betterment of their patients. But this is not the only problem, the biggest problem is that a handful of international drug corporations control the medical schools and any certification, directly or indirectly. Drugs are big businesses, bigger than the GDPs of many countries. If the drug companies make any medications, which will cure diseases, then they will go bankrupt. So they design drugs that will relieve the symptoms without curing, and they will keep the patients alive for a long time, so he uses their drugs for as long as he lives. You may have heard of side-effects of many of the drugs. Most of these side-effects have been created intentionally, so you will need more drugs to cure the symptoms of the first drug, and so on. These drug companies, using different tactics ensure that alternative medicines will never replace the allopathic medicines. For example, if any doctor saw a benefit in using homeopathy, or herbal medicines for their patients, then their professional bodies will cancel their certificates, and they will never be able to practice medicines again. These companies would run campaigns through university professors who receive research grants from them, to discredit alternative medicines. As long as these handfuls of drug companies remain strong, we will not see the public health improving or finding cures for major diseases. So there is a strong need for us to disassociate our medical profession from the Western control, so we could use any method or medicine to improve the health of our people.

There is a lot that I can write about disease and health, but more on that in another book. Here, I am going to offer some ideas that may help many people to gain good health. Firstly, we need to understand that, 50% of our immunity is in our digestive system. So if we look after our digestive system then our bodies will be able to tackle most of the diseases. The best way to do that is by keeping an eye on our digestive system by comparing what comes out from the other end, with the Bristol Stool Chart, which can be downloaded from the Internet. Our stools tell us everything about what is going on in our digestive system, which should be corrected if needed. Transit times of stools are another indicator of problems in the digestive systems. You would find more information on this on Internet. If we have a correctly functioning digestive system, then it will not only provide all the nutrients that we need but its 50% of immunity will be defence against many illnesses.

There are three fundamental things that will avoid disease and promote good health, clean environment, clean water, and avoiding pesticides. I have already mentioned that a lot of diseases are caused by our lack of sewage facilities, or poorly functioning sewage systems. If we want to reduce the number of disease incidents then we need good sewage and waste management systems. The government could reduce their healthcare bill by providing fully functional sewage systems or grants to those who want to install their own onsite sewage systems as I mentioned earlier.

Drinking unclean water or water polluted with chemicals is another major cause for ill health. The best thing to do is to either boil drinking water or use water filters. Government could provide people water filters free or at subsidised prices to promote good health and avoid diseases. However, another thing to watch out for is the chemicals in water, such as, chlorine or fluoride, which are added to municipal waters. They are also dangerous and cause the thyroid problems, which stress the Adrenal Glands in turn. There is a concern among some political theorists of using fluoride in water. They point out that fluoride is the drug that was used in Russian prison camps to keep the prisoners tame. They also accuse that some of the Western governments, such as, USA and UK increase the levels of fluoride in drinking waters when there is likely to be protests, so to keep the population tamed. Some of the European countries, who were using fluoride in their waters, have stopped using them. Some theorists even go as far as saying that through fluoride, the Western powers control the population. That is, they point to a link between fluoride use and decreased thyroid functions, which in turn affects many other bodily functions, including adrenals and testosterones. They argue that fluoride is one of the reasons the humans have lost sperm count over a very short period of time. By the way, chlorine has similar affect on human health as fluoride. I do not know truths in these claims but there are some powerful links to what they claim. I would say, it is better to be safe than sorry.

Another major problem we have from modern agriculture is their extensive use of pesticides. There had been a few deaths in UK where some people had eaten fruits with pesticides on. I never understood why in Pakistan we peel apples before eating. Pesticides on fruits are perhaps the reason. We should all be aware of pesticides on our vegetables and fruits. They should be washed properly before eating or cooking. I already mentioned that the pesticides actually mimic estrogens, perhaps another reason for reduced sperm count in males. But the biggest problem from pesticide ingestion is that they overload our livers, and it may be the very reason there is widespread liver disease in Pakistan.

Further, the exercise is the best defence against diseases. A daily walk of at least two miles, and yoga will keep anyone healthy and supple. We don't need many expensive gyms for good health. Here I would like to tell older people not to think of old age as a disease. If they behaved and stressed their bodies like younger people, then they will remain young and healthy. The reason older people lose bone density is because they do not stress them enough, so over time they lose bone density.

Finally, we have a lot of fake doctors in Pakistan who prescribe wrong medicines which could kill patients. If someone had been doctor's assistant or had worked in a pharmacy for a year or two, then they open their own clinics and prescribe medicines and injections which require the full understanding of human anatomy and bodily functions and how they would respond to these medicines. But these people don't have a slightest of knowledge of such things but readily prescribe medicines. This problem is widespread in rural areas because there are no doctors there, and people do not want to travel to cities and spend many hours just to see the doctor. So they consult these fake clinics. I think there would be a few deaths a day because of such clinics. I know of someone who had to had his arm amputated because of a wrong injections causing serious infection, a few deaths due to wrong type of drugs, a death by giving someone glucose intravenously who was diabetic, and a death due to someone injecting drug right into the heart of a patient. Unfortunately, the victim's family does not usually complain about these fake doctors either because other people ask them to let it go, or the victim's family puts this down to victim's fate. So these fake doctors get away with murder. In the West, the doctors are very caring and careful when treating their patients only because they know that they will be punished by courts if they were reckless or negligent. So it is utmost important to register cases of negligence and recklessness in Pakistan to get rid of fake doctors, and also to bring real doctors in line. But there is another problem in

Pakistan. Everyone thinks that they know better, and they try to treat themselves with drugs. They have known of complaints and names of drugs which other people had used and got better. So if they have similar complaint then they go to pharmacy and buy even the most potent of drugs and take them. This is very dangerous and must be stopped. Let me tell you how things work in UK regarding medicines, which will give us some ideas on how we could prevent drugs misuse in Pakistan.

In UK, we have 'over the counter drugs' and 'prescription drugs.' Over the counter drugs are those drugs that anyone could buy on the counter of a pharmacy without requiring a doctor's prescription, because they are deemed safe to use. For example paracetamol tablets. Even then you cannot buy more than two or three packs of 16 tablets at the same time to prevent someone overdosing and killing themselves. On the other hand, no one could buy 'prescription drugs' without doctor's prescription and the prescription must be printed on NHS[72] special paper, which will have all of the doctor's details. Further, the pharmacist will not return the prescription to the patient but keep it in his records. I think one purpose is to prove that they have not given out prescription drugs without a prescription. Now the UK system is moving towards electronic system where the prescription is sent straight to the pharmacy of patient's choice electronically, and they could collect their medicines after identifying them. We need a similar system to prevent misuse of medicines and hurting ourselves.

Lastly, I do not know what efforts has the Pakistani government made to prevent Dengue infection? I know it sprays insecticides and created special teams to deal with the virus, but I think it has not put its efforts to prevent the infection in the first place because treatment is very expensive. I think there are two effective methods which the government must adopt to reduce the infection because then it will

[72] NHS stands for National Health Service

save a lot of money on treating those people. Above all it will save people's lives and win more votes. Long-Lasting Insecticidal Nets (LLINs) could be purchased from UNO or WHO for about $2 to $3 per bed net. These bed nets could kill mosquitoes and protect people sleeping under them. Further, some people are already using Mosquito Repellent lotions to repel mosquito attacks. If these two methods of prevention is adopted by every Pakistani family then we will have almost zero infection from Dengue and we will save a lot of suffering and deaths. Even though the bed nets and repellent lotion are cheap, even then the government should provide them at subsidised price to public, so everyone is encouraged to use them. The extremely poor must be given these items free.

Public Education Issues

Just as the provinces set their health policy, by allowing each province the power to set its own education policy will yield different results. Local politics usually pushes the politicians to promote local language and local culture. If all the provinces chose to teach in their respective local language, then it will be a nightmare where no one speaks the national language. By each province following its own education policy will also produce different qualities of education in Pakistan. These are just a few of the likely problems but let us see what are the alternative solutions.

The easiest solution, without provoking the province's autonomy for health and education, is by the central government bringing the chief ministers of all the provinces into *Council of Common Interest (CCI)* to discuss and agree on a common health and education policy. The federal government should reduce provincial health and education budgets slightly, so it could spend this on monitoring and providing help to all provinces. If their budgets are cut slightly each year and the federation spends it on their behalf, then we could have a better centrally managed system for our health and education. If possible, the government could negotiate with all the provinces to give back health, and education to centre in exchange for some other incentives. If this happens then that would be the best these governments would have done. This could also be achieved when a single party, or a coalition, comes to power in all the provinces.

I could write a lot about our education system and how to fix it, but more on that in the second volume of this book. However, I will make some simple suggestion to improve our education system, which would create some of the best graduates in the world. Firstly, we need to go back to basics. You may have heard of the term GIGO in computer sciences. GIGO stands for, *Garbage In-garbage Out*. With regards to education, if we put incompetent teachers in our schools then we could only get dumb students out of these schools. We cannot expect any other results. My point could be proven if the government decides to give teachers the same exams as the students, then I can bet that half of them would fail, and the other half, which would pass these exams would not have achieved first class grades. In fact, we should give the same exams to teachers every year before the students take their exams, to see how well the teachers know their subjects. The private schools must not be excluded from such programme.

The next thing is that we should divide subjects into smaller chunks or levels, instead of matching them to a school year. I mean that if we have decided that by the time a child finishes his primary school, he should have learnt certain maths skills. Then we could divide these skills into simple addition and subtraction as Level 1, simple multiplication and division as Level 2, three digit addition and subtraction as Level 3 etc. It would be much better to divide the whole subject to many logical levels for the whole of primary and secondary schools. Then higher levels could be created for college and university etc. The division of subjects into many Logical Levels or Units, which represent certain skills, will have at least two important benefits. The understanding of subjects could be tested at the end of teaching for that level, which could be just in a month or two. So the several tests for several levels could be tested in a single year. This way, we do not need to wait a whole year before we could test a student's understanding, when it is too late. It will also improve student's retention of knowledge.

The second benefit from such a system is that the teacher will get a quick feedback and correct the problems as they arise, instead of the students failing exams at the end of the year. This simple strategy will increase the understanding of the subject and the pass rate will be higher and few failures, improving overall quality of our education.

Further, we could utilise video teaching technology to record each level of each subject by the very best teachers, in several languages, such as, Punjabi, Pashto, Baluchi, and Sindhi, and broadcast them regularly on TV and Internet. We could provide free DVDs of the video lessons to anyone who needs it. This will increase understanding and reduce the education bill for the parents as well.

DOOM

Almost all the countries of the world have a *Ministry of Defence,* suggesting that its only purpose is to *Defend* its territory in case of war. From its name, it seems that it has no offensive capabilities, or it shouldn't have. But I think that we should have a much clear and correct name for this ministry, *The Ministry of Defence & Offence.* We could shorten it to DOOM by rearranging the initial letters. I don't mean to change just the name and not its function. But I think that we should make a fundamental change to how our DOOM will work. We need to allocate special units in army, air force, and navy with a specific functions of offensive capability and operations. These units will develop their attacking capabilities to strategic and lethal levels, and they can never be used for defence. In a war, they should remain in their offensive operation even when the other units may be going for ceasefire or surrender. The reason for them to be operational in these circumstances is that they could turn the war in our favour.

My reasoning behind such a separate dedicated unit is that fighting a war on our soil is much more costly in terms of lives lost and destruction of our infrastructure. Offence is the best form of defence, and we must use it to our advantage. Have you ever wondered why USA has never fought a single war on its soil? The reason is that if they had fought a war on their own soil, then it would mean destruction of their infrastructure and loss of lives. Such a war will make people sceptical of wars, and their own citizens would prevent their rulers from waging unnecessary wars against other nations in future. You may recall the Cuban Missile Crisis, when Russia took their nuclear missiles to Cuba, right up America's ... USA quickly agreed to Russian demands but they didn't know that Russia did not want a war but was trying to fill the gap of their nuclear delivery capabilities because they did not have a suitable delivery mechanism at that time. America of course will never have a war on its soil, and it will always avoid a direct conflict with an equal opponent. America only fights with the countries that are much weaker than her, and are far away from its soil. It is a wise strategy. We cannot completely avoid a war on our soil, but if we utilise our offensive units then we may be able to take the war to our enemy's soil to reduce our losses and increase those of our enemies. That is why we should acquire ICBM[73] technology, so we have offensive capability to take the war to the soil of any country that attacks us remotely or brings a war to our soil.

---

[73] ICBM stands for Intercontinental Ballistic Missiles capable of reaching anywhere in the world.

Ministry of Lie (MOLE)

In his dystopian fiction, *Nineteen Eighty-Four*, George Orwell paints a picture of *Ministry of Truth*, shortened to MiniTrue, which was responsible for propaganda and revising the past to match it with the current party line. Those who are interested in politics will be amused by reading this novel. However, I am proposing a different type of ministry which will be called '*Ministry of Lie* (MOLE)', because it will become a very effective and useful Foreign Policy tool in the hands of an able minister. Let me elaborate how it will work.

The MOLE will have a simple declared policy 'To confuse the enemy, and to entertain own citizens.' Its functions will be many but propaganda will be the main function. The reason we need MOLE is because it is unacceptable for an interior minister to announce such things as 'we have caught three Indian spies in Quetta, who we have thrown into fire alive' and to tackle many other nasty issues. But if the Mole minister says this, and the world media protests, then our government only needs to laugh at it asking 'who said this to you'? They would say, minister of lies. Then we could ask them who should they trust? But if the above incident was actually true, then it will not only unsettle the Indian spies, but also their government, but they will also be helpless to do anything about it. By the way I am not proposing to throw Indian spies into fire alive.

The power of this ministry is in its name and its declared function, because they together generate paradoxes, which will truly confuse the world. Like the above example, we could achieve hundreds of foreign policy objectives through this ministry and get away with murder. But the MOLE should tell lies most of the time, and only pepper it with truth occasionally for a devastating effect. However, there must be one thing very clear that this should never be used to lie to our own people.

We have a very able person for this ministry already in Pakistan. Who would be more qualified than the former Interior Minister,

Rehman Malik, who made people believe that there was no such thing as target killing in Karachi, but only the girlfriends were having their boyfriends murdered? Many people claim that no one knows his true identity, and the name, Rehman Malik, does not tell us about his true identity. If someone is so intelligent to fool the whole nation, then there could never be a more suitable person than him for this job! Prime Minister Sharif should urge the Peoples Party to lend him Rehman Malik, to serve MOLE.

Military Reforms

To defend our nation, we do need reforms to make our armed forces the best in the world. Luckily, we have professional army whose soldiers have never been conscripted[74], unlike the US armed forces. Our forces have never been used to suppress its own citizens like the most Middle Eastern forces. Despite these qualities there are many signs of deterioration and sometimes it seems that it has not come out of its colonial past. For example, when I see military parades led by the *Band Master*s who are dressed in Scottish colours, and tartans, playing Scottish bagpipes, then a question comes to my mind, 'is it the army of an independent nation or of British Imperialists'? If in sixty years, we have not been able to change just the military band, then how is it possible that we would have made any innovations in military strategy or technology? Military officers are still punished today by transferring them to education corps to stop their promotions. If the *Army Education Corps (AEC)* is full of disgruntled officers then what will be the quality of education in our army? Education is extremely important area of services, and it must have highly motivated staffs that create the best officers. It must be made a privilege to serve in AEC instead of a means of punishment.

---

[74] When a nation forces its citizens to enrol in its armed forces through compulsory enrolment, then this process is called *Conscription*.

Another area related to education which needs the attention of Prime Minister and the President is the sending our officers to US and other countries for training. We know that most of the military takeovers around the world were supported by USA, and I already mentioned what the former Chief of Army Staff, Mirza Aslam Baig said in his interview. He told us on national TV that American embassy staffs were making lots of visits to the then Chief of Army Staff, Pervez Musharraf, just before his military takeover. We further know from Lt. General Shahid Aziz's interview on national TV that, when he was on training in USA, the US military officers asked him to work for them undercover. How many of our top officers would have been persuaded to become their Sleeper Agents[75], or how many Sleeper Agents do we have in our military presently?

Further, what is that they can teach us that we don't already know about war, strategy, and tactics? Or are we so naive that they will teach us about the real secrets behind their training or how they make strategic decisions? Even civilians like me, who are interested in war history or how the wars are fought, know the guiding principles behind US strategies, because they are observable. For example, we know that the relationship between the US generals and executives is mainly driven by Clausewitzian[76] approach. Naval strategy is influenced by Mahan[77], who himself was influenced by Nelson[78]. Other theorists who have influence on US military strategy are Corbett[79], Douhet[80], Billy Mitchell[81], and Warden[82] etc. We

---

[75] A Sleeper Agent is a form of a spy who is sent to a target country with the instructions to stay asleep and not act. He only acts, or is activated when there is a need for him to act.

[76] Carl Von Clausewitz was a Prussian soldier and military theorist whose military insights USA values and adopts.

[77] Alfred Thayer Mahan was US Navy officer, geostrategist, and historian.

[78] Horatio Nelson was the famous British Naval commander.

[79] Sir Julian Corbett was a British Naval historian and geostrategist.

know of the Warden's Five Rings in airpower theory, and we see this from US recent wars where they had targeted the inner rings to create physical paralysis. Let me briefly explain these five rings. Warden divides the country into five rings for an air attack. The outer ring is the enemy's armed forces, which he believed are less important, and should not be attacked first. The second ring is the population, meaning it is more important to attack the civilian population to win the war than attacking enemy's army. The third ring is the infrastructure and we know of its importance. The fourth ring is the System Essentials, the essentials that are necessary to wage war. The last and the inner ring is the enemy's leadership and he advocates in attacking this first because if there is no leadership then the war will be over in an instant. I think there is nothing new in Warden's airpower theory, because if we pick up the history books then we will find that when a king wanted to defeat another country, then he attacked the capital city of the enemy country and captured or killed the king and the whole nation would be defeated. That is why the kings always ensured that their capital was heavily guarded.

Our contemporary world is no different than the ancient times when it comes to war. Any country could employ two simple strategies to counter the Warden's strategy. For example, in the time of peace, we could decide that in war, the leadership will automatically pass down to the next level in case the primary leadership is killed or captured. For example, if the Prime Minister is killed or captured, then the leadership will automatically pass down to President, Foreign Minister, Interior Minister, Finance Minister in that order, and then to the Commander-in-Chief of armed forces, and his lower staff and so on. This way the enemy will have to attack the second ring and so

---

80 Giulio Douhet was an Italian general and Air Power theorist.
81 William 'Billy' Mitchell was US Army general and is considered father of US Air Force.
82 John Warden is a retired US Air Force officer and Air-Power theorist.

on. But if the capital is abandoned and leadership is spread around the country then the enemy will have to resort to attacking the further outer rings. To counter Warden's strategy further, instead of conventional formations where the soldiers depend heavily on continued supplies, we could turn everything into guerrilla formation including air force and navy, where small cells of military, air force, and navy has systems essential to support themselves. Many theories could be developed by our own civilians and military strategists without going to US or other countries for military training. By sending our top officers to US for training we will leave ourselves open to US, about our capabilities without gaining anything new from them!

The next thing that I want to discuss is that we may be wasting a lot of knowledge and talent from our armed forces, which could actually benefit us greatly. For example, when I heard of our soldiers and officers going back to their units after having fought on the highest battleground in the world, I was disappointed, because I am sure that we did not learn from their unique experience of fighting on the highest battlefield of the world, which we may never get from anywhere else anytime sooner. Let me explain my point with a real example.

In the Second World War the Japanese had some of the very best pilots who could shoot down American planes over and over without getting shot down for a long time. But still the Japanese fighter pilots lost. The reason was very simple. The Japanese command put their best pilots in the war until they were killed, while the Americans also put their best pilots in the war, but they ensured they came out of fighting and shared their experience and tactics with the new pilots. This way they built up huge database of knowledge, tactical information, and experience. This way, even the new US pilots could compete with the very best of Japanese pilots. On the other hand, the Japanese started losing their best pilots but they had not prepared their new pilots to the standard of their best pilots so they lost. Did we ask our soldiers and officers who fought on Kargil to come to Kakul and write books on their experience, create training manuals, and provide training to our future soldiers and officers? I doubt it! Our officers have also the tendency to dismiss the ideas of soldiers and low ranking officers, which is a big mistake, because they are the ones with the real experience on the front line and we could learn from them more than we could from officers. Further, did we learn from the soldiers and officers who carried out operations in Sawat and Karachi? Did we learn anything from the soldiers and officers who have been serving in Quetta and Karachi for many years so that we could build a knowledgebase? We need to ensure that we send our officers and soldiers to Kakul or any other suitable place for a year or two after they have just been on some special mission, to write about their experiences and advice for similar future deployment, and perhaps write books and training manuals. It should be made an honour to go to Kakul, or in training instead of a means of punishment. We should pay them all bonuses while doing these duties and give badges for coming up with doctrines and theories. We could bring the very best soldiers and officers from retirement into active service of sharing their knowledge so we could further improve our armed forces.

Film Industry & Cinema

Pakistan film industry had declined since the Zia era, and now only a few films are produced. As a result, people started watching Indian and Hollywood films. A new trend now is towards Turkish TV dramas. Many religiously minded people are against these because they think it is corrupting the youth, and our culture is invaded with Hindu and Western ideas and norms. They fear that our future generations would have lost their culture. Their first response to such cultural invasion is to impose a ban on these TV programmes and films. I deeply sympathise with them, but they have overlooked the actual reason that we are invaded by other cultures, which I will explain later. Let us now briefly survey what is happening in the film industry.

Indian cinema is just a copycat film industry, and I see them not even a tiny threat to our cinema or culture. However, the Hollywood is a tool for American Cultural Imperialism. Their objectives are to export their culture to the rest of the world, and to further their propaganda of depicting Americans to be the most cultured, intelligent, and technologically advanced nation on earth. They are trying to subdue the world psychologically, by their fictitious technology and weapon systems through their films. The sad fact is that, most people around the world have started to believe this propaganda, coming from Hollywood. The main complain I hear from ordinary people and from analysts, is the element of nudity and pornography embedded into Hollywood and Indian films. This also makes these films and TV dramas unsuitable for family viewing.

As mentioned before, many people miss the dynamics behind such cultural imperialism from abroad. It is our own fault for killing our film industry and not providing an alternative. People need entertainment, and if we prevent them from going to cinema, then they will watch foreign movies on VCR (then), and DVD. This way we lose control on what they watch. But if we made our own movies, which must pass censorship, then we had plenty of control over what the people may watch. So if we want some control over what our youth may watch, or if we want to stop the pornography and foreign cultural imperialism, then we must have a fully functional and thriving film industry and cinemas.

I believe the film industry is being revived in Pakistan but many fear that it will go in the footsteps of Bollywood and Hollywood, which is an outcome no one wants. I think that we would benefit more from following our own path rather than copying others. If we have an effective film industry then it could also be a useful Foreign Policy tool, just like the Hollywood is for Americans. The

Hollywood depicts the American President as a benevolent ruler, its military as the keeper of world peace, and its technology as the superior than any that could be found on earth or universe. But truth is quite the opposite!

Before we could talk about reviving our film industry, we need to clearly define what direction it must take in the next decade and next century? I think that our goal should be to create only the films that could be watched with the family, that is, to completely remove the pornography and profanity form our films. This way members of the family watching the films together will not need to be embarrassed. The second goal should be to become the best film industry of the world and make a lot of foreign exchange reserve from it. The last goal should be to use it as a foreign policy tool, to export Pakistani cultural imperialism. The films could also be used for shaping our society and politics. For example we could highlight the social issues unique to Pakistan so it creates awareness and constructive debate. Like Hollywood, we could raise the status of our politicians and paint them as benevolent rulers, which will push them to match public expectations. As Iqbal[RA] said that the responsibility of world leadership is on our shoulders, so we should export our ideas around the world through our films as well. In fact, many goals could be achieved through films as well as providing entertainment to our people. The next challenge is how do we organise our film industry?

Firstly, we should ensure that every province has its own film industry, including Baluchistan, FATA, Gilgit Baltistan, and AJK, who currently do not have it. We should organise them as Publically Owned Corporations (POCs) as mentioned earlier, so the public will gain from the profit. This way we would have a large source of investment for our film industry. We must never accept foreign investment for our film industry, or we will be influenced by their agenda. The biggest challenge in our film industry and stage drama had been that, it either attracts actresses of bad character who would sleep with directors and producers to get a role in the films; or it attracts men of bad characters, actors, directors, or producers, who push good women to sleep with them if they wanted a role in their films. Because of this, the film industry has had a bad name, and no one in the right mind will send their daughters to work in films, stage, or TV. If we want to succeed then we must completely reverse this trend and perception.

To make our film industry to have a good name in our society, we will have to make some very strict policies and then implement them fully. For example, to protect young women, we must have a powerful woman of good character overseeing the recruitment, auditions, and payments of actresses etc. Such a powerful woman could be a parliamentarian, or a parliamentarian committee which has more than 60% women as its members. The directors and producers must also be required to submit detailed reports with plausible reasons for why they had chosen certain actresses? Their claims must be checked for their validity to ensure that no favours are given, which is a sign of moral corruption. Many other safeguards could be built in to make it an effective and honourable film industry.

However, to achieve the third goal above, we must ensure that we make our films in six different languages at least, Urdu, English, Arabic, Chinese, Spanish, and French, so most of the world could understand our films. This will create markets for our films that the Hollywood had been unable to tap. When I say that we should make our films in different languages, then I do not mean to provide subtitles or dub them, because that is useless and viewers do not get a good experience. It is cheaper to make film into many languages at the time of shooting the original, because this way you do not have to create a set again for making it in other languages and the actors are aware of the story line at that point. I also do not mean just to translate the story into different languages because we know that a lot of meaning is lost in translation and the story and dialogues do not flow. We must hire the linguists, writers, and poets to rewrite the story in their own native languages for it to have an effect and for flow, because we would not know the underlying meaning. Translated words do not have the same effect as that used by the native writer because he understands the deep underlying meanings of words. For example, I used the Urdu word 'Gharjamai' in my fictitious story earlier on. It could be translated into English as 'a live-in husband who depends financially on his wife's family.' We could make the English audience understand the literal meaning of the term Gharjamai, but it will not have the same effect on English audience as that on native Urdu speaker, who understand that Gharjamai has many social implications. Gharjamai is not respected by the society because he is lazy and depends on others. His status is slightly higher than the servants of the family. He lacks the ego and self-respect etc. I am sure you would agree with me that literal translation of story and dialogues will lack the impact and force of the story.

Further, we must also hire the best linguist and language trainers from their respective countries for the best accent and dialogue delivery. We must not rely on our foreign language trainers because they will never be able to have the same accent as someone of the native country and culture.

With regards to acting, we ought to learn from many original trainers, such as, Sanford Meisner. I am not an actor but after watching him teach acting, I can now pick many mistakes even in many of the Hollywood films with the top rated actors playing their roles. One of his techniques for dialogue delivery, which I can remember, is what he called, *Pinch and Ouch*. This means that during acting, instead of an actor waiting for his turn to deliver his part of the dialogue role, he must react to the feelings in the dialogue of the other actor he is engaged in. It means that you should only say 'ouch' when someone 'pinches' you. It is pointless to say ouch before someone pinches you. There must be many other trainers like him, which may be worth learning from.

Finally, the government should encourage the film and cinema industry by not putting any tax on them for at least ten years, but a twenty-five years tax free film industry will grow very quickly, and a lot of investment will flow into it.

Afghan Refuges

Since 1979 Soviet–Afghan war and later US-Afghan war, the Afghan refugees have been pouring into Pakistan. There are about 1.7 million legal migrants, while there are about 1 million migrants who are living illegally in Pakistan. UN refugee agency (UNHCR) calls it 'the largest and most protracted refugee population in the world.' Now there are second and even third generation of Afghan refugees in Pakistan. These people have the right to go back to their homes and we should assist them in such a way that they are not disadvantaged when they go back home once the war is over.

Broadly speaking, there are three types of Afghan refugees in Pakistan; the very wealthy, self-employed, and the poor. It will be difficult to remove the very wealthy because of their business interests in Pakistan, and their likely influence and ties with Pakistani politicians, but we need a firm and open policy to remove them. We should not care too much about these refugees but we should worry about the Afghan refugees who are either poor or working in Pakistan. This is by far the largest group of refugees and they are most likely to suffer when going back to their country. Where we have hosted these refugees for more than 30 years, we should not abandon them now. They are our Muslim brothers and sisters, and also our neighbours. So we need to find ways to ensure that these people will be settled well in Afghanistan when they return in a few years? There are at least two things we could do to that end.

Firstly, before they go back home, we should ensure that they are all educated and trained for various professions which the Afghan economy needs. Secondly, we should ensure their continued financial support for at least five years when they need it after their return. We need to ask the current and the likely future Afghan government, what education and skills their economy will be needing, and then coordinate our efforts with them to provide necessary education and training to Afghan refugees. This will have two benefits. Firstly, when these refugees will return, they will have necessary jobs available to them. Secondly, the Afghan economy will get an instant boost because they will not need to waste time and money in educating and training their workforce.

To achieve our second goal of ensuring their financial support, we must set up a fund large enough to support every returning refugee for at least five years in case they could not get a job or setup a business etc. It would be morally wrong to push them back to their country without first ensuring that they will be able to survive there. The fund should be in the hands of an independent body that has the integrity, and that has the sources to dispense the support, and able to monitor it. Perhaps, a joint Afghanistan, Pakistan, and UNO venture could oversee this fund? The government of Pakistan and USA must contribute their shares, and a worldwide appeal should be made for this fund. I believe that we could raise millions of dollars for this fund when the donors know that it will be used well.

IDPs

In 2009, there were over 3 million *Internally Displaced Persons* (IDPs) in Pakistan, mainly from FATA. There are still over 700,000 IDPs needing to go back to their homes. These people were displaced from their homes due to military operations and tribal conflicts. The UN refugee agency UNHCR is helping our IDPs but it is not enough. We need to help our own people and not rely on outside assistance. When there are disasters like earthquakes or floods then we instantly get together as a nation and assist our brother and sisters in distress. Is it not a disaster for the people who were forced to flee from their homes nearly a decade ago? Are we going to leave them to suffer?

Perhaps, we did not care about IDPs because the media did not highlight it enough, or we thought that government will help them. Whatever the reason, we should now understand the plight of our displaced people and help them. We should create a permanent fund for IDPs apart from resolving the current issues, because natural disasters will continue to strike, and we will have new IDPs who would be forced to leave their homes due to natural disasters.

At this stage we need more female workers helping IDPs, because the displaced women from FATA do not seek help due to their strict observance of Pardah[83]. So they remain out of reach from any help. Similarly, older and ill people are also unable to seek help due to their immobility. Our Khyber Pakhtunkhawa families are helping IDPs, but it is the responsibility of the whole nation.

Regulating Media

Most people in Pakistan now claim that the Media has emerged as the fourth pillar of state, after parliament, military, and judiciary. It is a very powerful position indeed. However, I think the media does not have a fixed place in power dynamics in Pakistan, but its position is quite fluid. It sometimes holds the dominant position, and at other times it retreats to fourth position, depending on the vacuum left by the other three pillars of the state. We saw media to be in the dominant position when there were stories of corrupt politicians circulating. It is now in a retreat in the early days of the new government, which still holds moral authority. Despite this, Media

---

[83] *Pardah* is a Persian word meaning 'curtain'. In Muslim societies women observe pardah, which has three main components; veiling of women, segregation of sexes, and women's moral conduct.

still holds huge power since no government has been able to collect billions of rupees of due tax from a very large media house. No politician, whether in government or in opposition, dares to talk about this media house that it should pay it due tax. They all fear that a smear campaign will start against them if they spoke against this media house, and they may either lose their government or may not be unable to come to power again. So can we equate the media to Triple One, 111 Brigade[84], the King Makers and Breakers?

Well, no one can deny the positive effects the media had on public life; it has given the power to the weak and checked the power of the strong. But I still feel uncomfortable with media holding so much power without any check and balance! There is talk about some people in media houses acting as mercenaries, pushing foreign agenda in Pakistan. There had also been incidents when the media compromised our National Security. For example, by identifying a terrorist attacker being a Pakistani, which he was not, caused serious diplomatic issues with India. I also believe the media has played a prominent role in spreading Bhata Mafia in Pakistan, because they discussed it so much in too much detail, that the other criminals adopted it as an easy method to make money. Before media highlighted it, it was only a localised issue.

Similarly, the Western media is also responsible for promoting terrorism around the world by showing the success stories of Al-Qaeda. Then there is a serious problem of some media persons accusing politicians and others for corruption without providing any evidence. Further, there is personal bias of reporters and journalists. Media persons are driven by the *Ratings* of their programmes so they will use any means to get higher ratings. Finally, there is talk about media owners, who will do anything for those who provide them large advertisement revenue, whether they are businesses,

---

[84] *111 Brigade* is the army unit, which is sent to overthrow Pakistani government during military takeover because it is located near the capital Islamabad. So it is known as the *King Makers* and *King Breakers*.

politicians, or government. There are so many issues with the media that two prominent TV talk show hosts[85], Hamid Mir and Absar Alam, went to Supreme Court to request guidelines, so that media could self-regulate.

Even though I understand Hamid and Absar's frustration but I disagree with them on self-regulation, because self-regulation is no different than giving a prisoner the key to his cell, and then expecting him not to escape! We do have a media regulator, PEMRA, but it does not use its power for the reasons I mentioned above. PEMRA or *Pakistan Electronic Media Regulating Authority* perhaps does not have power to regulate print media as the name implies. So the first thing we need to do is to give it power to regulate all media through amendments to ordinance that gave birth to it, or through a new bill. Next issue is how to regulate it effectively?

The most effective way to regulate media is by regulating the most powerful man in every media house, that is, the owners. We do not need complex rules for such regulation. Instead we could create an eligibility criterion to own and run a media house, which should be same as for a parliamentarian. The exactly same rules should apply to media house owners as a parliamentarian, to submit yearly personal financial statements etc, and they should be required to appear in front of parliamentary committee to answer questions. If at any time the owner becomes ineligible due to corruption case, not paying tax, or for any other reason, then the PEMRA will have the authority to sell that media house, and hand over the proceed to its previous owner. This way, the owners will be liable for the actions of their staff, so they will enforce good practices.

To deal with National Security issues, for example, what is allowed to be printed or reported, and what is not allowed, the PEMRA needs to devise clear guidelines with the help of foreign ministry,

---

[85] TV talk show hosts are called *Anchor Persons* in Pakistan.

interior ministry, military, and ISI. Then these guidelines are given to all print and electronic media houses to follow. PEMRA should also have a single point of contact 24 hours a day, for any guidance if media house is not sure about a report conflicting with national security doctrine or not. This way, the problem of media accusing politicians and others will also resolve itself, because the owners will be answerable for their staff.

The problem of *ratings* effecting journalism could be resolved by removing the ratings generating equipments, or requiring it to be placed in such a way that it samples the entire population and not just the urban population.

The most important issue that affects journalism is the media houses giving more air time to those who pay the most in the form of advertising. But this is not where it stops, they even ensure that most of their programmes do not criticise too much the government that pays them more in advertising. The governments, having the largest budgets have been bribing the media houses and getting the favourable results during their election campaigns. From such practices the public loses out because they do not get the truth. We need to ensure that public gets the truth all the time and it can be done easily.

The PEMRA could make it into law that the advertising income for all media houses, for a single advertiser, must never exceed 7% in any month. The media houses should be required to submit a report with a breakdown of all advertisers and amounts received. The reason I suggest we use a monthly limit is because if it was an yearly limit then all political parties and governments will use all of their advertising budget near the time of elections, effecting results.

Further, if a government in power is advertising its projects, but at the same time, the same party is also advertising from its party budget, then they should both be counted as one advertiser and not two, because they are the same. Similarly, the media houses that have more than one TV channel, and also newspapers etc should be seen as a single entity for application of this rule. They must be required to calculate the advertising income for the whole group and the total revenue received from any single advertiser must not exceed 7%. These distinctions are necessary to prevent any misuses by advertisers advertising in different mediums of the same media house and breach the 7% limit. If these suggestions are implemented then the media houses will automatically become independent as they will have no incentives for bad journalism. Further, by putting a 7% limit for a single advertiser, the advertising will become cheaper and smaller businesses will also be able to advertise, giving people more choices and reduced prices.

PBS & Truth

Pakistan Bureau of Statistic (PBS) reported a consumer price index (CPI) of 8.3% and 9.6% for 2013, and 2012, respectively, measured in the month of July. In other words, the PBS is telling us that, if someone was spending Rs.10,000 a month on food, clothing, housing, and other necessities of life last year, then now he only needs to spend just Rs.9870 per month to buy the same things due to deflation. But is it true?

Of course not! People are crying out on the price rises, and tens of people are committing suicides everyday because they cannot cope with the inflation, and make ends meet. Then how the inflation could just be 8.3% a year? The true inflation would be in the region of 20% to 30% a year or higher, if we consider the rate of people becoming poor from being in the middle class a few years ago! The reason PBS does not tell public the truth is because PBS is answerable to government, and their top officers are chosen and promoted according to their subservience to government. So they will fiddle the numbers as the government wants. The country could have a financial chaos, but the PBS indicators will show that everything is hunky-dory.

PBS produces many other statistics including GDP, and Social Welfare statistics etc, which only mislead Pakistanis and the world. PBS is the very important department and it must tell the truth to the public. If it tells us that everything is fine, when it is not, then it is not serving its purpose and must be closed down. Unfortunately, the system forces all the bureaucrats to follow the government's line, which is not good for the country. I believe that all the bureaucratic governmental departments should be made independent, but if I had choice of just the one department to be made independent, then I would choose the PBS.

Our colleges and universities can play an important role here by setting up their own Statistics Think-tanks, to counter the governmental propaganda coming from the PBS. There is no need to spend huge sums of money on creating think-tanks, but only a few Mathematicians and Statisticians from a few colleges and universities around the country need to get together to draw up a plan on how they will collect, organise, and publish their statistics. They could use their students to collect CPI, GDP and other financial data for the specialists to analyse. They could then publish their data on their websites. If they work diligently and honestly, then the major newspapers may publish their data regularly as they earn credibility. This will help people to make their decisions based on correct information at next elections, and the public will be able to choose the right people to lead them.

Index